CRIME AGAINST CHILDREN

CRIME AGAINST CHILDREN

Editor

Arunaima Baruah

PUBLICATIONS

KALPAZ PUBLICATIONS

Delhi - 110052

Crime Against Children
(Crime)

ISBN: 978-81-7835-082-0
Rs. 990

Reprinted in 2013 in India by
Kalpaz Publications,
C-30, Satyawati Nagar,
Delhi-110 052
E-mail: kalpaz@hotmail.com

Printed at: G. Print Process, Delhi

CONTENTS

PREFACE

There has been a kind of revolution of awaking regarding the state of children in our society. With this there has been an immense growth in the production of literature or Child Affairs, in general and Child Abuse in particular. Significantly, book have came to light on these subject needing immediate treatment mid 1960s. The government formulated laws and the society, as a whole has begun to respond to the issues and problems, related to children.

The million dollar question is: what is Child Abuse? Is it a syndrome or a symptom? There may be several different answers to these questions. In fact present study is a serious effort towards searching for an appropriate answer.

The author of this book has collected material quite painstakingly and presented it in an organised form for further use of scholar, researchers, social activists and for the general readers.

This book deals, rather successfully, with all the aspects, related to the abuse against children; child labour, sexual exploitation and child battering among others.

Here we specifically need to mention chat child battering a new phenomena coming to light has infact been in practice since long time through so called emotional border prevalent in Indian family set up. Though the subject began to be examined in America, U.K. and other western countries as early as in 18th century, it has drawn attention of Indian researchers and reformers very recently. That is why we have incorporated a separate full-fledged section on their aspect of child abuse which is almost each time perpetuated by none other than the parents themselves.

The author has very optly divided the work into different sections, for a clear presentation. The problem is there and an effort to seek a solution is also been made through the present piece of work. In that endeavour, the book emerges as a strong voice against the victimisation of children and advocates for their cause.

I hope, this book will certainly stic the column waters and would succeed in creating a new awareness in society regarding neglected lot, which the children are.

Arunaima Baruah

INTRODUCTION

Since ages, children have been victimised by one abuse or the other. It is not wrong to say that they are a neglected lot. For children there has never been a golden age. Throughout the history of our society, children have been bought sold, enslaved, exploited and killed. They have been abandoned, severely beaten and physically abused. In fact, the more we go in history we find that the lot of childrens had been houshes, and crueler. Poverty and man situation have especially led to killings of children.

Ironically, the children have hardly ever enjoyed complete protection from the adults in society. There has been a widespread evidence of child ill-treatment seen everywhere. If we go deep into the pages of history, we would find a catalogue of abuses from which children have suffered in the past.

Truly speaking, the victimisation starts from the birth of a child itself. For instance, the practice of infanticide or the willful killing of new born babies was widely accepted among ancient and prehistoric people as a legitimate means of dealing with unwanted children. The same has taken the shape of foeticide with the advent latest scientific and technological instruments.

Abandonment was another ill treatment, noted out to children. Poor parents used to leave their newly born babies at deserted place, in order to get rid of them. It has been the practice in Europe, Africa and in India. The unowed mothers also threw their illegitimate infants in dustbins.

Sexual exploitations is another abuse, which children have faced over the centuries. Out of last adults would modest them to their appeasement. Poverty and illiteracy has played great role in facing children to be exploited in order to earn their meals, a day.

Children have been used as slaves and bonded labourers in all societies. In India, the children, coming from the lower strata of society served the mighty and wealthy. They served, served and died.

Although times have changed and the miseries of children have been reduced with the help of passage and implementation of certain laws yet their lot as a whole has not improved much. Even today, the children are forced to work against their will, as labourers, only meet to bounded over, if not slaves. Fortunately, the infanticide is not in practice, scale—though stray cases cannot be ruled out—but, there are instances, where unmarried mothers still abandon their unwanted babies, in fields, large dustbins and pits and tanks etc. Children—both girls and boys—are exploited sexually, even now. The newspapers are full of news about rapes of minor girls and the inhuman attitude of adults towards young boys.

This is the true picture of the harsh relations.

However, there are sings of hope. Now, the society is far becoming more aware about the state and status of the children. The governments have framed lower to stop in victimisation of these. There are a number of social workers, activists, all over the world, who are committed to the welfare of children.

In India, too state of affairs, regarding the lot of the children has begun changed for batter. Apart from the Government, a number of non-governmental organisations (NGO's) are engaged in their pursuit of child welfare through various social, health and educational activities.

Section—I

THE PERSPECTIVES

1

THE PERSPECTIVE

When we talk of child rights, the first thing that came to mind is denial of human rights to children. No single cause can be attributed to the problems. But to begin with, the population explosion is the must dominent one. Continuous population growth in slums and backward areas where notions of large family to have many hands for earning/increasing family income, family planning programmes do not reach easily. Therefore, a large group of poverty-ridden population, ready to adopt any means of livelihood, perpetuate to continue, putting children even on dangerous work which boundary wall is full of danger and darkness. India is the second most populous country in the world after China. As per 1991 census, total child population in India was 29.77 crores and the figures for 2001 are expected to be 30.72 crores. According to a survey made by an autonomous institute under Department of Women and Child called NIPCCD. About 92 million children still live below poverty line. Female infant mortality ratio continues to be 119 in rural areas and 62 in urban areas. Girl literacy rate is reported to be 19.63 per cent as compared to 30.09 per cent male literacy between the age group of five to nine years and again 36.44 per cent in female children as compared to 62.42 per cent male children between 10 to 14 years. Similarly, in the age group below 18 years in rural areas, two-third children are illiterate and in urban areas, literacy rate in this age group is just little more than one-third per cent as estimated in 1984. Infant mortality rate calculated for 1990 by NIPCCD in rural areas was 66.6 per thousand; in tribal regions, 74.0, whereas in urban side, it was 81.3 per thousand live births.

WHO survey reveals that mortality in children between 0 to 12 months of age is 200, between one to two years is 145, between two to three years is 100 whereas between three to four years, it decreases to 80 per thousand live births. Nearly half of the total deaths (47 per cent) have been recorded in the age group of 0 to four years. About one-third of all deaths take place in the first year of life. Nearly 20 per cent of all deaths occur in the first month and about 10 per cent of all deaths occur in the first week. On other words, two-fifths of all infant deaths occur in the first month and nearly half of the deaths in the first month occur in the first week.

The constitutional provisions of India especially included in chapter IV on Directive Principles of State Policy indicate the commitment of our Government towards the well being and proper development of children. Article 15 (3) of fundamental rights indicates that nothing in this article shall prevent the State from making any special provision for women and children. Article 24 prohibits that the child labour by saying that 'no child below the age of 14 years shall be employed to work in any factory or mine or engaged in any other hazardous employment'. Article 39 (C) of DPSPs lays down 'the health, strength of the workers, men, women and the tender age of children are not abused and that the citizens are not forced by economic necessity to enter a vocation unsuited to their age or strength'. Article 39 (F) states that 'childhood and youth are protected against exploitation and against moral and material abandonment'. Article 45 says 'the State shall endeavour to provide within a period of ten years from the commencement of the Constitution for free and compulsory education for all children until they complete the age of 14 years'.

Child Labourers

As per the census survey India has the largest number of child labourers in the world. As per ILO figures, about one-eighth of the children in the age group of 10-14 years are at work, and further one-third of rural children are seen working.

There has been recorded a continuous increase in the work participation rate of child workers in the previous years. Moreover, studies conducted have revealed the non-stop increase of child labour population in different forms. During the 1971-81, decade census shows that over 90 per cent of child workers come from rural areas. In total, there has been 3.91 per cent increase of child worker from eighth to ninth decade. Of the total increase, 25.64 per cent are in urban areas whereas in rural areas, this increase is just 2.21 per cent. The rate of increase is further higher in case of girl child workers in both rural as well as urban areas i.e. 30.48 per cent and 47.06 per cent respectively. In case of male child workers, there has been rise of 19.67 per cent in urban areas whereas their rate participation in rural areas is as low as 8.24 per cent.

Regarding literacy rates, the data indicates that in 1981, 63.1 per cent male and 77.0 per cent female child workers were illiterate in urban areas, whereas in rural areas, the per centage of illiteracy had been 80.0 per cent and 89.0 per cent for male and female child respectively. Sector-wise participation on per centage basis shows that in the year 1981, male child work participation in primary sector was 84.63, girl workers 86.39, while in the secondary sector, the participation per centage of male children was 9.18 and of female ones 9.7; in the tertiary sector, it was 3.91 whereas male workers participation was 6.19 per centage points.

Table 1.1

Number of Male and Female Child Workers in Different Sectors and Age Groups in India

Sl. No.	Sector	Age group	Main Workers			Marginal Workers		
			Person	Male	Female	Person	Male	Female
1.	All categories	All ages	2,22,517	1,77,544	44,973	22,089	3,357	18,552
		0-14	11,169	7,413	3,756	2,424	684	1,740
2.	Cultivators	All ages	92,523	77,591	14,932	10,362	1,474	8,888
		0-14	4,013	2,912	1,101	1,183	352	831
3.	Child Labour in	All ages	55,500	34,732	20,768	8,864	1,178	7,686
	Agriculture	0-14	4,774	2,783	1,991	1,007	240	767
4.	Livestock, forestry,	All ages	4,992	4,160	832	435	130	305
	fishing, etc.	0-14	704	563	148	67	34	33
5.	Mining and quarrying	All ages	1,264	1,101	163	19	8	11
		0-14	27	16	11	3	1	2
6.	Production and repair units							
	(a) Household sector	All ages	7,711	5,647	2,064	862	107	755
		0-14	424	—	229	195	69	17
	(b) Sectors other than	All ages	17,432	15,834	1,508	587	189	393

	household	0-14	541	400	141	40	14	29
7.	Construction Mark	All ages	3,565	3,207	358	141	69	72
		0-14	80	52	28	11	1	7
8.	Trade and Commerce	All ages	13,929	13,012	917	365	172	193
		0-14	245	224	21	20	13	7
9.	Transportation, Storage	All ages	6,069	5,899	170	73	61	12
	& Communication	0-14	34	31	3	1	1	—
10.	Miscellaneous	All ages	19,530	16,360	3,170	381	149	232
		0-14	327	204	123	24	9	15

Source : Census of India 1981, Series I, India Part II Special Report and tables based on 5 per cent sample.

Besides other factors commonly discussed here and there, the priority of employers to employ children with profit motive has raised the extent of child workers because of which they are now found to be seen in almost all states and, by and large, in the same areas where adult workers are working Table 1.1 indicates the number of workers by type, sector, age group and sex in India in 1981. Table 1.2 explains the employment, status of the children (age 5-9 and 10-14 years) by sex and residence.

Table 1.2

Per centage Distribution of Children (Age 5-9 and 10-14 years) by Principal (Usual Activity) Status, Sex and Residence in India 1987-88

Sl. No.	*Usual activity (Principal) Status*	*Villages*				*Cities*			
		Male		*Female*		*Male*		*Female*	
1.	Working (or employed)	5-9	10-14	5-9	10-14	5-9	10-14	5-9	10-14
2.	Worked in household	0.5	9.0	0.4	7.2	0.3	3.1	0.2	2.0
3.	Salaried/Waged	0.1	1.6	—	0.5	0.1	2.3	0.1	1.2
4.	Casual labourers	—	0.1	—	0.1	—	—	—	—
5.	Casual wage labourers in other type of work	01	3.8	0.1	4.8	0.1	19	0.1	1.3
6.	Total no. of working children	—	0.5	—	4	—	8	—	0.2

A comparative figures of child workers participation between 1971-81 given herein reveals the growing rate of their participation in both rural as well as urban areas and in both the years, the participation rate of employed worker is more in comparison to those working in household.

Table 1.3

Number of Children (5-14 years) in the Labour Force by Residence and Sex in 1971 and 1981

Sl. No.	Area	1971 Total	1971 Male	1971 Female	1981 Total	1981 Male	1981 Female
1.	Rural (percentage)	9.97	7.28	2.69	10.19 (+ 2.21)	6.68 (- 8.24)	3.51 (+ 30.48)
2.	Urban (percentage)	0.78	0.61	0.17	0.98 (+ 25.64)	0.73 (+ 19.67)	0.25 (+ 47.06)
3.	Total (percentage)	10.75	7.87	2.86	11.17 (+ 3.91)	7.41 (-6.08)	3.76 (+ 31.47)

After having a glance at the table above, it becomes clear that over 90 per cent child work-force comes from rural area. As far as the employment criteria between 1971-81 is concerned, it remained same in both the years. Some interesting observation were made in case of change in number and composition of child labour. In total there had been 3.91 per cent rise; in rural areas, it was 2.21 per cent and in urban areas it was 25.64 per cent. Again, in urban areas, because of factors mentioned earlier, there has been an increasing trend. Similarly, there has been prominent increase of workers from 1971 to 1981 in rural as well as urban areas. Also out of the total child labour force, 84.63 per cent of female children and 86.89 per cent of girls engaged in tertiary occupations were 6.19 and 3.19 respectively. Wages they get are exploitatively low not even half of the daily wages given to an adult.

It has also been found that participation rate of child workers also differ from state to state and from one organisation to another. For example as per a survey conducted in 1978, male child worker' participation rate varies from one per cent in Kerala to 11.7 per cent in Andhra Pradesh. In the case of girls, the participation rate even in the same area varies from 0.3 per cent in punjab to 10.5 per cent in Andhra Pradesh. However, the appearance of child labour in organised sector is reported to be abolished. Statistics of the Ministry of Labour show decrease in the average daily employment in the registered factories from 7784 in 1950 to 3592 in 1986. However, these figures do not underestimate the presence of child labour in the organised sector, still, there is hardly any doubt that child employment is mainly concentrated in the unorganised and semi-organised sectors and small scale industries. For evidence, (UNICEF, 1984) in Mirzapur carpet weaving belt, child workers are reported to be more than 40 per cent and in Sivakashi, 60 per cent of the child labourers were girls. Of total worker in mica and shellac factories, the per centage of children is 30 and 10 respectively.

According to an ILO study, about 35 per cent of workers in Firozabad glass bangles industry were children which are now concentrated in house hold units of sample work after Supreme Court order. A study (NIPCCD,1977) reveals that 18.7 per cent of children start working before they complete an age of 12 years. In urban areas, a large number of children are working in small establishments like ships, way-side restaurants, domestic help, brick kilns construction sites, stone breaking, garage, metal workshops, handloom and handicraft industries etc. It is in addition to those who work as self-employed, in marginal and low paid activities like shoeshining, newspaper vending and ragpicking. These children are engaged in different types of activities and the conditions in which they work hampers their mental and physical development. As pointed out earlier, in rural areas, children are involved in family occupations where they earn alongwith their family members. In urban and township areas, on the other hand, children are engaged in wages-type establishments like in dhabas, road side restaurants, domestic servant in big towns, glass and bangle industry in Firozabad, carpet industry in Mirzapur-Bhadohi, Jammu and Kashmir, diamond industry in Surat, bidi industries in Madhya Pradesh lock industry in Aligarh and notorious match and fireworks industry Sivakasi.

Street Children

The issue of another group of neglected and so-called street children deserves equally serious treatment. The reasons for increase of their problem are rapid changes in the social system, unplanned urbanisation and pitiable state of the rural population. Out of the total 884 million (1991 census), 217 million reside in urban areas, and every third person living in urban areas is below poverty line. Out of the total urban poor population in 1984-85, 68 per cent were women and children. It is further assumed that in six cities of Bombay, Calcutta, Madras, Hyderabad, Bangalore and Kanpur, there are approximately 5 lakh street children.

A UNICEF (1994) analysis reflects that on an average, 47.4 per cent street children spend their nights on the open street. It is further observed that 58.3 per cent of these children are working out of the total employed, 56.6 per cent are self-employed as porters, street hawkers, shoeshiners, newspaper sellers, parking attendants etc. About 32.7 per cent are reported to be working in shops and other establishments. A majority (90 per cent) of street children are exposed to dirt, smoke and other harmful objects and do not have bathing or toilet facilities. They are often nabbed by police for crimes and put under lock-up for vagrancy, gambling, street brawls or are sent to remand homes. According to a study analysis of Street Children, 1989, total number of street children in Delhi alone is 1,00,000 and 45,000 in Bangalore, 25,000 of whom are homeless. A situational analysis (Lima, D., 1989) of neglected children in Bombay shows that majority of street children were denied education, those who got opportunity to attend the school dropped out without even before the primary level.

These street children are primarily engaged in informal sector which do not require technical skills and money. Some of these children are engaged in more than one kind of work during the same day. Their work in some cases is changed from one season to another. The total working hour in which they mark have wide fluctuations. In some occupations they work only in the early morning and late evenings, e.g., selling of newspapers, flowers, balloons, etc. Further, it has been noticed that most of the children work for long hours (8-10 hours) and there earnings are between Rs. 10 and Rs. 15 per day. ragpicking and scrap material collection brings higher daily income (Rs. 30 to Rs. 50). In fact, these street children are deprived of getting bathing and toilet facilities and are forced to live in unhygienic condition leading to various health hazards. The nutritional and health status of these children is poor because of inadequacy of food and non-availability for medical care. These children (Lima, D.; 1989) are also physical abused, extorted by older children, adults and local dadas. Some occupations like ragpicking have health hazards arising out of getting hurt from sharp pieces of metal and glass and the risks of insanitary conditions and they also run the risk of sexual abuse. Another study (SPARC, 1991) observed that some of the street children had to seek support and protection of local gangs to survive in cruel adult world and learn the survival tactics. As their backgrounds are unknown, they are not trusted and society does not recognise their dignity and values, being young citizens. Their existence is just tolerated but not recognised. They are deprived, marginalised, unprotected and alienated from the stable life who do not have their own family to live and, therefore, live in their own groups.

Some Efforts for the Rehabilitation of Neglected Children

After having done a detailed study of the nature and extent of the problem and are as of support they need, a rehabilitation project was started in the areas of beneficiary's needs and priorities. The first effort was made to help the children's families to know the real price of rags which their children collected. The Mysore Paper Mill was contacted by the Centre for the disposal of rags collected by these children which was purchased at 70 paise per kg. instead of 50 paise per kg. which middle men paid to these children. This raised the children's income. The second step was to help the children in saving 10 per cent of their daily income in their small savings accounts. After that the children were motivated by trained social workers to gather at a common place where they could have rest, clean up themselves tide up their hair and clothes. They were told stories and were entertained by playing games etc. Later on, the Centre started formal education in the form of writing and reading in their own languages. Gradually, the Centre started formal evening schooling from 3 pm. to 6 pm. for those who were not going to formal school. Health and hygiene was considered one of the important programmes for which the Centre employed a doctor. Vocational training in carpentry, tailoring etc. was given even on stipend. Formal discussion with the parents of these children was also considered a useful part of the project and after improving their foundation, they were helped in getting the jobs of peon, cook, carpenter, helper in other departments and most of them have been engaged in this very centre which is being run for their rehabilition.

Factors Responsible for Child Work

The specific reasons compelling children to join work vary from one family to another. Generally, it depends upon several factors like educational, financial status of the family, employer's motivation to employ children, availability of adjustable job in nearby community, and parent's tendency to neglect children's responsibility and use them as labour to support the family income or to prepare them for adulthood. Some of the important factors compelling children to join labour force, are being discussed here detail.

(i) Monetary Hurdles: The leading factors is economic compulsion which continues to increase the size of children in the labour market. In fact, on the one hand, we see the rich who continue to be richer because they do not have shortage of resources and the area they wish to continue for their further development welcomes to see their systematic approach. On the other hand, we have a large number of rural and urban poor people who are not aware of their privileges and rights and because of that, they are experiencing every type of injury, abuse and exploitation. Their life has become full of risks and their severe poverty compels them to do any type of work irrespective of their age and sex.

Undoubtedly, poverty alleviation programmes have been introduced by the government with the help of voluntary organisations, but because of the limited coverage of the programme and defective service delivery policy, benefits do not reach the deserving section of the society in the sense their backwardness requires and they perceive to overcome the poverty they are experiencing. As a result, the poor, needy, weak and fearful children who cannot go against their parents are ready to face neglect, abuse and exploitation, when they deserve to have special security and care as they do not have the physical, and mental maturity to face hardship. The Ministry of Programme Implementation (PTI) in its annual report of 1990-91 pointed out that there were 29.9 per cent population in 1987-88 below the poverty line and it was assumed that the per centage will go down to 25.8 per cent by 1989-90. But unofficially, we know that still there are more than 50 per cent of the population below the poverty line, but out of these, the per centage of children, as stated earlier to be below poverty line, is very high. A study conducted by A.N. Singh, 1990, reveals that as high as 38.5 per cent child workers acted as labour because of poverty and 20 per cent to enhance their family income. The motivation for 18.5 per cent employers to prefer children is that they prove cheaper.

Various studies have also proves that increasing economic compulsion has been noted as a pull factor for migratory rural children. A study conducted in Bombay (Singh, M., 1979) restates that 63.2 per cent of children migrated to Bombay is search of employment due to scarcity of family income. Absence of the adult earner's another factor which leads to child labour practices. A study conducted in Varanasi, Badhoi and Mirzapur belt (singh, A.N., 1990; 114) establishes that one of the major compulsions for the majority of children to mark has been the inadequate income of the family earner. Further economic compulsion is increasing due to unemployment, under employment, large number of dependants, little or no skills and absence of productive assets due to which children have to work.

(ii) Growing Population: A developing country like India needs to have systematic planning to ensure a risk-free and secured future. Undoubtedly, some effective efforts have been made from time to time by the government and voluntary agencies to mend minds of those who believe in large family size. In fact, the problem needs in-depth information dissemination of population problem of implications of populations growth, complications which people (women and children) are likely to undergo in the absence of resources of different kinds which they require and the country feels to promote for the better quality of life. However, importance of family welfare programmes and their implementation at different levels has not achieved popular its acceptance; therefore, rural, urban and tribal people still continue to believe in large family size. For these poor unexposed and backward families, children are not a burden on them. Rather, they understand that more children means more income of the family. In fact, to check the problem, it needs overall planning at every level in the way people perceive to accept it. As mentioned earlier, large family size in a poverty ridden society puts the parents in a different situation where they fail to perform their responsibilities towards family and force their children to work even at a tender age. Their ignorance encourages them to hold the view that children are God-gifted and we have no control on it.

Child Labour as Employer's Priority

Another major factor is that employers want to get more profit on limited expenditure. Moreover, they are aware of the economic compulsions of the families in the extreme poverty. They watch out for exploiting the parental economic compulsions when they learn that children of backward families are more tolerant, can be put on difficult jobs for long hours, even on lower wages. Secondly, they have come to know of the productive quality of children who do not raise grievances pertaining to their working conditions. A study conducted by A.N. Singh, 1990; in Varanasi states that 33.5 per cent employers prefer children as they work hard. For 18.5 per cent, child labour is cheaper; for 15 per cent they can be assigned any job, for 15 per cent, child workers create less trouble; for 15 per cent, they can work for longer durations etc. These aspects establish the importance of employer's willingness to employ children which further becomes an important reason for increasing child labour in the country.

Parental (or Parent's) Illiteracy

Overall literacy per centage in the country continues to be very low. In the areas where the rate of child labour is higher, illiteracy is also comparatively higher. This indicates the interrelationship between illiteracy and encouragement of child labour practices. It is a well established fact that educated, aware and exposed parents plan the future of their children and make every possible attempt to ensure all round development and protection to their children from insecurity and risks of life. It is seen that the parents who are illiterate are satisfied with their present happy life of the family and never think of the future. They believe in employing children rather than planning their future. The study by A.N. Singh, also indicates that 83.8 per cent of the child workers' fathers were illiterate, 12.8 per cent were just primary and rest of them were middle and high school. Similarly, another study (George, K.N.; 1977) tells that most of the children who came to labour force belonged to lower literacy group. About 44 per cent of child workers' parents were illiterate.

Other factors like rapid urbanisation, home environment, broken homes etc. have been found responsible for child labour However, the employment of children holds both positive and to employ children whereas negative aspects obstruct children's development, motivate them do develop evil practices which become areas of worry for the researchers, social thinkers, Government and society in general to feel concerned about the problem.

Advantages of Child Labour

(a) Physical fitness: For the proper physical, mental, social and spiritual development of child, along with availability of education, nutrition, love and affection, physical activities keep their own place which need priority. Lighter work in the interest of children's physical health when they become capable to do work, should be encouraged with the care that its interests remain only the development ones.

(b) Faster Learning Capabilities: The child has vision to observe and learn to think in short time if it is made interesting to him. He has more flexibility of arms, fingers and body as compared to adults which helps them learn the work skills easily and develop a sense of responsibility and confidence.

(c) High curiosity levels: By and large, a child takes more interest in knowing and learning a thing. In this way, a curious child, by nature, slowly becomes trained in different skills provided it is made more purposeful with availability of all possible developmental condition.

(d) Hardships Develop Tolerance Against Employers: Children who assist in the family occupation or work with their relatives do not have the same kind of the problem and treatment which employed children are receiving at the hands of their employers and adult co-workers. Therefore, these self-employed children have freedom to express their grievances and difficulties they face while working. As a result, work is not that much burden on them as employed children feel and experience.

(e) Some of Responsibilities and Self-dependence: The aim of education and training institutions is to help the people to become more responsible and self-dependent. Work environment, if development, provides a kind of climate which makes children sincere, punctual and disciplined.

Disadvantages of Child Labour

(a) Early Work Affect Child's Overall Development: Being young and the future architect of the nation, the children deserve to have overall protective, progressive and developmental opportunities in the areas of their interest. Compulsion of work, when they are young, defies them of their rights and is unjustified to humanity and the future of the nation.

(b) Health Hazards: Long hours of work at work place alongwith morning and evening hours of work at home is fatal to their growth and development. Night work, continuous standing or sitting or use of single set of muscles in poor working environment where they carry heavy loads, pressure of speed of work, contact with the industrial poisons etc. cause harzards to health and provide harmful conditions for the future of child workers.

(c) Psychological defects: Compulsion of work performance in a given time with controlled supervision leads furthermore to problems relating to the tensions and mental alertness of working children.

(d) Children denying bad habits: Children, while working, get liberty from the parents and are given importance when they suppose the family or give a helping hand to their family. This kind of parental freedom provokes these children to take up independent decisions which further leads them to spend more of their earnings on their own and start smoking, gambling, and join gangs which can hamper their future development.

(e) Exploitation of Children: Employers' attitude to have more and more production on less expenditure encourages them to put the children in exploitative and abusive conditions and mature them in a watchful/tight administration which results in the form of occupational diseases, physical deformity and handicap.

(f) An Expensive Affair: It is felt by some of the employers who employ children that output of the child worker is comparatively less profitable as compared to the adults. According to them, child requires more supervision and care and chances of destroying raw material are higher expecially when they learn to work.

(g) Decreases Employment Opportunites for Adults: Children, while working, decrease the value of adults in the labour market and increase the risk of adult

unemployment. If further moves with a lot of psychosocial, moral and physical implication for children, economic consequences for adults and a blot to the society at large. These deserve in-depth study of the problem, reality of their situation, responsible reasons encouraging them to continue the practices and to have disirable and percieved corrective strategies.

While talking about the methodology research of any kind, proper, systematic and in-depth understanding of the subject one is going to select for study is required. Therefore, for selection of the problem, which is new and need based deciding on the pattern of studies in the field introduced by the researches and to have an all dimensional understanding of the problem, one has to go through the previous studies conducted on the similar aspect. Consultation of related literature helps the researcher to have an adequate, comprehensive understanding and uptodate knowledge of the subject. More so, it brings enough clarification of doubts one finds in the process of study and also generates sufficient guidelines which enable the researcher to conduct his study without experiencing hurdles which could come in the absence of its consultation. It is because of these reasons, an attempt has been made herein to review and analyse some of the relevant studies in the area of interest indicated under the objectives of the present study.

A Brief Description of Some Research Studies on Child Work

A study on working children in urban Delhi (ICCW, New Delhi, 1997) has tried to examine the extent, reasons, and consequence of child labour practices in Delhi. The study observed that most of the children were employed in work- shops and the children employed in tea stalls, dhabas and as domestic servants come from the states of Uttar Pradesh and Bihar. The average monthly income of their families was Rs. 321.50 and the average size of the family with working children was 5.5. The number of working children per household generally increased with bigger family. The daily working hours in most of the establishments were 6 to 10; and were violating the provision of the maximum of six hours (for young persons between the ages of 12 and 18) laid down in the Delhi Shops and Establishments Act. Almost 50 per cent of the children in registered tea stalls and dhabas worked for more than 12 hours a day. The environment and working conditions are unhealthy and most of the establishments are situated in the walled city and are located in lanes and by-lanes. The lighting and ventilation in these working units are just sufficient to carry on the work but sanitation and hygiene cannot be simply provided in such conditions. The children engaged in manufacturing and servicing earned less than Rs. 60, domestic workers earned Rs. 26-50 and those in shops and dhabas earned Rs. 26-50. The child labourers in auto repairs and cycle repair shops are being paid Rs. 30 as wages. These children have to be satisfied with low status, occupations and/or low wages with unfavourable working conditions.

In another report based on study of child labour (Labour Bureau, 1979), it was revealed that out of six tea factories surveyed, the total employment was 1,484. Of these 434 were adolescents and 171 were children. The rates of wages of children differed from Rs. 2.99 to Rs. 3.05 per day. Children were also entitled to subsidised ration. In addition, free medical aid, free cooking full and tea leaf (250 gm.) were also provided. In these factories, children were working for more than the prescribed duration of work, i.e. four hours. No special welfare facilities for children existed there. In the match and fire works factories nearly 40,000 to 50,000 children below 15 years of age are working in Sivakasi and surrounding regions. The reason for such high number of child workers in these areas was that these areas happened to be labour intensive and where the entire process of activities is done manually and 60 per cent of the country's matchboxes and 90 per cent of its fire works are produced here. Similarly, in bidi industry, of the total workers, 40 per cent were children below 14 years. The average minimum and maximum income of child workers ranged between Rs 1 to 1.50 per day. The working conditions in these industries were unhealthy and pitiable. The work places were extremely crowded, dark and dingy. The workers were residing in small and congested houses situated in the slums of the town and were forced to work for long hours to earn their livelihood.

A survey based research study conducted on "Working conditions of children employed in unorganized sector-child labour in Sivakasi" (CSR, Madras, 1984) found that majority of the children working in match units were girls. Working children were found to be main bread winners in most of the families in Sivakasi. The study further observed that 36 per cent of the families have more than two children employed in match units. It is reported that 95 per cent of the child workers took job in match units because of the financial reasons.

According to the report given by the Chamber of Match Industry, the industry is paying 35 per cent to 50 per cent more than the minimum wages fixed by the Government. But the findings show that the wages of child workers are less than what is stated by the Chamber of Match Industy. Moreover, child workers were seen to be working for long hours in ill-ventilated places without basic amenties like water and toilet and rest pause. The affects their health and retards their physical growth. The welfare facilities provided to the child workers and their working conditions were not commensurate with the growth and monetary turnover in the match industry. Health and nutrition of these children had been completely neglected by the employers. The toilet facilities were almost non-existent even in their homes. 15 per cent of the children stated that they are forced to work inspite of their poor health conditions. These children work for more than 10 hours per day. Out of all the child labourers, 11 per cent said that they were treated harshly by their employer, 88 per cent stated they are abused when committed mistakes, the rest are beaten on such occasions.

In four villages of Mahendragarh and Rewari Districts of Haryana, Satish Chander and Devi Lal conducted a study on child labour. Data analysis revealed that 89.5 per cent parents in the child labour families were illiterate, followed by six per cent who could merely read and write. The overall educational status of their families was very miserable. About 49 per cent child labour had never gone to school whereas 40 per cent had discontinue education. About 56 per cent parents expressed favourable view regarding the children's education where as remaining 44 per cent doubted the utility of school education for their children. Caste playing a dominant role, it was observed that a major number (39 per cent) children belonged to Chamar families alone. The greater burden was on the shoulders of children belonging to nuclear families, (70 per cent) more than on those of (30 per cent) joint families. The maximum number (66 per cent) of children came from the most common family size. The study also confimed that small family reduces the necessity of sending children for work in rural areas.

According to K.D. Gangrade and J.A. Gathia's report on women and child workers (1983) in unorganized sector indicates that India has the maximum number of working children. The brick kiln sector of Stwarigaon near Delhi attracts poor rural families who work from Oct. - June when there is no agriculture work. Families are paid on a piece work basis ranging from Rs. 18 to 21 per 1,000 bricks. So they use their children to raise their production quantity. The children risk injury from the work as well as silicosis of the lungs after three of four years of exposure to brick dust.

Carpet weaving work in states like U.P., Kashmir and Tamil Nadu are flourishing centres of carpet weaving. Varanasi, Bhadohi Mirzapur are big centres of carpet weaving. In Mirzapur belt only, 50,000 workers are engaged in this work of which nearly 20 per cent are child labourers. Match industries of Sivakasi in Tamil Nadu employ thousands of children from the age of 5 for over 10 hours a day. Women and children come mainly from Harijan landless families. They are paid on piece rate basis. In Sivakasi, of a total 1,00,000 workers, the child labour population is guessed around 45,000. The child labour is essentially a problem of poor and destitute families, where parents cannot afford education of their children.

At TISS, Bombay, Gopunjkar, V. Pratibha and V.S. Dhole conducted a study on working children in a tribal area of Maharashtra. It said that children are the source of cheap labour to employers. The poverty ridden parents also welcome whatever the child can bring in an add to the meagre household income. Child workers are paid in cash and in kind against jobs they perfom. Form many cases the wages which children get are lower than what is due to them. It is also found that except for a few activities like saldari, children enjoy a real free life and do not think it to be the constraints of work. The hours of work are nor rigid and in some cases maltreatement does exist. School facility is available for the children and existing health facilities are inadequate to fulfil the needs of people. Disease are resulting out of malnourishment and unhygienic conditions. The Special Nurtrition Programme (SNP) was found to be satisfactory.

For all over findings on phenomena of child labour, a study conducted by the Institute of Economics and Market Research on Child Labour in Himachal Pradesh assessed that one-third of 10-14 years' old children in rural and one-eight of those in urban areas are at work. In agriculture they work for about 280 days in a year. In villages, children were kept in as bondage and as contract labour in urban areas. Economic condition of the family was the main reason for children to take up jobs. Employer wanted to have child labour because they were easy to manage and also they had to pay less wages. Of the working children 36.79 per cent belonged to Scheduled Caste/Scheduled Tribe families, another 20.75 per cent to lower castes. Most of the children worked for less than a year but child labour engaged in tea plantations was more stable. 41.10 per cent children were doing temporary jobs and 30.14 per cent seasonal. The job they got was on the basis of personal relations and quite a few through newspapers etc. About 37.59 per cent parents conceded and working children were getting better treatment at home in the shape of nutritious food, clothes etc. It was also found that working children were sober and better bahaved. However, bad habits like smoking, gambling had been acquired and some become disobedient. A large number of children were working for long hours. About 5.26 per cent worked for more than 15 hours and 18.31 per cent for 10-15 hours. In Kangra 76 per cent of children had to labour for 7-8 hours and 9.07 per cent mentined about poor safety conditions, but mostly did not think it as a problem. A few complained that their work affected their lungs etc. The working conditions of these children are without doubt very unsatisfactory. Children continue to work in places which lack proper sanitary and ventilation facilities. Medical facilities are also not provided.

Regarding education of child labourers, a report of the committee on child labour (Ministry of Labour, Government of India, December, 1979) reported that in our country, the tradition of educational learning outside home was confined to the upper caste, the previleged classes.Children of the producing classes learnt the required work skills and work in the family. Step by step these children get fast in the ethos of labour. Thus poverty and child labour always make each other and continue to reinforce themselves in families and communities. For a number of tasks discussed in previous pages, employers prefer children to adults. In fact child workers are not organized on lines of trade unions which can furiously fight for their cause. Child labour is also justified on the ground that it trains the child's fingers in the required skill. The cases of child labour are the highest in Andhra Pradesh where it accounts for about 9.0 per cent of the total labour force, 9.2 per cent of the total child population and 3.7 per cent of the total populaton of the state.

In the findings of Mendelievich Elia edited book for working children shows that the age of children's entry to various jobs varies according to the place and the occupation. Children, only at six years of age have been found working, although the usual age of entry into employment is from eight to nine years. In agriculture child worker are usually unpaid. There seems to be no particular division of work among men, women and children in agriculture family undertakings. The report of the National Commission of Labour, Employment of Women and Children (Government of India, 1969) has found that in many cities large number of young boys work hard for long hours and in strict discipline. Even children five year of age may be found in some of these places working without adequate meal, intervals or weekly off, and 10 to 12 hours daily for as low as 2 annas in the case of those of tender age. The Labour Investigation Committee (1946) found that due to scarcity of inspection staff, has become difficult to enforce the relevant provisions of law.

Highlighting another aspect of child labour, the Labour Bureau's study stated that legally banned hazardous industries such as match manufacture, cashewnut processing, bidi making, carpet weaving employment of children below 14 years either uncertified or having false age certificates continues. The gradual reducation in the employment of children since independence is partly due to expansion of educational facilities by the state and also relatively due to the implementation of statutory provisions relating to child labour.

A research undertake by Musafir Singh, V.D. Kaura and S. A. Khan on working children in Bombay by (NIPCCD, New Delhi, 1980) brought to light the difficult conditions of working children who were residing in slums and backward areas.The majority of the families of working children had five to eight members, the average being 5.8 per household. Out of 703 children in the age group of 6-15 years as many as 319 (45.4 per cent) were found working. Out of total, 403 (57.3 per cent) were boys and 300 (42.7 per cent) girls. The minimum number of hours a child worked was four and the maximum 14, the average being 8.7 per cent. As many as 54 per cent did not express any problems in the performance of their jobs. Similarly, 88.6 per cent of the children were satisfied with the treatment meted out to them by their employers and 14.4 per cent were not satisfied with their salary, 66.6 per cent with the duration of their work, 5.9 per cent with the facilities and benefits available, 10.2 per cent with the jobs security 3.9 per cent with the treatment of their employers and 2.4 per cent with the treatment of their colleagues. A similar study on child labour-a socio-economic perspective (Singh, A.N., 1990; 113) said that besides economic conditions child workers' families which forced them to undertake carpet weaving, 14 per cent of the child workers' parents put their children in labour market because they were getting into bad company and in case of 13 per cent child workers, they themselves wanted to earn and live like their colleagues in the community. A majority of children (62.1 per cent) were illiterate and in remaining of them education varied from first standard to eighth standard. Of the total child labour force, 72.5 per cent of child workers came from backward communities, 19.1 per cent from Scheduled Caste and

5.5 per cent from High Caste families. The employers' preference to have child labour shows the various reasons previously mentioned e.g. that 33.5 per cent preferred to employ children they work hard, child labour is cheaper than adult workers; and that they can be put to any job. It is also brought to fore that income of child workers some earned between Rs. 151 and 200 per month, others between Rs. 101 and 150, and still others between Rs. 51 and 100.

There were children who earned Rs. 50 or less whereas 18 respondents did not earn any thing. The data analysis further reveals that a large no. of the child workers accepted that they worked for 11 or more than 11 hours per days. This statement was also supported by 73 per cent of the parents of child workers and 11 per cent of the employers. Similarly, 28.8 per cent of child workers admitted that they worked dalily during night. Forty-two per cent accepted to work for two hours per day, 28 per cent for the three hours whereas 1.1 per cent informed about working four hours daily during night. It has been found that 30 per cent of child workers have spoken about their cordial relationship with their adult workers and the rest of them have non-cordial relations. In the same way, 24.3 per cent child workers have told about their cordial relationship with their employers and the rest of them did not have cordial relationship. Their participation in work with the major co-workers leads to unwanted behaviour, as their behaviour patterns including bad habits become adult like. This also hampers their socio-physical development.

A university dissertation on the working and living conditions of ragpicking children in Delhi by Bhatia, Minakshi Bhatia 1988-90 found that of the highest no. *i.e.*, 67.11 per cent were from Tamil speaking belt areas, 27 per cent from Hindi speaking be whereas 39 per cent from Rajasthan. 9.2 per cent boys and 66.67 per cent girls were from nuclear family. Fifty-six per cent felt their work as heltic and 27 per cent did not feel so. Visual handicaps was found in the respondants between 5-10 years and in 11-15 years. Seventy per cent of the respondants did not use oil. Forty-nine per cent had bath on alternate days and rest once a week and did not use soap. Similarly, 60 per cent showed interest instudy, 65 per cent were not happy with work they took up. Seventy per cent boys and 50 per cent girls did not get pocket money. One more dissertation more dealing with another aspect i.e. on situational analysis of girl rag-pickers in Delhi (Aggarwal, Ritu, 1989) found that the daily income of ragpickers are between Rs. 4-6. On an average six to eight members had been found living in the families of rag-picking children. They pass their leisure time watching T.V. and remanining in the rooms. Girls are permitted go for collection of rags along either with elders of the family and they work for three to four hours in a day. NIPCCD study conducted in 1986 on rag-picking children in Delhi found that 90 per cent children came from nuclear families. A large number i.e., 90 per cent lived in houses owned by them. Every three out of four lived in katcha houses with minimum civic facilities. These respondent were migrants from the States of Haryana, Rajasthan, Tamil Nadu, Uttar Pradesh and West Bengal. Regarding education, 37.7 per cent attended school. Out of them 40.7 per cent had dropped out before completing their primary schooling . One-third of the members of the families studied were engaged in rag-picking. They contributed to the extent of 31.24 per cent of the total monthly income of the families. The circumstances which forced them to get into this work were poverty, non-availability of suitable work for children and family occupation etc. According to their parents, 90 per cent of child rag-pickers took up this work willingly. The average frequency of cuts and injuries as told by parents and their children was six times more than average which occurs in a month. Every fourth parent/guardian did not felt about any change in the habits and behaviour of the children engaged in rag-picking.

Indeed, a number of enquiry committees, commissions were established by the Government Surveys in the field were conducted to assess the difficulties of the problems in different areas of children's employment. But these are primarily based on the problem of child labour who are employed and working under the strict controlled administration except few which rag-picking children are experiencing. Therefore, the present study has been concieved to assess and evaluate the overall aspects of the problem of employed children also along other aspects which need special treatment.

To sum up the conceptual part of the problem which itself is by no means exhaustive to be dealt with, child workers are undergoing hardships of various kinds but true pictures cannot be presented through such studies and enquiry committees reports as these children are working under the strict control of their emplyoer. The only section of child labourer it is more vocal in rag-pickers since they work independent of strict discipline of employers. The following section will give a more detailed presentation of not only the problem areas of child worker but will also deal with the safety measures available & being implemented to redeess the situation.

2

EXPLOITATION THROUGH THE AGES

In the ward of Hobbes, in the state of nature, man is bruite, nustry and selfish and what can be more brutish than exploitation of the most Hindu creatures of nature, i.e., children. It will not be wrong to say that for children there has never been a golden age. Throughout the history of Western societies, children have been killed, abandoned, severely battered and sexually abused. They have been the biggest victim of societal disturbances. In fact, the further beyond we go in history, more brute and crueler appears to have been the lot of children. Considered the property of their parents or the state, children in the past had little recourse or protection from adult society, which hardly rationalized abusive behaviour as being for the good of a child. To a large extent, contemporary concern with child abuse and neglect is the result of relooking at child-rearing practices that have been occurring since time immemorial. In the widespread evidence of child maltreatment in the part, the documentation shows what it is the girl child who has been the bigger sufferer that because of her sex. Hints perterining to them are too high to be reproduced on any single bank, while discerning the child abuses and atrocities, the one mentioning a few of then.

Child Infanticide

The practice of infanticide the desired killing of newborn babies, was widely accepted among ancient and peoples as a legitimate means of dealing with unwanted children. Because resources were few and there was a need to limit family size, any child that cried too much; was sickly, deformed, less than perfect in size or shape; or otherwise failed to conform to the standards set by the medical practices, was vulnerable to being killed. Furthermore, girls, twins, or children produced one of illicit relations were frequent victims of infant murders. Methods used to dispose of children included exposure, drowning, beating, mutilation, putting lac of salt in throat, suffocation, 'potting' in jars, and being thrown into dung heaps or buring pits. As we have already said, the most vulnerable victims were girl children. An economic burden to their families because they required a dowry and shifted to their husband's family after marriage, females were at high risk of being killed. It was reare in some cultures for more than one female to be kept per family, and the greater frequency of female infanticide was exercised in a large imbalance of males over females, which survived at least through the Middle Ages and possibly into early modern Europe, where the historian Mols noted a "curious" surplus of boys over girls between 1450 and 1750. In ancient society, the *Patria Potestas* (Father as absolute authority) granted a father the control of life or death over his children. The Greeks and Romans both destroyed their weak and deformed offspring in the hope that only the strong would survive. The survival of the fittest was advocated by Plato, Aristotle, Seneca, and others as necessary means to strengthen the race, and was reinforced by the Roman Law of the Twelve Tables which forbade the rearing of defective children. Dead father of children were expected to be revered by their children as if they were gods. Children themselves had no legal rights separate from their fathers and, due to their dependent status, did not enjoy an protection. As Aristotle wrote, "The justice of a master or a father is a different thing from that of a citizen, for a son or a slave is property and there can be no injustice to one's own property"

If we look into the age prior to Christian era, a child in some societies was not considered human until certain ceremonies were performed, after which infanticide was forbidden, to exemplify, the Egyptian midwife prayed or the soul to join the new born child, imparting his spirit to the child. In Athens, the *amphidroma* ceremony was performed on the fifth day, from the birth of child when the baby was carried around the ancestral hearth by its nurse to receive consecration and a name. Receiving a name was very important to a child for it confirmed his identity and his right to life. If the father did not want the child, it was compulsory that he dispose of before the *amphidroma.*

It is frequently assumed that since the ancients freely condemned many of their infants to death, they had little regard for child life and child rights. In reality, however, the conditions of life were so hard and resources so scarce that the ancients appear principally to have been concerned with bringing up the offspring who had a reasonable chance of survival. This attitude, on the other hand, stimulated great concern for child care in the ancient world in order that children could grow up to be strong and healthy child sacrifice, was also practised not only as a method of population control or agencies, but as a means to get rid of evil and ensure good fortune for the community. In China, India, Mexico, and Peru, for example infants were cast into rivers as offerings to water gods to ensure good harvests. The Egyptians, Phoenicians, Moabites, and Ammonites also sacrificed their infants in order to please avenging gods. Sealing children within building foundations was a traditional practice which endured from the time of the Creation of the walls of Jericho in 7000 B.C. to sixteenth-century Europe. It was believed that the foundations would be strengthened by the interred children.

Unfortunately, infanticide did not stop throughout the Middle Ages and, by 1527, the latrines of Rome were said to "resound with cries of children who have been plunged into them". A high rate of offsprings killing continued to exist throughout the eighteenth and nineteenth centuries among both legitimate and illegitimate children, although the practice was more common for the latter. Legal prohibitions did not stop infant murder; rather, they altered its methods. After the fourth century, abandonment became a dominant alternative of troubled parent-child relations.

Abandonment

Throughout the Middle Ages, thousands of children were exposed and abandoned by their helpless parents. As one writer noted, "It [exposure] was practiced on a gigantic scale with absolute impunity". The practice was considered easier by the hope that the founding would be rescued, although that happened infrequently at best. Those who were saved were often sold into slavery or prostitution; some had their teeth extracted for sale to the rich; and others were deliberately maimed to instill pity, thereby making them more effective beggars.

In the hope of saving the lives of abandoned children, foundling homes were established in the eighth century. The first such home was begun by Datheus, Archbishop of Milan, in 787 A.D. Other foundling shelters later opened in Montpelier in 1010, Marseilles in 1199, Embeck in 1274, Venice in 1380, and in 1421, Florence, where the famous *Ospedale Degli Innocent* (Hospital of the Innocents) was started. These institutions ultimately proved ineffective, since many infants died from overcrowding, poor child care, and an insufficient number of wet nurses.

Large numbers of foundlings have characterized most of European history, especially in times of social and economic crisis and war. In the late seventeenth century, St. Vincent de palu, the patron saint of charitable societies, got married over the great number of infants left on the steps of Notre Dame and appealed to the ladies of the court to finance an asylum for abandoned children. Applying the biblical principle. "Thou art thy brothers's keeper," St. Vincent de Paul charity among all of society's fateless and established in the public mind the needs of the for care and protection. Similarly, in eighteenth-century England, a retired sea captain named Thomas Coram became so hurt by the tiny infants thrown onto the dust heaps of London that the spent 17 years soliciting support for a foundling hospital. Established in 1741, the London Foundling Hospital sought to prevent child killing and the "inhuman custom of exposing new born infants to perish in the streets". Baskets were kept outside the homes to receive the children, and the 'tour' of turning box was built to keep the identity of the mother secret and to save her from shame and harassment.

In the United States, founding hospitals were not established until the middle of the nineteenth century when the New York Founding Alsylum was established on Randalll's Island in 1869. Before that time abandoned children were taken to almshouses where they mingled freely with the destitute. The renowned social photographers Jacob Riis and Lewis Hine were instrumental in awakening late nineteenth-century America to the plight of abandoned and neglected children. They say that the New York City alone some 100,000 homeless urchins were said to wander the streets.

Though established with good intentions, foundling homes were no panacea for the problem of abandoned children. Even in the best homes, it was common for more than half the infants to die within their first year. Nonetheless, demand for admittance to the homes remained high. In London, after the Foundling Hospital accepted an open admissions policy in 1756, pressure for admittance became so great that it led "to the disgraceful scene of women shouting and fighting get to the door, that they might be of the fortunate few to reap the benefit of the hospital". But mortality was so high that foundling hospitals, "instead of being a protection to the living, became, a charnel house for the dead". Although many of the children of couples unable to support them.

Wet Nursing

Another form of institutionalized abandonment common throughout history was mercenary wet nursing. Wet nursing had been rejected since antiquity by physicians such as Galen and Hippocrates, who pleaded with mothers to nurse " with your own unborrowed milk". Nonetheless, most parents who could afford it, and even many who could not, sent their babies to rural wet nurses immediately after baptism. Kessen wrote that a persistent theme in the history of the child is the hesitation of mothers to nurse their own babies. Until the eighteenth century, when attitudes began to change, breast feeding was considered crude and below the dignity of the middle classes.

Indicative of the extent to which wet nursing was exercised, is the fact that of 21,000 children born in Paris in 1780, 17,000 were sent into the country to be wet nursed, 3,000 were kept in nursery homes, 700 were wet nursed at home, and only 700 were nursed by their own mothers. Even among those mothers who kept their infants at home, pap (grain and water) was usually fed them rather than lactation. There were many reasons given for the practice of wet nursing. e.g, a mother may not have been able to produce an adequate supply of milk; she may have had the fear that nursing made on her sleep, social lifc, and ability to work; or she may have scared that breast-feeding would impair the shape of her breasts and her sexual attractiveness. It appears, however, that men were important factors in discouraging maternal suckling:

Men often feared that a nursing child would be in competition with them for their wives' attention. Mainly, however men sought the services of wet nurses because they were reluctant to sleep with their lactating wives since sexual intercourse was said to "troubbleth" the blood, and thus the milk. According to Mary Wollstonecraft, wet nursing was practiced till as late as the eighteenth century due to the desire of fathers to maintain sexual relations with their wives. History tells that although country airs was believed to be good for infants, the terrible poverty that motivated rural women to take in nursings created an environment that was helpful to neither good care nor survival. Wet nurses were often more concerned with their fee than their nursing, and charges of brutality and neglect were quite common. The mortality rates of babies given in nursing were extraordinary up to double of infants who stayed with their mothers. For foundlings sent to wet nurses, mortality was even higher. A child might suffer form a lack of food, clothing, and unhygienic conditions or from unscrupulous wet nurses who, on receipt of their fee, murdered their charge. Nurses were known to replace a dead child with another live one without informing the parents about the matter.

According to historian Edward Shorter, the eighteenth-century mortality rate of legitimate infants in the French city of Rouen was 19 per cent, 38 per cent for those legitimate offsprings sent to rural wet nurses and 90 per cent for foundlings sent to rural nurses around Rouen. Moreover, the children of wet nurses suffered from maternal neglect and died in large numbers. Same time after they were abandoned by their mothers.

Swaddling

One more child-rearing practice closely associated with the abandonment was *swaddling,* which resulting in "entirely depriving the child of the use of its limbs, by enveloping them in endless bandage...; and by which the skin is sometimes excoriated; the flesh compressed, almost to gangrene; the circulation nearly arrest; and the child without the slightest power of motion". Swaddling can be dated back at least to Roman times, and is so closely associated with infancy that the American Academy of pediatrics, when deciding on an official insignia, chose a picture of a swaddled baby modelled after the Della Robbia mediallins that adorn the *Ospedale Degli Innocent* in Florence. Swaddling was practiced as a means of keeping babies warm and as protection from air, sunlight, and soap, which were thought dangerous to the child. Moreover, swaddling was deemed necessary to help the infant's bones growth straight. Without swaddling bands, it was feared that an infant might get scared at the sight of its own limbs and tear its eyes and ears out. Or it might touch its genitals, or crawl around the floor and remind its parents of its affinity toward animals.

To some extent, Swaddling bands may have protected children from abuse as it appears that swaddled babies were rarely beaten. When swaddling was stopped, however, toilet training became necessary. Swaddled babies were frequently left in their excrement because it was considered that clean linen and fresh clothes would "rob them of their nourishing juices". The decline of the practice swaddling can be seen as the beginning of the struggle between parents and children over control of children's bowels.

Nevertheless, the there is little to suggest that swaddling itself created physical or mental disabilities. The key to understanding swaddling is in the symbolic realm, for it provides a way of understanding how parents thought and felt about their children. Swaddling without doubts restricted a mother or wet nurse from hugging, cuddling, or caressing a baby, and it reduced the interaction of infants with their parents. Furthermore, swaddling greatly affected the baby's demand for attention from mothers and urses, who were frequently preoccupied with other tasks and not especially interested in the routine chores of child rearing. When the baby was tied up, it could be left alone for long periods of time.

Apprenticeship

Sometimes, children, rich and poor were sent at about 7 years of age to apprenticeship which is the service to learn useful skills as well as proper behavior. Although masters were expected to be kindly but firm in their teaching, quite often children suffered violence at their hands. Master were allowed wide discretion in "correcting" their charged, as long as they did not cause permanent handicap or death. The medieval institution of apprenticeship, which survived into modern Europe and America, was apparently started with the fear that parents would be unable to provide a proper education to their children since excessive parental involvement or affection might interfere with children's productivity.

Early Parental Sentiment

In the Middle Ages, parents had little "awareness of the particular nature and behaviour of childhood" for "as soon as the child could live without the constant solicitude of his mother, his nanny or his cradle-rocker, he belonged to adult society". Parents thought the world of children to be an uninteresting one. According to Stone, aloofness, the acceptance of God's will, or sending one's children away from home were three ways in which parents managed with the high rate of infant mortality. Children were consequently caught in a vicious circle: they were neglected because they might die, and they were more likely to die because they were neglected.

Beginning of the Era of Renaissance

From the period, western civilization began to awaken from the intellectual and social stagnation that typified the Middle Ages, glimmerings of a new concept of childhood as a distinct phase of life came to existence. After the fourteenth century, a tendency to express in art, iconography and religion (in the worship of the dead) the personality which children were soon acquire, and the poetic familiar significance attributed to their special nature began to develop. This special nature was expressed in the sixteenth- and seventeenth-century practices of making infants wear clothes that were distinct from adult clothing, providing children with their own games and toys, and making them the centre of special attention, especially by portrait painters. For the first time, children in the Renassance were represented in art as children rather than as miniature adults. But, above all, a great concern for the child's ethical welfare and development replaced the medieval period's seeming indifference toward children.

The period of the sixteenth and early seventeenth centuries was vastly more messy than of medieval Europe. The Protestant Reformation had destroyed the unity of Christianity. To preserve the social order, children needed to be properly educated and disciplined, for it was through them that system would be restored and a godly society came to be created on earth. Children were now seen as a dependent class in need of protection from the vagaries of society. Due to their immaturity, children needed to be prepared for life. They had to be given a special treatment, a sort of quarantine, before they were allowed to join the adults. This on process teaching and learning would begin at home.

Thus, changed eithics of the Renaissance stressed the importance of the family and the special responsibilities of parents in teaching proper behaviour. Family discipline had to be strict and hard as there was a fear that children would be spoiled by excessive indulgence or coddling. In all aspects of behaviour children were expected to show regard to their parents.

Among the upper classes, children addressed a parent as "esteemed parent," "honoured Sir," and "Madam." It was ritualistic for them to bow before their parents each morning to ask their blessing, and they were not allowed to speak lest spoken to first. Such acts of deference in the home conformed with the behavioural norms of society as a whole.

The early Puritans were very much concerned with establishing a high standard of family discipline that they awarded the death penalty for disobedient children, although there is little evidence that it was actually ever invoked. Nonetheless, parents were expected to control their children, and they risked having them taken away from their custody if they were unable to fulfill their obligations. The authority of the father in disciplining his children was strengthened by the rising power of the nation-state which spewed forth a flood of official propaganda putting greater emphasis on the need for authority and obedience and the Protestant Reformation and its concern with suppressing the innate sinfulness of children. Calvinist principle concerning original sin held that severe discipline of children was needed to defeat the Devil, punish cunning and strip the "young viper" of his innate wilfulness and depravity. Salvation depended on the ability of parents to maintain family discipline, authority, and order.

Flandrin also saw in Catholic France from the sixteenth century onward a desire of the monarchy to re-establish the authority of parents. One French writer proposed that fathers be considered "gods on earth." Reverence of children for their parents was considered foundation for future obedience between citizens and their sovereigns. The strict subordination and repression of children was paradoxically the consequence of a greater interesting children. Parents, especially fathers, took quite seriously their duties of exacting obedience from their children, not only for their own sakes but for the children's as well.

But it acquired the most negative shape. According to Stone, physical brutality toward children reached its peak in the sixteenth and seventeenth centuries. Whipping had become so usual that when one theologian tried to convey to some children a sense of Heaven and Hell, Heaven was where children "would never be battered anymore" and Hell was a place "worse than a thousand whippings". The Biblical adage, "If thou smite him with the rod, thou shalt deliver his soul from Hell," became the core of educational theory in the school as well as at home. Flogging had become a daily punishment in schools for academic lapses and misbehaviour. Even great teachers such as Pestalozzi, Beethoven, and Milton regularly beat their students although a few exceptions such as Montaigne saw no effect of whipping other than "to weaken and cower the soul or make it more disasterously stubborn and antagonistic". As written in the History of Childhood a very large per centage of children born before the eighteenth century would today be called "battered children".

The Age of Real Enlightenment

By the eighteenth century, European society was becoming more child centered. Interest in proper care and management was increasing more children were being fed at their mothers' breasts no doubt saving countless lives; and swaddling was disappearing thereby leaving children free to interact with their caretakers. Popular family portraits showed children paying with their parents instead of than posing stiffly. During this period the formal deferential acts toward parents that were so much practiced in post-Renaissance family life were replaced by greater informality and less reliance on physical punishment to instill conformity. According to de Mause, it was the first evidence of children not being battered at all dates from the period 1690 to 1750. Before that time virtually all child-rearing tracts preached severe corporal punishment as a means of correcting the behaviour of children.

Ponting out changing attitudes, the Calvinist nation that children were innately depraved was superseded by the environmentalist theory that children were born neither good nor bad. Those who believed in environmentalist doctrine believed that a child was born a *tabula rasa,* a blank slate, to be shaped by human experience. John Locke, physician and philosopher, gave literacy and philosophical strength to this new conception of children in his seminal book, *Some Thoughts on Education* (1693). This treatise which had been reprinted 25 times by 1800, took a lighter view of flogging as an instrument of education. Locke taught that punishment was to be used in moderation only, and for very young children who had not yet achieved the powers of reason. He believed that greater reliance should be extended psychological punishments such as shame and guilt, or on moral persuasion. Locke urged that "fear and awe ought to give you the first power over their minds and love and friendship in riper years to hold it". Physical punishment was found not to be an effective tool of educating the young. The Geneven philosopher Jean-Jacques Rousseau took Locke's nation a step further by asserting the essential innocence of children. Although Rousseau assigned his own children to a foundling hospital, he played a crucial role in enhancing the place of children in society. One of the first writers of great stature to call attention to the special needs and rights of children, Rousseau stunned the world by not only disclaiming the belief that children were depraved but by claiming that they were born innocent and were corrupted by society's institutions. Opposed to child rearing practices like wet nursing and swaddling, Rousseau encouraged interest in the process of growing up, not merely in the end product. In Emile (1762), Rousseau teaches us to "love childhood, indulge its game, its pleasures, and its lovable nature.... why take from these little innocents the pleasure of a time so short which ever escapes them? .... Nature wants children to be children before they are men".

Child Labour

After the drawn of true renaissance, life may have improved by the nineteenth century for middle class children, existence was still hard for poor children. The Industrial Revolution increased the demand for cheap, unskilled labour, and many children were ideally suited working terribly long hours for meagre wages in taught conditions. Children as young as 4 and 5 years were regularly put to work in the mines and mills of England and America. Many risked their lives to health hazards. Abraham Jacobi, father of American pediatrics, became appalled at the plight of child life. He argued that, "Factory life is an abomination, and not only a cruelty committed against the individual child who is helpless, but a danger to the future of the republic, which cannot be expected to thrive while the physical and intellectual development of the future citizen is crippled by the greed of the manufacturers and the recklessness or partiality of legislatures".

These small tender creatures of the western countries especially of England and America who worked in the factories and mines fared little better than the chimney sweeps. Robbed of their childhood, very young children of even 5 years worked 16 hours a day, sometimes with iron rivets around their ankles to stop them from running away. To keep the working at a steady pace, children were dipped into cisterns of cold water or flogged by their employers. In the mines, thousands of male children worked as breaker boys separating coal from slate. Their hands would placed from the sharp stones; coal dust damaged their lungs; and, like old men, they had a permanent stoop. "You begin in the breaker," the miners said, "and end up at the breaker, broken yourself".

Attempts for regularisation of child labour were hindered both by powerful employers who needed cheap labour and by poor parents who needed the added income. Sometimes parents lied about their child's age in order to get him employment. It was a rare child, however, who retained any of his meagre wage. At the root of the problem of child labour was the severe poverty of the parents who were obliged to send their children to mills and factories. From with the struggle to curb child labour, many important social reforms evolved. As W. D. P. Bliss writes that, there is scarcely one subject in the whole range of social reform more important than that of child labour. Many of the reformers who opposed child labour, such as Homer Folks, Jane Addams and Florence Kelley, knew that the scaring institution could not be controlled without supplements to the family income of poor working parents. Some of the programs that stepped on the heels of child labour reform included mother's aid persons, workmen's compensation, minimum wage laws, and health insurance. The evolution of children's rights was so tightly tied to efforts to limit and control child labour that, when the United States Children's Bureau was established in 1912 as a governmental unit to assure the welfare and health of children, it was placed within the Department of Labour.

Pediatric Action Toward Child Abuse

Although physicians throughout the years have made many important contributions to improving the state of children, medicine as a profession did not officially recognize child abuse until the paper named. "The Battered Child Syndrome" was published in the Journal of the American Medical Association by C. Henry Kempe and his associates in 1962. The diagnosis of the "battered child syndrome" defended heavily on the work of pediatric radiologists who had observed cases of infants with bone fractures and internal wounds that could not easily be explained. Kempe and his associates criticized the medical profession for its reluctance to diagnose child abuse, which stemmed from physicians' emotional ties with their patients, denial of the facts, violation of their legal and moral responsibilities, and fear of being embroiled in controversy. Within a few years of the publication of this article, reporting laws were passed in all states making it compulsory for all health professionals to report suspected cases of abuse. Conferences and publications on child abuse multiplied, increasing public awareness and resulting in the passage of the Child Abuse Prevention Act of 1974. This act established a National Centre on Child Abuse and Neglect, and provided financial assistance for demonstration projects in the identification and treatment of abused children.

While summing up it is been said that when the United States Constitution was produced approximately 200 years ago, its authors made no mention of family matters, specifically relations between parents and children. This arrangement was neighter accident nor oversight as the founding fathers intentionally left it to the local communities to clarify the bounds of acceptable and unacceptable froms of child rearing. Communities were forced to question themselves what practices they considered abusive and harmful to children. Is corporal discipline acceptable? At what stage does it become abusive? What constitutes neglect? When should the state intervene in family matters to protect children from their parents? It is clearly this last question that devides those professionals and scholars who would limit state intervention only to extreme cases of physical abuse or sexual exploitation from those who would extend state intervention to include cases of the more unclear situations of psychological and emotional abuse and neglect.

If we look back into the pages of history, it is seen that the bounds of "reasonable" child-rearing practices have changed greately. Parents no longer have the power of life or death over their children. The difficult question is to decide what reasonable child-rearing practices should recognised be today. No society has gone beyond Sweden in limiting the prerogatives of parents in disciplining their children. In 1978 the Swedish Parliament passed laws restricting all forms of corporal discipline and verbal or emotional chastisement of children. While this law has not penalties for violators, it has set a new parameters for parent-child relations in that society. Child abuse has deep historical roots; it is interwoven the fabric of any society. A historical perspective allows us to appreciate how parents and other caregivers have behaved in relation to the values of their times. Contemporary confusion and conflict over the rights of children and the roles of professionals and the state in the lives of families are understandable in make of centuries of ambiguity about who children are and who should extent protection to them.

3

SLUMS: THE URBAN BIRTH PLACES OF CHILD ABUSE

As a citizen of India we all deserve equal rights provided by our constitution to enjoy against various risks of life and promotional opportunities as to enhance our physical, mental capacity and socio-economic status. Everybody needs a house, a important private rest place of human kind, which not only provides shelter but also keeps its own importance in nurturing and rearing of the children. In every house, children learns their first lesson of physical world. They get experienced, matured and become useful citizens of the nation. In fact, it is a place where birth, growth and death of its members take place. It provides opportunities to its members to enjoy the basic domestic life.

Children in a house, gets a separate or some sort of protected atmosphere where they are shaped according to the set values of the family. In a house parents and children both have opportunities to live together where they feel free in expressing their feelings and experiences without being formal to each other. Moreover, a house provides a kind of common platform to the members of the family to perform their roles in favour of the family's future and well-being. It gives opportunity to marry, satisfy sexual need, obtain family property, prosperity and happiness with the joint strength of the family.

Provision of good housing (Vagale, L.R. 1968) makes profound influence on community health, efficiency and social well-being of the people. Therefore, the significance sector needs to be emphasised. Experience show that housing has made easy locating welfare and developmental services at common place in an organised way to the individual, family and the people as a whole.

Shortage of Housing Developers

Under article 21, of the Directive Principles of State Policy, special provision has been indicated which says that the state shall secure adequate means of livelihood, raise the living standard and ensure economic justice. Here lies the significance of housing in an individual's life. However, the problem of housing is still a serious challenge to the policy-makers, planners and the agencies working for promotion of housing. The issue of housing shortage was also brought before the academicians for study, debate/discussion from time to time so that a low cost effective housing system can be evolved. But the problem seems to persist throughout the country with a different set of local issues related to it. The problem has become more serious in the metropolitan cities. As per census report in 1971, there were 14.5 million dewelling units which rose to 21.1 million in 1981, 24.7 million in 1985 and estimated 29.2 million dwelling units in 1990. Further, the break-up of rural-urban housing shortage was revealed in that it was 11.6 million in 1971 which rose to 16.5 million in 1981 in rural areas whereas in urban areas the shortage of housing was 2.9 million in 1971 and 4.8 million in 1981. It means the increased per centage of housing shortage from one decade to another was just double. According to the estimate made by National Building Organisation, in 1985 housing shortage in the country was 27.7 million of which 5.9 million was in urban areas. It was found that 50 per cent of the households live in one room and 27 per cent in two room units. In Bombay, about 77 per cent households occupy one room houses with common amenities. It has been reported that 35 million are living in slums in various parts of the country out of which over 13 million reside in metropolitan cities. In Bombay alone, about 50 per cent of its population reside in slums.

Study clearly indicates that we have acute shortage of housing in our country. (Chandramouli, M., 1981) has estimated that in urban India the homeless per lakh population is 374 whereas in rural areas it is 269. Similar views have been expressed by a National Sample Survey report. It further reveals that in urban areas 44 per cent households keep only one room and 28 per cent two rooms. 25 per cent household have plinths, walls and roofs of mud. Per capita floor space occupied by 21.10 per cent households comes on to 87.7 sq. ft. Only about 43 per cent households have supply of tap water. Poor housing and poor health-hygienic of the huts create more health problems to its occupants. A study led by the Planning Commission through academic institutions in certain cities (Chandramouli, 1981 reveals that majority of families lack basic civic services such as water supply, drainage, sewerage, latrines and conservancy services.

Surrounding Slums

Slums have become a universal phenomenon today. Although, the problem is considered to be a scene of filth and squalor as the area is covered with dingy streets, unkept rows of dilapidated houses, of overcrowding in tiny rooms without ventilation and most essential civic services. Even pacca built slums are found to be overcrowded, single room tenements, ill-ventilated and in an extremely poor state of habitation. Kacha huts that one finds in industrial sites have been constructed in an unplanned and congested manner on given land, with little or no essential services. Indeed the non availability of civic services is the basic problem for slum dweller and the others in their surroundings.

Slums Defined

The changing characteristics of slum-dwellers from one place to another and from one age to another has made definition also change. Therefore, the subject has been described in various terms according to the characteristics of the slum's locality.

On the basis of available literature on slums and definition given by the authors on the subject two set of approach is clearly seen in practices. A group of authors have defined the term on the basis of huts, there conditions and various essential facilities that slum lakhs. Another group of authors definitions are based on the characteristics as well as life-style of the slum dwellers and their dependents. Let us discuss the views of those authors first whose definitions are based on the quality of slum surroundings.

The Oxford Dictionary's meaning of slum is "as a street alley court, etc. situated in a crowded district of a town or city and inhabited by the people of low income class or by the very poor; a number of these streets and courts forming a thickly populated neighbourhood of a squalled and wretched character" of untidy crowded houses. It indicates that slum is a locality which is loaded with squall, definitions, dirt and disease, overcrowding and low-income group population.

As per UNESCO definition, "a slum is a building, a group of buildings or areas characterised by overcrowding, deterioration, unsanitary conditions or absence of facilities of amenities which, because of these conditions or any of them/endanger the health, safety or morals of its inhabitants or the community" (quoted by Anderson, 1960: 191).

In the words of Bengal, slum can be characterised as an area of substandard housing conditions within a city. Another in 1955 said, "a slum is always an area. A single, neglected building even in the worst stage of deterioration does not make a slum".

Clinard defined slum as inadequate housing, deficient facilities, overcrowding and congestion. Further he points out that it is a ways of life, a subculture with a set of norms and values which is visible in poor sanitation and health practices deviant behaviour and characteristic attributes of apathy and social isolation.

Government of Karnataka, Slum Clearance Act Karnataka

(i) any area is or is likely to be source of risk of life, safety or conscience of the public of that area, of its' neighbourhood, by reason of the area being low lying in hygiene, squalid, over crowded or otherwise.

(ii) the buildings in any area, used or intended to be used for human habitation areas:

(a) in any respect unfit for human habitation and

(b) by reason of dilapidation, overcrowding, faulty planning and design of such building, narrowness of faulty arrangement of street, lack of ventilation, light or sanitation facilities or any combination of these factor's threatening safety, health and moral. It may by notification declare such area to be a slum area:

Some definitions given by authors, based on quality and characteristics of the slum dwellers life are as below:

In the words of Contant, "in each one (of the largest American cities) one can find neighbourhoods composed of various minority groups, many of these areas are now designed as culturally deprived or 'culturally different' but earlier they could have been more simply designated as slum".

A Washington conference in 1931 explained that slum area is visible area of disintegration and disorganisation.

It is, however, not only the decaying and dilapidated houses, the filthy alleys and streets, nor the unlimited number of children and poverty stricken adults which make up the slum, the slum is more than an economic condition. It is a social phenomenon in which the attitudes, ideas, ideals and rituals play an important part.

One more definition by Zorbaugh is that, "the slum is distinctive area of disintegration and disorganisation. It is an area in which encroaching business extents a speculative value to the land. But rents are low: because little business has actually come into the area, it is no longer desirable for residential purpose".

On the basis of the study of slums in Latin America Oscar Lewis has developed a new concept which he says as culture of poverty and further states that culture of poverty can be seen as it is:

(1) Lack of effective involvement and integration of the poor in the major institutions.

(2) Low wages, unending unemployment problem and under-employment, lack of income, absence of saving food etc.

(3) They are aware of middle class values but do not live by them.

(4) Poor housing conditions, over crowding, beyond the standards of the nuclear and extended family.

(5) Early entry to sex, free unions or consensual marriages: a high level of abandonment of wives and children.

(6) Feeling of helplessness, dependence and inferiority and backwardness.

(7) High incidence of material deprivation, weak ego levels, strong feeling for present time, no hope for future and high tolerance for psychological pathology of all sorts.

National Sample Survey Organisation (1976-77) mentioned the following important conditions relating to slum:

(1) Density of human habitation in the slum as compared to the city, i.e., overcrowding.

(2) Tenurial pattern of the area whether rented or possessed by the residents.

(3) Pattern of ownership of dwelling units.

(4) Availability of basic amenities and facilities like water, approach road, electricity, latrine sewerage system etc. unsatisfactory.

(5) Economic condition in the slum as compared to the city, i.e., poverty for want of avenues, incapacitating the residents to look up in life.

A number of terms have been used to define the slum area which differ from one city to another. Jhuggi-Jhopri or JJ. colonies katra in Delhi; dhakka and deha basti in Kurukshetra; bustee in Calcutta; cheri and chawl in Bombay. In foreign countries—calumpass in Brazil; favellas alagados in Mexico, etc. Academicians and planners on the basis of slum conditions, have used different names to refer the slum habitats. Some of the commonly used terms are: blighted area, deteriorated area, inner core area, lower class neighbourhood, low income residential area, marginal area, unplanned settlement, uncontrolled settlement, spontaneous settlement, provisional settlement etc.

On the basis of definitions given by the author and the agencies, it indicates that slum is not a kind of condition which does not emerge spontaneously but it is a gradual creation that develops out of the socio-economic and cultural conditions of the people in a particular settlement which one finds in the form of physical, mental, moral and social backwardness of the human kind, overcrowded, dilapidated, unhealthy conditions of locality which lack proper facilities of health, water, sewerage, latrine, education etc. Some important characteristics on the basis of previous definitions are listed below:

(1) Improper facilities of housing, water, sanitation, road, health, education, electricity, latrine and welfare services for dependants and handicaps.

(2) Highly populated, lack or ventilation, proper street and unhygienic locality, loaded with subcultural norms of their own culture groups that differ from one group of Jhuggis to another even in the same locality.

(3) Sub-standard socio-economic condition. By and large their work, relationship, standard of living and future, etc., are guided by their own tradition. They kept sub-organisations even at community level, prepared to pick up even anti-social means available for their livelihood and they face underemployment and unemployment. They plan for present, not for future, pick up lower means of income and have mobile life-style.

(4) Feelings of helplessness, dependence inferiority, insecurity, sense of resignation, high level of tolerance, higher ignorance and visible abuse of women and children in the pockets.

Difficulties Associated with Slums

The major motivation for people's migration from rural to urban area has been to look for work for their livelihood. Other factors that one notices are increasing population pressure, decreasing availability of shelter and love of the parents to their unemployed and defendants in poor rural families. These are the factors which force the needy and poor to leave their families and move towards cities where there is availability of job opportunities. There are some more factors like desire for higher education, pleasant city climate and some other better facilities have been found responsible for people's migration to urban areas, but the helpless migrated people who find it expensive only to live in rented houses give birth to slums. Due to these reasons only during 1941-51 there had been largest migration to Madras involving more than 17 lakh people. Next comes Bombay slums with 16 lakhs. The higher increase of urban population has been noticed in Tripura which comes 93 per cent among males and 93 per cent in females as compared to 47 and 60 pe rcent respectively in Delhi.

Division of India in 1947 has been found another important occasion when about 62 lakh Muslims left the country and nearly 70 lakhs migrated from across the border. Delhi and other big cities were accessible to them. In Delhi alone a high number of migrated population squatted on roads, footpaths and on unauthorised government land. This has caused the problem of slum in the city. Along with the shortage of accommodation on cheap rate in the city and perpetual poverty which prevailed all round, complete ignorance of urban life style, community and caste solidarity have been the important reasons which led the migrated population to remain in compact basties which helped them to maintain the village neighbourhood pattern in the area. Gradually, slum basties have sprung us as migrant pressure and beyond the scope of civic bodies to improve it. An estimate shows (Gupta, G.R. 1983: 2480) that one-fifth to one-fourth of the population of any Indian city lives in slums. During late 50's, nearly 24 per cent of Delhi population lived in katras and basties (BBB, 1958: 1911:93). During 60s, 71 per cent people had only less than 50 square yards area (Rao and Desai, 1965: 432-488) in Delhi.

According to Planning Commission (Task Force) estimate, in 1981 slum population in India was between 32-40 million which constituted 20-25 per cent of the total urban population. The National Buildings Organisation (NBO) in 1981 estimated nearly 19 per cent of Indian population are in slums. In class one cities the per centage of slum population is 18.12 of the urban population.

Bombay Municipal Corporation held that there were 85 slum localities before the Second World War which rose to 206 zopada-patty colonies with 108 to 273 huts in 1969. Bangalore city had 195 slums in 1973 which increased to 287 in 1982. The total slum population that is more than 3 lakhs had been packed into 3451 areas or 11 per cent of the total corporation area of the city.

Calcutta is another slum populated city in the country where some of the basties have often one water tap for over 200 persons (Sen, 1960: 160-161). Another sample survey report submitted by District Authority (CMDA) reveals that 33.8 per cent house had no permanent wall.

In the case of Ambedkar camp in Nehru Place in New Delhi, a population living in about 17,000 huts clustered together for the last fourteen years. They have been labelled as encroachers for whom Capital has yet to plan out resettlement issue. Till then, they live without basic facility that is imperative for life. A survey (H.T. 1994) sponsored by the C. Achutha Menon Foundation and conducted on behalf of (HDFC) has found that only one-fourth of the male population had regular employment. The broad division of employment involved the formal sector occupations in the public sector and large private sector concerns. Whereas caste occupations like shoe-making or pottery had a little in number. The rest of them get employment only casually at construction sites, repair or other manual jobs.

Slum people do not live in illusions, as far as the problems of their daily lives are concerned. Even after repeated requests, they have not been provided with electricity and consequently each one of them has illegal connections. The slum wing has provided some hand pumps, but each one of them dried up within months of installation. The female population mostly works as domestic help in the surrounding bungalows. Most of the women are the sole breadwinners in the family consisting of at least three generations as the parents-in-law also usually live with them. The average income varies from Rs. 1,000 to 15,000 a month. Most of the families have settled here permanently as they have nothing to hold back to their roots. Most of them are not even able now to trace out their own migratory background. Despite all this, there is an obvious attempt to maintain their own regional identity. The clusters mostly consist of people migrated from the same area and sometimes from same caste origin. The scheduled caste people prefer to live with their own community, so do the OBCs and other castes.

In human living conditions of these unsung, unknown heroes are far from being enviable. Their huts are so small that they enter them only when too tired or ill to move out. The plot of land has been given to them by the former settlers at the cost of Rs. 500 to 1000. Sometimes they manage to construct two rooms to sublet one on a rent of Rs. 200 to 300. These dwellings have neither ventilation nor any outlet for filth. Consequently, the gullies, that are hardly a meter wide, are always slushy and it is unimaginable to walk without saving through the filth. Some of them have small ditches at their doorsteps which serve as the dirtcans never to be cleared. Children play around in the dirt with relish though many of them have got severe skin infections.

Speaking about health aspect, out of each family in the area, atleast two persons are suffering from chest diseases, malaria, diarrhoea, tuberculosis, and viral fever. Several cases of AIDS have also been sighted but there has been absolutely no effort to generate any awareness against these dreadful diseases. The patients usually go to a far off Government hospital or to registered medical practitioners who charged them high but can offer no respite.

A social worker of slums, Balram, complained that the Government hospital in the adjoining area could not provide him with proper medication, and he was forced to stretch beyond his financial limits to get his father treated. Balram himself is suffering from fever and skin problems, but is undeterred in his attempts to find respite for the jhuggi dwellers. Preeti is a two-year old who suffered from chicken-pox a year back. Now she has a bloated stomach and wounds all over her body. She is unable to walk or talk. There are several cases like Preeti waiting in vain to grow in a world that hardly cares for them. These kids are left to themselves as their mothers have to go out for domestic helps.

There are supposed to be twelve anganwadis and according to records, eight are working. But in reality, only two are functional with attendants paid only scantily. There are three Government schools around the area, but none of them is less than two kilometres away. The school going children cannot afford to take a bus always, so usually they have to walk. Most of them fall ill frequently on the regularity cannot be maintained and once the process in disrupted they either opt to join their parents in their work or sit at home. As a result, crime rate is also going up alongwith the other vices like drugs, etc.

In some areas, flesh trade is also quite common. These areas are not only visited by the hutment dwellers but also other sections of the society. Kidnapping and trading of the fair sex is also not unusual though people usually hesitate to talk about such incidents. The hutments are built around a ditch which is atleast 250 ft. in diameter and 20 ft. deep. The slush from the ditch spreads into the huts during rainy weather and people have to live in the muck itself.

When the slum wing of DDA was contacted on the issue, their blunt reply was "try to live with the filth, because if the ditch is cleared, it would be barred for the local residents who are actually encroachers into the green belt area". There have also been cases of agencies approaching them with dream like proposals of housing societies. One of them made collection of Rs. 180 each from 300 hutment dwellers. But two years have passed and they have not returned.

Due to the unauthorised character of the area, the residents cannot get bank loans. In moments of financial crisis, they depend on the local treasurer who charges quite high interest rate.

Inspite of all this, the inhabitants have not lost their sense of belonging to the main street of the capital. The socially claim their share in the urban neighbourhood of the metro cities that remains antagonistic to their existence.

According to a survey (Rao, V.G. Prasad, 1975), "one-third of city population lives in slums". In Ahmedabad as per 1971 census figure, there were about 2,50,000 slum dwellers and 9000 pavement dwellers. Nowadays one finds that almost every city country is suffering from the problem of slum dwellers in one form or the other. Sixth Five-Year Plan estimate showed Indian slum population at about 20 per cent of the total urban population. National Building Organisation estimates that 39.77 per cent of slum dwellers live in metropolitan cities, 34 per cent in cities (which comes between 1,00,000 and one million) and rest in other areas. Some more detailed information available on slum population given below provides clarity about its extent in some of the major cities in India.

No. of Slums Dwellers Year and Citywise

Year	Ahmed abad	Bangalore	Bombay	Calcutta	Delhi	Madras
1976-77	5.4%	1.7%	6.6%	5.5%	7.6%	9.9%
1981	8.0%	3.0%	28.3%	32.3%	18.0%	13.6%
1990	11.1%	10.4%	41.3%	43.9%	32.1%	21.1%

Source: India Today, Jan. 31, 1998 quoted in Shankar, J. *Social Problems and Welfare in India,* Ashish Pub. New Delhi, 1992, p.300.

Statistics shows in the table reveal gradual increase of slum dweller population from one year to another in all the cities mentioned in the table. In some cities rate of increase is as high as about eight times in Calcutta seven times in Bombay and ten times in Bangalore from 1976-77 to 1990 which requires attention of the programme planners and policy makers for its control, clearance and rehabilitation.

(A) Slum Rehabilitation of Slum Dewellers

In order to bring change in the total environment of the slums and to provide new houses the Indian Government has initiated the following three types of schemes:—

(I) Slum clearance or rehousing to the slumdwellers.

(II) Improvement of slums clusters.

(III) Sites and Services.

In the year 1952, the Government of India introduced the subsidized scheme of house construction for workers with 50 per cent capital subsidy and remaining 150 per cent loan by the Government which was extended to slim dwellers in 1957-58. Upto 1969 only 72584 dwellings were benefited against 1,13,550 units sanctioned under the scheme. Houses for weaker sections were later integrated with the scheme. Under this scheme, provision was also made to give loan and subsidy to state housing agencies. For the construction of houses at subsidised rate upto 1997, a sum of Rs. 125 crores was spent which constructed more than 1,85,000 houses under the scheme in.

However, after experiencing some difficintly in the scheme 1977, it was thought to transfer the scheme to the occupiers at actual cost on hire purchase basis. The scheme introduced for re-housing of slum families having income upto Rs. 350 per month by the construction of single multi-storeyed tenements in metropolitan and other big cities. Constructed about 1,69,000 dwellings in many big cities including Bombay, Pune, Solapur etc. However, in of low rent and maintenance problem, constructed tenements were shifted to the existing occupiers. Prof. Willizz (1963) who was formerly with the Ford Foundation in Calcutta did great work in slum rehabilitation and said "for slum clearance and rehousing scheme the Government of India grants direct subsidies and low-interest loans to State Governments. They also stipulate specifications for re-development schemes, suggest tenant classifications and set maximum rents. At present the programme (now being considered for upward revision) sets the ceiling for construction at Rs. 6600 per family in Calcutta in Units of 232 square feet. The maximum income of an eligible family is set at Rs. 250, per month and the maximum rent is Rs. 21.50 per month. In short, the Government of India stands ready to shoulder part of the slum clearance and rehousing costs provided that the costs are kept within reasonable time. Housing must conform to decent standard, so that old slums are not replaced with publicly built new slums. Ceilings are set on the income of the families and rents to ensure that poor people benefit from the programme. However, survey report (Bhardwaj, R.K. 1974) prepared on the programme revealed that after slum clearance not more than 30 per cent and the slum dwellers settle in Basties, denying estates and the rest for reasons of earning go to the slums in the adjoining areas.

(B) Betterment of Slums Areas

One more scheme which has been introduced by the Government after experiencing the sheer inadequately of effort regarding huge magnitude of the problem, organisational and financial constraints, and the appropriate nature of the salvation of the housing problem in the slums was slums improvement. The scheme was started in 1972. Under this scheme, State Governments get financial assistance to provide basic amenities such as community water supply, community toilets, store-water drains, street lighting and paved pathways. This scheme is subsidized by the State Government. The implementation of the scheme is done by the respective Municipa; body of the city and the State slum clearance Board. In 1985 about 15 million persons got basic amenities out of an estimated 33 million population. Now, under this scheme, aid for home improvement has been added. Under the 5th plan, cities having population of 3 lakhs or more were included in the programme. Now the scheme is under State Control and experiencing some problems in its proper implementation. Since the scope of the scheme is limited, there are some cities/areas which have been left out of the programme.

(C) Previous Sites and Services

With the purpose of generating a large number of dowelling units and encouraging people to construct their own houses on incremental self-help basis, the State Government has decided to change its stress to construction of dwelling sites rather than puçca houses to the needy and the poor. The World Bank approved a major project in this regard for Bombay and Thane where 65,000 sites were proposed to be started by 1985-86. Similar projects under sites and services scheme have been taken up in some other major cities. Under this scheme, plots are made available to various income groups at affordable price with an initial payment and the balance repayable over 20 years. In order to provide financial assistance to the beneficiaries through HUDCO or cooperative housing finance societies under the active supervision of the MHADA, DDA undertook a massive operation of clearance of squatter colonies and rehabilitation of 80,000 families in 27 newly developed colonies. Similarly, by 1976, 70,000 more families were shifted and 70,000 sites were identified under the programme. Besides, the programme has been responsible for socio-economic problems faced by the slum dwellers while shifting from one settlement to another and adjusting in new areas. The scheme has also been extended to the industrial areas where needy and poor workers are in need of this facility. Workers engaged in bidi-making and handloom weaving are being benefited under the scheme by the Government. A major project for construction of 3000 houses for Bidi workers in Sholapur has been initiated by the Central Labour Ministry and State Government. Similar projects have been sanctioned for other sites/slums like Pune, Jalna, Kamit etc.

What else, the General Assembly of the United Nations had officially declared 1987 as the International Year of Shelter for the Homeless with the purpose "to improve the shelter and neighbourhoods of some of the poor and disadvantaged by 1987, and particularly in developing countries according to nation priorities and to demonstrate by the year 2000 ways and means of improving the shelter and neighbourhoods of the poor and disadvantaged". The limited IYSH funds were spent to support and stimulate national and local action through actual shelter demonstration projects. Such project which already in existence for the pre-1987 period, new approaches to such basic problems as improving or providing; drinking water supply, sanitation and waste disposal, betterment environmental health conditions and services, and providing low-cost constructing techniques and materials with use of local skills, methods and materials.

To strengthen these programmes, a number of improvement trusts are set-up in housing colonies and cities like Delhi, Madras, Bombay, Calcutta etc. These trusts are involved in acquisition of land in identified areas, land development and disposal of plots at the rate of pre-determined prices. Further' on the positive achievements of the trust, it was decided to set up State level specialised agencies for slum clearance. This will help to have accurate number of houses for various groups of needy by mobilising funds available from various sources. The Housing Board has been established in all the States by the State Government and some of the State Governments have set up additional agencies for special group like slum habitants weaker sections and for the rural people.

The resettling of the jhuggi dwellers in planned colonies was conceived in 1975 by Sanjay Gandhi at the time of Emergency. The squatter settlements in Nizamuddin, Shahdra, Ajmeri Gate, Delhi Gate and some other areas were cleared by the concerned authorities and the slum dwellers were shifted to these resettlement colonies. Each one of them was paid Rs. 2000/- as bank loan to construct a one room house in a 25 sq. ft. area. They were given electricity, water connection, open spaces for green belt and especially in Trilokpuri, a sprawling park with a lake named after Sanjay Gandhi. Each house holder was supposed to pay a rent of Rs. 8 to the DDA and the houses were given on lease to the dwellers. However, after almost two and a half decades, the scenario has changed drastically. The sprawling park has turned into heaps of filth, the lake is spoiled and cannot be used in any way except for mosquito breeding. Electricity supply has become so scant that almost every house has illegal connections.

Regarding ownership also, in Trilokpuri resettlement, a major section was no more owned by the original allottes. Most of the houses that were built 25 years back at the cost of Rs. 10,000 or so are now being sold at Rs. 75,000 and more. Most of them are double storeyed and some of them have even beautifully shaped terraces with flower pots, etc. Almost all the households have sublet a room or two. There are also plots that were connected together, sold and boundary wall had been erected around the area with a locked gate. The population residing here have a higher literacy rate that other areas. Along with beldars, masons, tailors, the—lawallahs, rickshaw pullers and the fourth grade employees of various public and private sector concerns, other higher class professionals like clerks, school teachers, journalists, etc. have also came to live.

Area of Trilokpuri is a perfect sample of the changing character of the urban poor. They cannot be categorised exactly as the backward sections of the population as almost every house has a television set, sofas, coolers and quite often a fridge also. Their growing aspirations can be noticed in the changes in their life style with a notion of a comfortable living space decorated with curtains, flower posts, etc. Many of them have their own scooters too.

More important is to note that though the average income of the population does not exceed Rs. 3000 to Rs. 3500 including the earnings of the female population that usually work as domestic help, the living standard are much better than the other slum areas. The aspiration to privide a better life to the family makes each of them to work after their regular hours. Some of them drive three whellers and rickshaws while other have vending *thelas* and small vegetable shops where they work in the evening. The regular employees in public sector and other big concerns to prefer to use profitably their personal skills as painting, white washing, scooter repairing, etc. in their extra time. The process of modernisation has offered the new roots a basis on which they are yet to recreate their own new values and norms. They are no more from the lower depths as they are taking active part in the creation of a new superstructure that promises drastic changes in the status quo. They will be form a world without exploitation or with equality in distribution but the sufferings will be shared by the collective as will be the dreams.

In nutshell, all the three types of programmes introduced for the better housing of the slum dwellers do not meet the need of the increasing population of slum dwellers in the Indian cities. Therefore, programmes deserve rethinking in their planning and execution at different levels. In order to overcome the housing problem of slum inhabitants accessible programme needs to be developed. In the absence of an effective programme, the problem continuous to persist in most of the Indian cities where the quality of life of slum dwellers has been lowering and is likely to be fully covered with risks and dangers. Slum dwellers' participation in the programmes initiated either for environmental improvement, or resettlement and welfare of children, youth, old persons, handicapped and other dependents would be a great salvation to the present difficulties of the neglected slum dwellers in the country.

Child Survival in Slums

It is a well established fact that a human being is the product of his environment that he receives in the family as well as in the community in the stages of his development. Among these two agencies, family comes as the first and an outstanding social institution which constitutes community and plays a significant role in the socialization of its young and dependents. Carr (1950) has written "functionally adequate home encourages growth, confidence, respect for personality, ability to face reality. It means functionally adequate home is an emotionally healthy home."

Slum family is unfortunately loaded with poverty and some more problems of one or another nature, where slum dwellers are led to avail any type of its profits. Zorbaugh (1929) observes: "slum is a distinctive area of disintegration and disorganisation. It is an area in which encroaching business lends as speculative value to the land. But rents are low. For while little business has actually come into the area, it is no longer desirable for residential purposes". A slum is an area of freedom and individualism. Over large stretches of slum people neighter know nor trust their neighbours. A majority of the native population is transient prostitutes, criminals and outlaws. By and large, slum children are grawn in kind of traditional and defective social environment in which they set motivation to pick up anti-social characteristics such as smoking, gambling, alcoholism, stealing, abusing others and disrespect towards their parents. Sutherland and Cressey (1955) observed that "no child is so constituted at birth that it must inevitably be law abiding and family is the first agency to affect the direction which a particular child will take".

Improper constructions and compulsion of 6-7 members (including adult and the children) living in a single hut, provide opportunities to the children to learn adult behaviour which their age, maturity and development should not have received otherwise. Similarly, disrupting community health and hygiene due to non-availability of basic civic services in the Indian slums, the health status of children seems to be extremely undergrowth and they suffer from the problem of malnutrition. Mumford (1970) has rightly observed "that the main elements in the new urban setup were the factory, the railroad and the slum. The slums present a sense of filth and squalor with dingy streets, zigzag rows of dilapidated houses, over-crowding in tiny rooms and totally inadequate basic services."

These slums have unhealthy consequences on the individual and community. The effect on health is ruinous, the general health rate is poor and infant mortality rates are very high; a higher per centage of children and adolescents suffers from many deficiencies and diseases. Decent family life is virtually a dream. The facilities for healthy recreation are poor and the level of community services is low. By discussing the problem of payment dwellers including their children Venkat Raman (1978) says that they are suffering in their eyes, misery in their face and hunger in the stomach, they present a miserable picture. They live in great distress and strain and traverse great distances before they get job to make a living.

People living in slum have picked up the work of casual labourers, rickshaw pullers, hawkers, car drivers, shoe-shining children, casual workers employed in small establishments and men without any work. An important urban sociologist Gist and Hadbert (1956) writes, "slum is an area of poor houses and poor people. It is an area of transition and decadence, a disorganised area occupied by human derelicts, a catch-all for the criminal, for the defective the down and out". Often, children in these slums do not go to school as their traditional belief and mobility characteristic do not motivate them to receive education. Those who attend, in absence of an approachable school, poor parent's motivation and their own negative mental make up on education, they drop out after two or three years of their schooling. Then either they are put at work to supplement the family income or those who do not find work to earn, join the gangs of the delinquent children which nourishes delinquency into them. Those who come from broken families even after working, in the absence of partial control and guidance to regulate their behaviour and manage their earning, they gct encouragement to develop anti-social characteristics. Girls rarely attend the school. Even of they attend they drop out earlier than boys due to possibility of marriage, care of young or siblings the family and doing household chores. Children of physically handicapped spiritually despair parents inherit their total lot of the disappointments and anger. Overpopulation (Rai, A. N. 1973) is the characteristic of slum life and is a psychological challenge to child's sense of individuality because he is so rarely alone. He does not find a contented life. Brought into unavoidable contact with adult weakness and greed, children find it tough to build up identification with hero-parents and other ideals. Overpopulation and talk of privacy makes the physical aspect of sexual life primary instead of realising it as largely the symbol of idiomatic personal relationship. A study conducted by Thakur and Dhadave (1987) in Gulbarga city, Karnataka observed that by and large family in these slums consists of 6-7 members. Slum dwellers are engaged as domestic servants, vendors, hawkers, drivers of bullock carts and tongas, unskilled and semi-skilled workers and as beggars.

To sum up, all this indicates over all defective environment and quality of children's life, where they are face hardship, advertises, denials, deprivation, cruelties, injustice and neglect which have adverse impact on their ability to live happily in their adulthood and the foundation of future society is weakened. Unless the problem is undertaken significantly with adequate resources, there are chances of meeting hundreds of millions of child labour and more members ill, handicapped, delinquents, neglected, and abused children in the years to come.

Section—II

CHILD LABOUR

4

CHILD LABOUR: GENESIS AND DIMENSIONS

Evil pertaining to children have persisted world over, in all societies and all communities irrespective of any regional barriers. The most prominent of these has been child labour which first came into existence in a wide spread form in Europe especially England after the industrial resolution. But it does not mean that India is devoid of it. We, the people of India have been practising it on a very large scale.

It was in practice in Indian society from time immemorial but the nature and extent of severity was different. Children gave helping hands to their parents in the household chores and also in family occupations. Various Sanskrit books have shown how children in Indian families shared the work-load of their parents and of their teachers during their Brahmachary period (study-life). The famous story of Krishna and Sudama clearly tells that children (students) were used by their gurus for carrying out certain household chores.

In the modern period with the advent of new industrial culture, this practice has assumed an alarming proportion only to draw the attention of social workers, philanthropists and social activists to its various drawbacks. It was never a problem till children were used as helping hands. The need for more production at cheaper costs and the motive to earn more and more resulted in using the helping hands as hard working hands. Various social organisations and reformers took serious notice of this practice and raised hue and cry. Consequently, it attracted attention of the gout. Parliamentarians and social scientist who made tremendous attempts to understand this problem from different angles.

A number of studies have been conducted in different sectors and states to determine the origin, nature and extent of child labour. Regarding its origin, it is difficult to give any specific date or time period when it would have come to existence. But various studies undertaken to discover the causal factors and others aspects of child labour themselve throw light on its origin and evolution:

(1) Back ground of child labour.

(2) Child Labour: A Glimpse.

India has the largest number of child labourers in the world. 70-80 million children in India begin work at a very early age. Child workers toil, at an average, for 12 hours every day and each are contributes 20 per cent of India's GNP. In return they receive an average salary of Rs. 90 a month; emotional and often physical abuse; incalculable damage to their health before they are even 14; limited access to education, food, water and shelter; the complete loss of their invaluable childhood; an underpaid or unemployed status as adults; and an entire lifetime of frail health and penury.

Defining Child Labour

"Child"

According to the constitution of India, anyone below the age of 14 is a child.

The United Nations Convention on the Rights of the Child says, anyone below the age of 18 year is child.

"Child Labour"

International Labour Organisation. "Child labour includes children prematurely leading adult lives, working long hours for low wages, under conditions damaging to their health and to their physical and mental development, sometimes separated from their families, frequently deprived of meaningful education and training opportunities that could open up for them a better future."

Encyclopaedia of Social Sciences. "When the business of wage earning or of participation in self or family support conflicts directly or indirectly with the business of growth and education, the result is child labour. The function of work in childhood is primarily developmental and not economic. Children's work, then, as a social good is the direct antithesis of child labour as a social evil."

Some Voluntary Groups. Any non-school going child is a child labourer.

Campaign Against Child Labour. (A national network of organizations working to cradicate child labour), Child labour includes children prematurely leading adult lives, working with or without wages, under conditions harmful to their physical, social, emotional and spiritual development, denying them their basic rights to education, health and development. This includes children working in any sector, profession or process, including the formal and non-formal, organised and unorganised, within outside the family.

The estimates on the magnitude of child labour in India may vary for different sources but the fact in that they are always on the rise.

13.06 million : The 1981 Census

17.36 million: The Planning Commission, 1983.

44 million : The Operations Research Group, Baroda, 1983.

20 million : Labour Minister, August 1994, when he announced a plan to "liberate" 20 million working children in hazardous employment.

All these estimates fall short of the actual figure for a number of reasons. There are, multiplicity of definitions; by difference authorities; different methods of computation; diverse sources of data; lack of information on the large unorganised sector of the economy which, in fact, employs the most children; non-inclusion of domestic workers. Recent estimates are based on ,the number of families living below the poverty line.

As per the finding of the Balai Data Bank, Manila, if nearly half of India's over 800 million population lives in poverty, the number of working children in India is likely to be over 100 million. According to the estimates of the Commission on Labour Standards and International Trade, Government of India, population of child labourers in India is 77 million, in 1995. Estimate have been computed on the basis of families living below the poverty line; and NGO's networks on child labour in India, estimate that there are 70-80 million child labourers, based on the number of non-school going children and families living in destitution.

Various Dimensions of Child Labour

Child labour is an unbiquitous phenomenon as evident in the following table. Child labour can be broadly classified into the following categories:

(A) Child labour covered by legislation

(B) Child labour falling outside the legislative framework

(a) Agriculture and allied activities.

(b) Informal, unorganised semi-urban and urban sector.

The other aspects of child labour which are not exclusive include, child labour in bondage; child labour

Trends in Index of Child Labour in India : Prominent Industries, 1961-1991 and Projections to 2001
Index Box : 1961=100

Industries	*Rural Male*				*Rural Male*				*Urban Male*				*Urban Female*			
	1971	*1981*	*1991*	*2001*	*1971*	*1981*	*1991*	*2001*	*1971*	*1981*	*1991*	*2001*	*1971*	*1981*	*1991*	*2001*
Cultivators	72	68	76	65	24	35	39	34	80	96	122	121	19	35	47	47
Agricultural Labourers	170	157	174	149	110	137	156	133	227	285	356	355	132	205	275	273
Household Industry	18	21	23	19	23	32	36	31	66	79	100	100	41	60	81	81
Manuf. (other than household)	133	246	272	232	139	271	307	261	128	194	244	243	127	261	375	349
Construction	90	112	126	108	76	155	169	143	105	142	180	180	80	104	144	143
Trade and commerce	113	129	140	120	47	72	76	64	193	226	283	283	87	128	172	171
Transport, storage and Comm.	118	112	128	109	247	164	354	301	205	183	226	226	282	118	200	199
Mining	91	70	77	66	75	76	87	74	79	73	93	93	75	74	103	102
Other Services	45	26	29	25	30	23	26	22	61	58	73	73	82	108	145	144
Total	90	82	91	78	49	63	72	61	107	131	164	164	72	109	145	144

Source : Chaudhri D.P., *A Dynamic Profile of Child Labour in India - 1951-1991*, CLASP-ILO, New Delhi : p. 45, 1996.

within and with families; girl child labour; child labour separated from families; child labour which is itinerant.

(A) Child Labour Covered by Legislation

The laws cover 15 per cent of the child labour force who are in the formal, industrial sector, in occupations identified as "hazardous" under the law and working on plantations. In the chapter on concerns for child labour, we shall discussed various legal provisions of national and international level pertaining to child labour. Except in the process of family based work or recognised school based activities, children not allowed to work in occupations that are hazardous. These are:

1. Passenger, goods, mail transport by Railway
2. Carpet weaving
3. Cinder picking, cleaning of ash pits
4. Cement manufacturing
5. Building operation, construction
6. Cloth printing
7. Dyeing, weaving
8. Manufacturing of matches, explosives, fireworks.
9. Catering establishments in railway premises or port limits.
10. Beedi making
11. Mica cutting, splitting
12. Abattoirs
13. Wool cleaning
14. Cashew and cashewnut descaling and processing.
15. Soldering processes in electronic industries.

In certain occupations, the number of child labour is so high that according to estimates, the number of child labourers in the Tea Plantations of West Bengal, Assam and some parts of South India only stands at 82, 140.

Estimates of the number of children employed in Sivakasi's fireworks industry range from 30,000 to 70,000. Children the match industry of Tamil Nadu, aged between three-and-a-half and 15, work in dark and grimy sheds, in a horrified position, handling dangerous and poisonous chemicals. They are carried in buses from their villages to the work sites from 3 a.m. to 5 a.m. and dropped back at home between 6 p.m. and 9 p.m. During the busy season a weekly day off is refused. Children are exposed to numerous hazards which include: the possibility of getting burnt while making the matches, inhaling lungfulls of toxic fumes, high degrees of intense heat and the risk of serious injury in fire accidents. Children in the carpet making sector work for 12 hours daily, sitting on their haunches or with legs dangling down pits to get close to the thread. Unventilated workplaces ruin their eyes, they are at risk of lung diseases from inhaling wool fluff, knotting makes their hand joints stiff and arthritic; by the age of 30, they are unemployed.

Industries like zari-weaving, glass manufacture, lock-making, gem-polishing, rag-picking, cleaning sewers, and many others are "non-hazardous" by law, but are in reality highly harmful. The most hazardous job for children is to carry the molten glass on a long rod. They have to run at a fast speed on a floor which is full of glass pieces and naked wires,.so that the molten material does not get cold. Children sit on the floor for hours in front of the flaming furnaces, melting and fastening glass bangels and beads. No child worker is given protective equipment. They have to constantly inhale toxic fumes emanating from the boiling glass, the colouring material, and the coal furnaces which damage the lungs, liver and other vital organs. Prolonged exposure to the extraordinary heat causes various grades of skin burn and irreversible visual damage. Children also suffer mental retardation and genetic damage. In 1992 only, India exported more than $ 2 million worth of glass and glassware to the United States.

(B) Child Labour Falling Outside the Legislative Framework

Existing legislation do not cover the majority of child labour who are to be found in, (I) the unorganised, rural sector of Agriculture and allied activities which employs 86.4 per cent of child labour according to the 1981 Census. The absolute number of urban male child agricultural labourers in 1961 was 33,180. It grew to 75,369 in 1971 and to 94,642 in 1981. According to estimates the number in 1991 is 118,153 at an all India level. Its distribution across the states varies enormously. The absolute number of urban girl child workers in 1961 was 28,510. It rose to 37,557 in 1971 and to 58,553 in 1981. The estimated number for 1991 is 37,271. The two combined are about 150 thousand urban child agricultural labourers whose work must be considered at least as hazardous as that in some of the most difficult urban industries. Female children are primarily engaged in collecting fuel/fodder, Fetching drinking water, weeding, poultry keeping, and food processing. Boys are primarily engaged in ploughing/Digging, threshing/harvesting, grazing cattle, tool-related activities, carrying goods, purchase/sale in markets. (II) A major section of the workforce in urban India is "unorganised": Workers who have not been able to form unions. Children in factories are not regarded as workers because their employment is illegal. The vast unorganised sector manages to evade all laws (such as the Factories Act of 1948) and legislation covering such industries because of the small size of the units or by falsification of records. Many of these units or industries, in spite of their known unorganised status, are highly organised or have direct links in a vastly organised system. Exploitation of child labour in these units is infact perpetuated by the involvement of the bigger and formal sector.

The list of occupations in the informal, unorganised sector given below is not exhaustive:

(a) Construction Labour

(b) Couriers

(c) Domestic workers

(d) Porters

(e) Sweepers and waste re-cyclers

(f) Factories/Workshops (e.g.) hosiery units

(g) Tanneries

(h) Vendors

(i) Helpers in restaurants, shops, canteens, garages

(j) Shoe-shiners

(k) Sex workers.

Bonded Child Labour

Bondage is enslaving; it enables the employer to assume ownership rights over the child. The child is 'sold' for a small amount of money, borrowed for various purposes. Once sold, he/she gives away all basic rights. Rural indebtedness is one of the most important causes of child labour in India. Children are bonded with families to work on farms of landlords to return debt or as domestic and menial labour for moneylenders as repayment of loans. Children may be pledged by parents to factory owners or their agents or middlemen in exchange for small borrowings. Children may be sold off and lured into prostitution, pornography, begging, illicit liquor/drug peddling, petty crime.

A 1981 study of the agricultural sector conducted by the Gandhi Peace Foundation and the National Labour Institute in 10 states found that out of India's 2-6 million bounded labourers, 8.1 per cent were children. Upto 73 per cent of child labourers are mortgaged into work by their own parents or guardians. A survey conducted by the Central Social Welfare Board in six major Indian cities in 1991-92 revealed that 29.38 per cent of all prostitutes were below 20. According to another estimate, 300,000 minors are engaged in sex work in India.

Child Labour within and with Families

Children work alongside their parents in agriculture, on their farms or farms and plantations of others; in the informal, unorganised sector's home-based units; as domestics; in handicraft-based industries such as painting brassware etc.

Female Labour

The girl child requires special mention in the context of child labour. She is a child, a girl and labourer and she faces discrimination at all levels. In almost all areas, rural and urban, where children are employed, the per centage of girls is higher than boys, according to the 1981 Census. Besides, in both urban and rural India, girls are also often put to care of younger siblings, cooking, cleaning, fetching water, fodder and fuel. These activities deny them of several rights but are often not considered labour because they are non-remunerative. The number of female child workers in absolute terms has gone up from 2.8 million in 1971 to 3.5 million in 1991. Girls constitute 70 per cent of child labour in the weaving industry and in the match industry 90 per cent of the workers are girls and women.

Child Labour Separated from Families

Street children working as rag-pickers, waste re-cyclers, hotel workers, vendors, couriers, shoe-shiners, at garage and petrol pumps, fall in this category as also bonded children. It is estimated that there are 314,700 street children in Mumbai, Calcutta, Chennai, Kanpur, Bangalore and Hyderabad (IPER, 1991) and 100,000 in New Delhi (Nangia and Panicker-Pinto, 1988). Working in garbage is extremely destructive to self-growth. It is also obviously unhygienic. Rag-pickers are exposed to skin infections, cuts from glass and metal bits in the scraps and possible tetanus, intestinal diseases due to eating leftovers, collected from the garbage, physical and sexual abuse, drug addiction. And all this is done with absolutely no prospect of medical or any other form of assistance.

Migrant Child Labour

Child labour who are not confined to a particular geographical area who include those who migrate with their families such as in agricultural labour, work at construction sites, brick-kilns and mines; circus, jatra and street performers; street children and especially those working on, for instance, trains, cleaning compartments or singing jingles.

Causative Factors

Since we have already seen in first chapter that no single cause can be isolated for the prevalence of child labour. It is inherent in the evil of poverty, unemployment, underemployment and low wages, caused by inequitable distribution of resources, unleashed by a centralised and lopsided economy and the backward nature of agriculture.

In some places, the dominance of a particular community engenders exploitation like bonded labour. The largest number of child labourers infact belong to the scheduled castes and tribes.

The non-availability or *the lack of access to schools*, an irrelevant school curriculum and the costs incurred for education leads to children being thrown out of schools into the labour force.

Children are employed because they provide ***cheap labour***— a force that can be easily exploited, bullied into obedience and because they are not able to organise themselves into unions against exploitation in the way that adults can. The persistence of child labour depresses and contributes to adult unemployment. At the same time, it increases child labour and children grow up into unskilled, debilitated adults, not even employed in the industry where they worked earlier.

While India has a number of laws pertaining to child labour, the most recent being The Child Labour (Prohibition & Regulation) Act, 1986, the legal framework operates from the paradigm of regulating child labour and has a number of *procedural and legal loopholes.* Moreover, poor implementation of legislation results in the continuing exploitation of child labourers. Public indifference and apathy is another factor for the perpetuation and child labour.

The New Economic Policies. With its market dominated paradigm has further led to deregulation of labour laws accelerated retrenchment, caused depression in adult wages and higher inflation, pressurising vulnerable families to compel their children to enter the labour force.

Conclusion

Child labour is thus both a cause and effect of illiteracy and of ignorance. Poor standards of living and levels of family and community life and cultural attitudes aggravate the problem. The issue of child labour is therefore inextricably linked with the overall need for social and political improvement, land reforms and alternative models of development. However, the fact remains that children cannot wait, there is an urgent need to tackle the problem immediately.

5

CHILD LABOUR IN PRACTICE

In the chapter on Genesis and Dimensions, we have seen that child labour is being practise in India and other countries of the world since times immemorial though its nature and extent has differed according to the period and geographical area the present chapter presents some of the case studies about child labour being exercised the chapter will discuss not only cases of national but also of international level for child labour.

The many manifestation of child labour can be broken down into seven main types for convenience of understanding none of which is unique to any one region of the world. There are: domestic mark; forced or bonded child labour; profession of sexual exploitation; agriculture plantation and industrial sectors; street work for the family and females work. Though it is difficult to discuss at the seven categories one by one since there is no water tight compartmentalisation in categories of child work, still, we shall try to present cases studies in as many as areas as possible.

There might appear same repitition of findings of various study as the aspect of child is being discussed from chapter I onwards, but the fact is that child labour and for that matter problems, difficulties associated with it are universal. Repitition of findings rather strengthen the cases for discovery of strong redressal measures.

Studies on Child Labour in India

A survey of working children in urban Delhi conducted in 1977 tried to examine an extent, causes and consequences of child labour in Delhi slums. It estimated 21,000 child workers in Delhi alone in 1973. Out of 1992 households surveyed, only 60 families had working children numbering 18. Most of the local children had been employed in the workshops. Children working in tea stalls, dhabas and as domestic servants hailed from the eastern and north-eastern parts of Uttar Pradesh and Bihar. The average size of their household was 5.5 and the average monthly income including the earning of their employed children was Rs. 321.5 per month approx.).

Another study by the Committee on Child Labour (1979) appointed by the Ministry of Labour, Govt. of India which examined various dimensions of child labour in different occupations, revealed that the cases of child labour were highest in Andhra Pradesh where it accounted for about 9.0 per cent of the total labour forces, 9.2 per cent of the total child population and 3.7 per cent of the total population of Andhra Pradesh in 1971. The child labour was prominent in rural areas than in urban areas. A higher per centage of children (5.31 per cent) in rural area were child workers whereas this ratio in urban areas was only 1.82 per cent. The participation of children in the labour force in the age-group of 10-14 years was very more (28.9 per cent) for males as compared to females (20 per cent).

If we go by the census figures 1971, they also reveal that out of 10.74 million working children, 36.03 per cent are cultivators, 42.70 per cent agricultured labours and 8.24 per cent are involved in live-stock, forestry, fishing, etc., 0.22 per cent in mining, and quarrying and 6.08 per cent in manufacturing units, 0.54 per cent in construction, 1.95 per cent in trade and commerce, 0.39 per cent in transport and 3.7 per cent in other services.

Another study of child workers conducted in rual parts of Haryana (1979) which was based on a sample of 200 child labour families in four villages, found that 89 per cent parents of child labourers were illiterate, about 49 per cent working children had never been put to school, 40 per cent had dropped out and only 11 per cent child workers were regular in carrying on the burden of schooling and livelihood both. In Rewari Tehsil, under study 70.7 per cent were male and the rest were female children, 19.4 per cent were between 6 and 8 years of age and 47.6 per cent were of 11-14 years of age; 305 per cent of them belonged to Rajput castes and Yadav each and the greatest number of child workers consisted of Chamar (Scheduled Caste). The family size of the majority of these workers was 6 to 8. The greater burden was on the shoulders of children belonging to nuclear families (70 per cent) than to those (30 per cent) of the joint families.

One more study which targetted at Problems and Social Services Needs of Child Labour in Agriculture sector in Uttar Pradesh (Singhs, 1982) revealed that the average age of the child workers was 13.6 years while the majority of child, workers (70.2 per cent) were from age-group of 13-18 years. The large number of them was from non-tribal Hindus and Scheduled Castes. The maximum number of child workers who dropped out from school the studies were in the age group of 8-12 years. Similarly, another study on the working condition of children employed in unorganised sector done by CSIR, 1984 which was based on a huge sample of 900 male and female child workers below the age of 16 years, indicated that the majority of children employed in match units in Sivakasi were females (67 per cent). Only 8 per cent were children below 8 years of age and a majority of the child workers (71 per cent) belong to the age-group of 13-16 years.

Another study on the working children in Bombay (Singh M., 1980) in the age group of 6-15 years observed that most of the working children belonged to low income groups in urban centres who generally live in slums and depressed areas. This study was conducted on 203 boys (67.7 per cent) and 97 girls (32.3 per cent) : three per cent of them were from the age-group of 6-9 years, 25.7 per cent to the age-group of 9-12 years and 71.3 per cent to the age-group of 12-15 years. Out of these 300 working children 211 (70.3 per cent) worked with the employer and 89 (29.7 per cent) were self-employed 287 lived with their families and 13 with guardians and other relatives. The majority of the families of the working children (63.8 per cent) had 5 to 8 members, the average being 5.8 per family. There higher number of male members than female members in these families. Out of 703 children in the age-group of 6-15 years almost 50 per cent i.e. 319 (45.4 per cent) were found working. Out of these 703, 403 (57.39 per cent) were boys and 300 (42.7 per cent) girls. Out of 319 working children, 200 (62.7 per cent) were boys and 119 (37.3 per cent) girls. The child labourers from Hindu families were more than those from Muslim families. The per centage of the working children grew with age, 9 per cent were in the age-group of 6-9 years; 39 per cent in 9-12 years; 78 per cent were in 12-15 years. Most of the children came into the labour force by the time they were 10 years. It was found that though male children shouldered the family's economic responsibility to a large extent than the female ones; but irrespective of sex, the eldest child in the family invariably had to work, the per centage being 96 per cent boys and 90 per cent girls.

In the hilly state of Himachal Pradesh, a study on the problem of the working children had revealed that about 1/3rd of the children of the age-group of 10-14 years in rural and 1/8th of those in urban areas were at work as child labourers in India. Children employed in agriculture and in households on an average worked for 280 days in a year. The most important finding of the study watchout in villageses, children were used as bonded labour and as contract labour in urban areas. Of the working children, a major part of them i.e. 36.79 per cent belonged to Schedule Castes and Scheduled Tribes, and 20.75 per cent to lower castes. Thus, cases of child labour is much higher in economically backward communities, and we can say without doubt that it is directly linked to poverty.

Another report (Gangrade, 1983) found that the states like Uttar Pradesh, Jammu & Kashmir and Tamil Nadu Varanasi, Bodhi, Mirzapur have flourishing centres of carpet weaving. It is in Mirjapur only where 50,000 workers are involved in carpet weaving of which nearly 20 per cent are children. Similarly, another survey (Gerry, 1981 shows that carpet weaving is growing in the states of Madras, Travancore, Uttar Pradesh and Kashmir. Employment of Children in activities suited to them keeps the production expenditure very low. They also work as apprentices. In household work of carpet weaving enterprises children are considered indispensable as helpers and as trainees who continue the craft.

If we have a look at that reasons which are behind consequence and flourishing of child labour it is obvious that the problem of child labour in India is the result of traditional attitudes, urbanisation, industrialisation, migration, lack of educational infrastructure or the reluctance of parents to send their children to schools, etc. In the ultimate analysis, main causes are extreme poverty and agriculture being the main occupation of the majority of population requiring more hands. But now growing urbanisation changed lavish life styles have contributed their own share to the problem. The institutions of child labour is essentially one of the poor and destitute families, where parents can not afford to provide education to their children. A study of the working children in Bombay (Singh M. 1980) observed that 20.6

per cent of the interviewed employers were employing children because they were quick and efficient, 12.6 per cent preferred them because they found them more amenable to discipline, some found them better suited for some types of jobs, 30.5 per cent said that their conditions had greater sentimental appeal, 9.3 per cent were in favour of them as they were cheap and 1.9 per cent had them due to their honesty. Out of 287 respondents (parents), the majority (170 i.e. 69.2 per cent) stated economic compulsions as the main factor. As many as 74 (25.8 per cent) mentioned that the child was sitting idle and doing nothing. Therefore he was put to work to save him from the bad company . There were 69 (24 per cent) respondents who said that the child had left the school and there was no alternative but to put him to labour to keep him busy. Sixty two of them (21.6 per cent) attributed the early entry to work of their children due to death, disease or loss of job of the earning members of the family. A few did not mention any special reason or circumstances but said that child labour was their family tradition. 17 of the respondents (6.0 per cent) said that their children were slipping into delinquency so they had to put them on some job so that might develop a sense of discipline. Twelve of the respondents mentioned that the child himself was keen to earn; so they did not stop him from getting into work. A few (10 per cent) said that the child was alone at home and, therefore, he was not safe to ensure his safety they put him on same job.

Study conducted in Hisar on the working children (Sharma 1982) found that a majority of the child workers joined the labour force due to acute poverty of their family, death and chronic illness of the earning members and there was no alternative to supplement their family income. Children migrated from different States. About 4/5 of the children came from the families whose average monthly income was less than Rs. 300 and the no of family members was 8 on an average. The social circumstances which also motivated the child workers to seek jobs were company of friends, rude behaviours of parents and elders and lack of affection in the family, etc.

A survey of the working conditions of children employed in unorganised sector, in Sivakasi (CSR, 1984) found that children were the main bread winners in most of the families there. A majority of families depended on the income from match units either as main source or as supplementary source of family income. About 36 per cent of the families had more than two children working in match units. Most of the children were forced to work due to poverty. A majority (95 per cent) of them took up jobs in match units because of the poor financial conditions of their families. Another 6 per cent of them were willing to continue their studies but were forced by their parents to work to support their families or to supplement the family income.

Similarly another study on Child labour in Himachal Pradesh observed that it was the economic necessity which compelled the families to send their children to work. Increasing incidence of debts created more pressure for sending all possible hands to work for money. Employers preferred child labour, because it was easy to manage them and also they had to give less wages to them. About 14.67 per cent employers expressed their opinion that children should be employed but 82.67 per cent answered in the negative. It was also found that in certain handicrafts like Zaribrocade, carpets which need training at the early age, children are preferred to adult workers.

Dr. M. Singh's study (1980) conducted (Singh M, 1980) in Mumbai City presents the working conditions of both self-employed and employed children. Self-employed child worker were seen to be working for 10 hours a day who earned around Rs. 82 per month on an average. The lack of fixed place of shelter, inadequacy of equipment and harassment by employer's were the main problems in carrying out the job smoothly. According to some parents, work developed a sense of responsibility in their children and made them sober, considerate and better behaved. The findings about the employed children revealed that one was asked to show a certificate of medical fitness by the employer nor the employer got him/her medically examined. A large no of them were getting a monthly salary of Rs. 100 and below. The Children engaged in construction work arts and crafts and production earned the highest wages whereas those in households and restaurants were paid the lowest emoluments in terms of hard cash. Out of 205 children who were earning, as many as 133 (64.9 per cent) got pocket money, 64.9 per cent, i.e., 133 children worked on regular basis and the remaining on daily wages. The minimum number of hours a child worked was a 4 hours and the maximum was 14 hours, the average being 8.7 hours. Out of the representative sample, 5.10 per cent working children had no fixed rest duration. Similarly, 35 per cent of the children did not get an off day during the week. Nearly 33 per cent of the parents did not visit the work places of their children. According to employers, protection against sun and rain was provided to 79.9 per cent of the working children, separate rest places to 20.6 per cent, proper lighting to 88.7 per cent, medical facilities to 41.2 per cent, drinking water and bathing facilities to 79.4 per cent, security against job hazards to 52.9 per cent, proper ventilation to 83.8 per cent, recreational facilities to 17.2 per cent and toilet facilities to 57.4 per cent. As many as 54 per cent children did not mention any difficulties in the performance of there jobs. Another 88.60 per cent of the children were contented with the treatment accorded to them their employers and only 11.4 per cent were not satisfied.

Similarly, if we look at the employer satisfaction, 68.1 per cent of the employers were satisfied with the work behaviour of the children and 6.4 per cent were not happy. According to the parents, none of the employed children ever met with any accident at the work place. It was further found that 47.3 per cent were satisfied with their wages, 66.6 per cent were satisfied with the length of their working hours, 13.7 per cent with the physical arrangement work, 5.9 per cent with the facilities and benefits available, 10.2 per cent with the job security, 3.9 per cent with the behaviour of their employer and 2.4 per cent with the behaviour of their colleagues. Another 36 per cent of the children had to perform household chores also in additions to the regular job. Statistics shows that the for total working children in two units of the carpet industry in Srinagar, wages varied from Rs. 2 to 10 per day for weavers. The wages were Rs. 2 to 4 per day when fulls kill of the trade was available. In both the units, children were required to work for the same duration as fixed fro adult workers. There were no special provisions for education, recreation, social security and other welfare amenities for children.

One more survey based study was conducted to find out various dimension of child labour and occupations where children are employed. The study found that chronic poverty was stronger factor than tradition for child labour. The income generated from child labour might be a pittance but it played a crucial role in saving the family from a shipwreck. Accordingly to this report, children, too in many cases were scared of being discard by their parents, if they failed to earn and prove that they were useful to family. In case of parental in ability, children become the sole bread winners. The child workers are not organised on the lines of trade unions which can fight for their interest. Child labour is also justified on the ground that it trains the child's fingers for the required skill.

One more research study (Gopunjkar 1980) on the working children in the tribal areas of Maharashtra, conducted with a view to preparing a detailed note on different types of child workers, did revealed that children participated in all the occupations/jobs available to them and activities of home family occupations and kept themselves working through-out the year. The child starts working from about 5 to 6 years of age. The income from the work of the child is both in case and in kind. Wages in cash are governed to some extent, by the Minimum wages (amendment) Act of 1979. But in many cases labourers are paid much less than what they deserve. The wages in kind are given at rates in accordance with the local practice. Except for a few activities like Saldari, children enjoy real free life and do not feel the constraints of work. They are not over loaded and feel free in the working atmosphere. However proper eduction and health facilities are not provided to them. Diseases resulting from malnourishment and unhygienic conditions and practices are very common.

Study based child labour in Himachal Pradesh based on a sample of 438 children, 419 parents and 337 employers found that most of the children worked for less than a year but those engaged in tea plantational (Kangra) were more stable. In the same manner, agricultural jobs appeared to be more stable than non agricultural jobs. As reported, 41.10 per cent children were having temporary jobs whereas 30.14 per cent had sessional jobs and 42.85 per cent of child workers slay within one kilometre radius from their places of work. Others had travel 1 to 5 kilometre. They got their jobs on the basis of personal contracts and a few through newspapers, etc. Less than half (37.59 per cent) admitted that the working children were getting better treatment at home in the form of better food, clothes etc. A majority of the children were working for long duration, e.g., 5.26 per cent for more than 15 hours and 18.31 per cent for 10-15 hours. In Kangra 76 per cent of the children laboured for 7-8 hours. About 9.07 per cent reported about the poor safety measures but most of them felt no problems. One complained that their work affected their lungs.

Mr. S. Singh study (1982), on problems of social service needs of child labour in agriculture in U.P. observed that an average monthly income of the child worker had been Rs. 68, Rs. 86 which came to about Rs. 2 per day. A majority of child workers were found in carrying water, house watching, buying domestic things, cattle grazing, working at night on irrigation sites and crop watching, etc. Approximate monthly income of the child workers was Rs. 60.86 and in the most of cases, payment was made directly by the employers and received directly by the child workers. Child workers were also suffering from minor ailments caused by seasonal variations are they were exposed to various serious disease also. A majority of the child workers stated that employers did not exploit them for over work. The health of the majority of the children was poor and their guardians were illiterate without any technical skill. The entire monthly earning of children was between Rs. 200 to 400 an average.

Cares of Child Labour from International Studies

It is said that children domestic workers are the forgotten children, which is why it is worth considering their condition before that of other, more familiar groups of child workers.

If we look at a day in the life of a little Marie, from Haiti. She is restavek—Creole for rester avec-the local term for a type of child domestic worker found all over the world, one who has been handed over by a poor family to stay with and provide domestic 'help' for a usually urban, well off family. She gets up at five in the morning and begins her day by fetching water from a nearby well balancing the heavy jug on her head as she comes back. She prepares breakfast and serves it to the members of the household. Then she drops the family's five-years-old son to school; later, at noon, she brings him home and helps him change clothes. Next, she helps prepare and serve the family's lunch before returning the boy to school. Between meal times she has to go to market and urn errands, tend charcoal fire, sweep the yead, wash clothes and dishes, clean the kitchen and— at least once a day— clean her female boss feet. She is not allowed to bathe in the water she brings to the household. She is regularly beaten with a leather strap if she is slow to attend to a request or is considered disrespectful. Needless to say, she is not allowed to attend school.

A survey of middle-income households in Colombo (Sri Lanka) revealed that one in three had a child under 14 years of age as a domestic workers. A study of a lower-middle-class residential area sin Nairobi (Kenya) observed that 20 per cent of households employed children in 1982, though by 1991 this had reduced to 12 per cent, perhaps due to falling living standards. A survey of domestic workers in Uruguay found that 34 per cent had started at working at very early age 14. A survey in India, nothing that 17 per cent of domestic workers were under 15 years old, found that girls aged 12 to 15 were the preferred by 90 per cent of employing households. Children are of often preferred to adults precisely because they can be dominated more easily and, of course, paid less.

The impact of a life like marie's on a child's development is profound. An obvious negative is poor nutrition, since it is rare that child domestics share equally in the family meals. A peruvin girl says:

In domestic set up, sexual abuse is often regarded by the employer as part of the employment terms. Jeanne, a 15-year-old working in Cotonou (Benin), has the routine heavy workload, is unpaid and is beaten when her employers are unhappy with her work. But her greatest problem is the family's 23-year-old son, who rapes her regularly. If she resists, he creates situations that led to her being beaten.

But the situation of some children goes far beyond the acceptance of poor conditions. They find themselves in effective salavery. In South Asia, this has taken on a quasi-institutional form known as 'bonded' child labour. Under this system, children, often only eight or nine years old, are pledged by their parents to factory owners or their agents in exchange for small loans. Their lifelong servitude never succeeds in even reducing the debt.

In India, this type of transaction is widespread in agriculture, as well as industries such as cigarette-rolling, carpet-making, matchstick-making, slate and silk. The most notorious of these is the carpet industry of Mirzapur-Bhadohi-Varanasi in Uttar Pradesh. According to a recent study, the thousands of children in the carpet industry are "kidnapped or lured away or pledged by their parents for paltry sums of money. Most of them are kept in captivity, tortured and made to work for 20 hours a day without a break. Little children are made to crouch on their toes, from dawn to dusk every day, severely stunting their growth during formative years. Social activities in the area find it hard to work because of the strong mafia-like control that the carpet loom owners have on the area."

Of course, most worst-exploited children belong to the most marginalized segments of society. As in other countries, these caste based minorities and disadvantaged groups are routinely seen as having no rights whatsoever. Often they themselves have come to believe that they deserve no rights. This kind of virtual child salvery or bandage is usually associated with India, Nepal and Pakistan. But it is found in other parts of the world, too. In Brazil, for example, forced labour is found from the charcoal burning projects of Minas Gerais and Bahia to the sugarcane establishments units of Espiritu Santo and the north-east. Whilemost such labour is performed by adults, children are inevitably involved also. In 1993, a British Member of Parliament reported having found children working to cool down charcoal kilns with mud in Acailandia. Also in 1993, children as young as four were found working in the cotton harvest in Parana. In Mauritania, thousands of children are still born each year into effective slavery.

The underground nature of the multi-billion-dollar illegal industry in the commercial sexual abuse of children makes it difficult to gather reliable data. But NGOs in the field estimate that each year at least one million girls over the world are lured or forced into this form of mast hazardous labour, which can verge on slavery. Boys are also often exploited. When scandals about child prostitution in developing countries came in the international media, it is usually a story about the phenomenon called sex tourism in which holiday-makers from the rich world mainly, though not exclusively, men, visit places such as Brazil, the Dominican Republic, Thailand and else where in search of sex with children.

But we should not lose sight of the fact that many thousands of young girls in many countries serve the sexual appetities of local men from all social and economic backgrounds. And never ending child prostitution exists in industrialized countries. In the US alone, at least 100,000 children are believed to be involved. Direct links between the commercial sexual exploitation of children and other forms of exploitative labour are uncountable. Notorious in their own right for appealing working conditions, Nepalese carpet factories, where 50 per cent of the workers are estimated to be children are common sites of sexual exploitation by employers as well as recruitment centres for Indian brothels. Children are especially powerless to refuse abuse by employers, either as perpetrators or intermediaries.

Village loan-sharks often act as procurers for city brothels, lending money to the family on the grounds that the daughter's work must pay off. However it happens, almost all such children are cheated by those they trust and may end up trafficked long distances and across borders. Rescue and rehabilitation is difficult for children. They often end up being prosecuted by the very legal machinery that should be protecting them. Even if they make it home, perhaps having been deported as illegal immigrants, they may undergo stigma and rejection by their families and communities. Shunned, ignored and invisible, they often have no choice but to return to the brothel or the streets.

The problem is out in the open now, after decades of what has amounted to a cross-cultural conspiracy of silence. The World Congress against Commercial Sexual Exploitation of Children, held in Sweden August 1996, put the issue on the world's agenda for the first time. The Agenda for Action agreed upon by participants will guide governments in developing programmes to address the problem.

Regarding industrial and plautation work, all over the world, children work in hazardous conditions. The industries are numerous, from leter-working in the Naples region of Italy to the preindustrial brick-making of Colombia and Peru, which can involve children as young eight.

At times, are exploited in mining operations also that would be considered too hazardous for adults in the industrialized world— for example, in the diamond and gold mines of South Africa, and in coal mines Colombian. As a trend, the children work with the barest minimum of safety equipment and constantly breathe in coal dust. The respiratory problems faced by child miners are also common in other industries. Many of them develop tuberculosis bronchitis and asthma. Children working in earthenware and procelain factories, are often unprotected form the silica dust. In the lock industry, they inhale noxious fumes released by dangerous chemicals. In the brassware industry, children work at high-temperature furnaces and inhale the dust produced through polishing. The numbers of children exploited by plantation agriculture across the world may be just as high and the dangers associated with much of their work are no less appealling. In Brazil's sugar plantations. for example, children cut cane with machetes, a punishing task putting them at constant risk of mutilation. They make up a third of the workforce in some areas and are involved in over 40 per cent of the work-related accidents. Brazilin a children are also exposed to snakebites and insect stings on tobacco plantations, and carry loads for beyond their capacities. In Colombia, young people who work on flower-export farms are exposed to pesticides banned in industrialized countries.

In Africa, children work on the plantations that grow the export crops on which the continent's economies depends from the coca and coffee and sisal plantations of Tanzania. In Zimbabwe, children work a approximately 9 hours a day, picking cotton or coffee for about $1. An ILO study on child labour in Zimbawe found that the most prominent exploiters of child labour were found to be the large scale commercial farmers who have used children in their fields for decades, especially during planting and harvesting season. These commercial farmers also protested against the Government's draft child labour regulations in 1995, for the reasons that they would interfere with children's right to work. The same years, farmers asked a District Education Officer to close down the educational institution to allow children to help bring in the tea and coffee crops. The request, which was reported in the local press, was rejected.

In contrast with child workers, of previous categories, some children work in the most visible places possible—on the streets of developing countries towns. They are everywhere: hawking in markets and darting in and out of traffic jams, plying their trade at bus and railway stations, in front of hotels and shopping malls. They live on streets long with millions of adults, who regard them as nuisances, if not as dangerous minicriminals. What most of these children actually do on the streets is, of course, work. A report from the state juvenile court said that, on average, three street children are killed every day in Rio, many by police at the request of merchants who consider the begging, thieving and glue-sniffing a major nuisance.

Children who work on the streets often come from slums and migrated settlements, where poverty and precarious family situations are common, where schools are overcrowded and poor, and where safe places to play do not exist at all. Their numbers have increased in place experiencing armed conflict, like Freetown (Sierra Leone) and Monrovia (Liberia), as caretakers have been murdered the economy affected and family and community ties served.

Children working on streets, virtually unheard of prior to the transition to a market economy, is now a growing problem in the Russian Federation too. In Kyrgyzstan, in Central Asia, the numbers of children, working on the streets, selling food and other products, have rose dramatically over the last three years. Many have dropped out of school or never attended classes.

As per the finding of a servey, "the nature of their work is .... most unhygienic, dangerous, demeaning.... They develop several kinds of skin disease like ulcers, scabies etc. While collecting rusted iron pieces, they often receive cuts on their hands and become susceptible to tetanus. The broken glass lying hidden in the garbage may hurt their bare feet, which may develop into festering wounds. Many other diseases arise from exposure to extreme weather conditions, like cases of sunstroke, pneunionia influenza and malaria. Carrying heavy burden under the arms or on their back adversely affects the height, weight, strength and stamina. The lure of eating thrown away or leftover food... leads to digestive disorders and food poisoning."

Of all the work children do, the most common is agricultural or domestic work within their own households. Most families around the world expect their children to help in the household, whether preparing children to help in the household, whether preparing food fetching water or groceries, herding animals, taking care of younger siblings or more arduous work in the fields. This kind of work can be useful. Children learn from a reasonable level of participation in household chores, subsistence food-growing and income generating activities. They also develop a sense of self-worth from their work within their families. But it is by no means always beneficial. On the contrary, work for the family many demand too much of children forcing them to labour long hours that keep them away from school and take too great a toll on their developing bodies. Such work can stop children from exercising their rights and developing to their full potential.

The kind patterns of early labour are reported in a survey of five Latin American countries. In rural Colombia, for example, one in four children aged 6 to 9 and one in three aged 10 and 11 work, either in the home, tending the family vegetable garden, looking after animals, or helping in a grocery store or small business. In the big cities, one in six of 10 and 11-years-old children and one in ten of 6- to 9-year olds participate in the labour market in some way.

More importantly, much of this work, particularly by girls within their homes, is invisible to the statistician aiming to measure the scale of child labour. It is also not included from child labour legislation, partly because of the difficulty of policing child labour within the family. Yet to say that such work cannot be regulated equal to advise that hundreds of millions of children can have no legal protection.

According to ILO, 56 per cent of the 10- to 14- year-olds currently estimated to be working in the developing world are male children. Yet, if we were able to measure the numbers of girls doing unregistered work as domestic helpers, or working at home to support other family members to take up paid employment, the figures would show more female child labourers than male over. Girls also work long hours on average than boys, carrying a double workload - a job outside the home and domestic duties on their return.

In conclude Child Labour in visible in both inside & outside loves in ogranised & unorganised sector, another male & female children, on legal as well as illegal grounder whatever the case may be, ultimately the looser are children who remain deprived of their opportunities which can help them grow up at complete human personalities. Since the problem exists everywhere, it also wilds to be tackled at by national and internationa agencies. Following chapter will their light on legal & social efforts at eradication of child labour & promotion of education from them.

6

SOCIO-LEGAL CONCERN ABOUT CHILD LABOUR

The economic exploitation of children in India has always been an area of concern. While official sources estimate the number of child workers to be much lower, others have placed the figure at the much higher level. High as they are, even these figures do not bring to light the real tragedy of the working child in India. Most children work in highly exploitative conditions and all are deprived of even the most minimal living and educational facilities.

A child who does not attend a formal school in rural parts is a working child. Collection of water, fuel, household chores and taking care of younger siblings all form important elements of a child's life. While many of these activities cannot be defined as hazardous work, in as much as they affect the normal development of the child and in the child's ability to reach his/her true potential they violate the convention on the Rights of the Child to which India to has been a signature and a ratifier. In the typical environment in which Indian children develop the concept of a non-working, non-social going child simply does not exist. Any concern for the issue of child labour therefore has to address the question of education. In this following pages of this in this chapter we identify schooling as the single most important means of prohibiting child labour. To this extent we also view the promotion of education and the elimination of child labour as being mutually supportive processes.

Consequently, we believe that the prevalence of compulsory primary education to all lies in its potential to eliminate child labour. It is in the context of eliminating child labour that we examine the scope of appropriate legislation governing compulsory primary education.

At present, elementary education in India is characterized by fictitious enrolment, high drop-out rates and a constantly growing number of illiterate children. Figures show that although the number and per centage of children attending school is on rise and the number of schools has grown, India's share in the world's illiterates has also risen. In other words, the number of illiterates in he country is increasing as a result of the high drop-out rate among children in the first five years of school. Moreover, corresponding trends are reflected in the statistics of child labour flourish with more and more children enter of children into the workforce each year. It is against this background that the Government of India through its plans and strategies has been dealing with the problem of bringing children to school. From the beginning, the issue to which academicians and policy makers have addressed themselves is, "How does a poor country like India plan an education policy and strategy which will include the children of both the poor and the better off ?" In the process of answering this question policy makes and educationists have uniformly justified the prevalence of child labour and accepted the inevitability of children's contributions to family income through.

Provisions Made Under the Constitutions

Constitution of India provides for the protection of children against exploitation and moral and material abandonment. A Number of articles in chapter III & IV (Fundamental of Rights, Directive Principles of State Policy and else where have been incorporated for this). Article 24 of fundamental of rights lays down: No child below the age of 14 years shall be employed to work in any factory or mine or engaged in any other hazardous employment". Article 39 (e) of DPSPs states that: "the health and strength of workers, men and women, and the tender age of children are not abused and that citizens are not forced by economic necessity to enter avocations unsuited to their age or strength". Article 39 (f) establishes that: "childhood and youth are protected against exploitation and against moral and material abandonment." Article 45 that: "the State must endeavour to provide free and compulsory education for all children till the age of 14."

Legislations/ Enactments Against Child Labour

In total, there are 11 labour Laws which have been enacted in the country for the benefit of children and adolescents engaged in certain specific kinds of labour. These Acts, *inter alia,* prescribe the minimum age, minimum wage, certain working conditions and regulate their working hours. These are slightly elaborated below:

1. The Factories Act, 1948, amended in 1949 and 1954 establishes minimum age for employment, 14 years. The Act prohibits the employment of a child or an adolescent (15-18 years) unless he is certified by an authorised surgeon as to his physical fitness for work and holds a token to that effect while at work. Rest, shelter, a canteen, etc., are also to be provided for all workers including child labour.

2. Shops and Commercial Establishments Acts. (State Acts) provide the minimum age for employment 12 years in all States except in the case of Andhra Pradesh, Kerala, Punjab, Tamil Nadu, Pondicherry and Uttar pradesh, where the limit given 14 years. These Acts regulate, *inter-alia* the daily and weekly hours of shops and other establishment, payment of wages, overtime charges holidays with pay, annual leave, employment of persons etc: This Act prohibits the employment of young persons

during the night (7 P.M. to 6 A. M.) and the hours of work for children are also fixed (3 to 7 hours).

3. For Transport, there are two Acts relating to employment of children in this sector: As the per Motor Transport Worker Act, 1961; The minimum age provided for this employment is 15 years. Under the Merchant Shipping Act, 1958 amended in 1966, Children below 15 years cannot ordinarily be employed as seamen and this applies to all ships registered in India.

4. According to Mines: Mines Act, 1952 person below the age of 15 is employed on the surface. For those working underground, the minimum age is above 16 years and, in addition, a fitness certificate should be given by an authorised surgeon is essential.

5. The Plantations Labour Act 1951 amended in 1953 and 1960, fixes the minimum age for employment at 12 and employment of a child above 12 years requires a fresh fitness certificate from the appointed surgeon every 12 months. Schooling, housing and the provision of medical facilities are the responsibility of the employer.

6. For Wages and Bonus, Minimum Wages Act, 1948 amended in 1954, 1957 and 1961, provides for the fixing of (i) a minimum time-rate of wages, (ii) a minimum piece-rate of wages, (iii) a fixed time rate of wages, and (iv) an over-time rate of wages for different occupations, places or classes of work for adults, adolescents, children and apprentices.

7. The Beedi and Cigar Workers (Conditions of Employment) Act, 1966, fixes the minimum age for employment at 14 years. The employment of young persons between 14 and 18 years is prohibited between 7 P.M. and 6 A.M.

8. The Apprentices Act, 1961, amended in 1972, say that no person under the age of 14 is to be given training unless he satisfies such standards of education and physical fitness as may be prescribed.

9. Atomic Energy Act, 1972 prevents the employment of children below the ages of 15 or 14, in certain specified sectors of the industry.

There are two more Acts relating to protection of children one is, the children (Pledging of Labour) Act, 1933 prevents any agreement, written or oral, expressed or implied, in return of any payment of benefit received by parents or guardian against the services of the child (persons below the age of 15) to be utilised in any employment.

The second are, the Employment of Children Act, 1938 amended in 1939, 1948, 1949 and 1951 says that— No child who has not completed his 15th years can be employed or permitted to work in any occupation connected with the transport of passengers, goods or mail by railways, or connected with a port authority within the jurisdiction of the port. The Act also prohibits the employment of children below 14 years in workshops connected with occorpating like beedi-making, carpet weaving, cement manufacture cloth printing, dyeing and weaving, manufacture of matches, explosive material and fire-workers, mica cutting and splitting, shellac manufacture, soap manufacture, tanning and wool cleaning.

The basic argument which is accepted is that the family requires the wage of the child to supplement its income; it is in fact this income which keeps the family going. It would therefore unjust to deprive the family of its sources of income by forcing a child to go to school. Two major policies which came up of this conviction were the Child Labour (Prohibition and Regulation) Act, 1986 and the National Policy on Education, 1986. But in this chapter, we shall discuss the constitutional provision, supporting levels/enactments, Governmental policies programmes especially NPE, 1986, international laws and conventionally and last but not the least governmental and non-governmental efforts at national & international level to fight against the evils of child labour.

National Policy on Education

Understanding and identifying the 'need' for giving access to elementary education to those sections of the population who 'cannot' be educated in the local schools, the National Policy on Education, 1986 announced the continuance of non-formal education (NEE) for working children as a major thrust area. This constituted an expression of helplessness in the matter of confronting the issue of child labour and also gave legitimacy to the employment of children. It also restricted any further discussion on the issue of the abolition of child labour and the provision of compulsory education for some time to come. The only excuse offered with respect to child labour was to accept its existences as "hard reality". The exploitation of children's labour was thus not addressed and instead more and more ambitious and sophisticated policies of non-formal education were designed to reach working children. A closer look at the details of the NFE programme will help to highlight these observations.

The "clientele" for NFE was identified as "children in habitations without schools, school dropouts; working children and girls who cannot attend school." During the first two years these children, were to attain primary school Level through the NFE centres, and in the coming three years they were to complete the upper primary level. All instruction were to be provided by local youth who would to work be ready as teachers with a remuneration of Rs. 100 to Rs. 200 per month "with the provision of an annual increment of Rs. 50 after the completion of two years of satisfactory service till remuneration reaches Rs. 500 per month."

Apart from the Government, the work of running NFE centres would be done through voluntary organisations and panchayat Raj institutions. The NFE programme, in design therefore, incorporates all the elements which in the opinion of the policy makers constitute a "good" programme. It does not hamper child's work schedule and at the same time is extremely cost-effective. But still, can NFE really achieve what it has set out to do?

Looking out is without prejudices, the NFE Programme is a low-cost strategy devised more out of financial compulsion than conviction. It ensures the existence of a band of highly creative and imaginative local school teachers in living in every village, especially in backward districts, who can with commitment condense an eight-year course of elementary education of five years. They can accomplish that, too, with only a half-an-hour tution every evening or whenever convenient to children, at a salary which is less than one tenth of what regular school teacher gets. At the same time, conjures an image of working child who is alert and earnestly waiting to attend the evening classes just to grasp all that is taught within half an hour or even one hour, thus catching up with children in the better off formal schools who attend for six full hours.

Without doubts, it does not require an expert in education to predict the efficacy of this programme. While the NFE programme is not the only programme provided through the New Education Policy, we have focused attention on this system of universalising education mainly because it helps to only dramatically illustrate the consequences of the assumption that have shaped government policy. To what extent are these assumptions achievable. In order to examine this we will briefly touch upon the experience of the M.V. Foundation (WVF).

Hyderabad which has been working for the rehabilition of working children over last eight years through education and of bonded labourers. The initial thrust of the programe was almost entirely on the abolition of bonded child labour. The focus over the years has shifted to target elimination of all forms of child labour through universal primary education every year, the organization has been conducting mobilisation camps for working children in order to take them out from work and admit them at the appropriate levels in schools. The methodology adopted has been to awaken the men and women in rural areas, particularly parents of working children. Parent and Teacher Committees have been formed and awareness generation training is conducted to sensitise all those involved to the issue of child labour. Children's camps have developed apart from teaching activities, a programme of development of leadership qualities among children. Street plays and campaign movements by children themselves to motivate other working children to got to school have also been introduced. The MVF programme also involves a strong component of follow-up measures to check dropouts among those who have gone through the camp.

In the eight years since the programme has been in operation, over 1,000 children have attended these camps and 3.500 have additionally been motivated to got to school. The latest phase of the programme includes 6,000 children from over 36 villages. The camps have been a revelation and have provided quality material on the attitude of children, parents, and government officials towards the problem of child labour and illiteracy. They have also provided pointers to the basic elements that need to be incorporated in any scheme dealing with these problems. In the main, the camps have told the society that :

(i) Abolition of child labour and universalisation of school education are practically supplementary to each other.

(ii) Parents of working children are ready to make adjustments to enable their children to go to school.

(iii) The income of working child is not the motivating factor, in most cases, for the parents to sent their children to work but the traditional.

(iv) There is no alternative to using government institutions in order to bring about universalisation of education as NGOs cannot provide the infrastructure on the necessary scale.

(v) There is considerable scope for involving the whole village community in the process of universalising elementary education.

It is equally important to examine the implications of the MVF experience in the context to the Government stand to universalising primary education. The first significant outcome has been that a large number of working children have been motivated to join school. In fact, even children engaged in the most exploitative from of work e.g. bonded labour have been withdrawn from work and to put schools. Time and again, the annual camps of the MVF have showen that children who are normally assigned the status of victims of the "harsh reality" of child labour are ready to go to school. Importantly, parents are willing to make such sacrifices as are necessary to ensure that children continue education.

Though it would be difficult for the MVTF or anyone to claim that such results in any situation, the fact remains that over a period of eight years positive results have been observed with respect to 5,000 children by MVF efforts. Obviously the argument of the harsh reality of child labour has been overemphasized to protect the institution of child labours.

One more aspect which the MVF experience emphasizes is the creation of a demand for educations in rural areas even among parents belonging to the economically weaker sections of the society. Experience of field visits shows that parents have not only disposed of assets such as cattle to enable their children to continue in school but have also opposed the employers of the children when they attempted to enforce contractual obligations against loans offered. In the extremely feudal and backward setup that exists in the villages of the Rangareddy district of Andhra Pradesh where MVF activities are concentrated, this is no small sacrifice.

If we go by this experience of MVF, that we can assert that the failure of the NFE programme lies not in its faulty execution. In fact, its greatest failure is in its fear that labourers cannot be withdrawn from work and therefore have to be provided the benefits of education outside working hours. The fact that there is an unfulfilled demand for formal education even among the poor in village setup has been totally denied in this attempt to expand primary education. There is a singular absence of trust in the fact that people, even poor people, value education and learning and are ready to make even extraordinary sacrifices to educate their children.

If we analyse from all angles, the issue of compulsory education has always been something of nenigma. At the theoretical level very few disagree that all children should get education at least upto the primary stage, or with the fact that children should not be put labour. In fact, the State has committed itself not only to the universalisation of primary education but also to the abolition of child labour through various provisions, not the least of which are the Directive Principles of State Policy enshrined in fourth chapter of the Constitution of India. This committment has been further strengthened by the fact that India is one of nearly 150 countries to have ratified the UN Convention on the Right of the Child, which articulates a series of children's rights including the right to fee and compulsory primary education. Still, the general attitude of policy makers has been that India cannot afford the distraction of a compulsory education norm. A number of reasons are given for this, but two major question marks are worth mentioning. The first one puts into doubt the role of the State in be given education, and the second stresses the inability to translate into practice such legislation which would relegate it to legislation on paper only. As far as the first question mark is concerned, in a society where the State has always played a important role in shaping the social behaviour or citizens through enactments, it is difficult to question the desirability of the State's intervention with respect to education. Today, in our country there one laws on issues ranging from minimum age of marrage to protection of civil rights and abolition of the social blat of untouchability. For the State to legislate on an issue concerning a child's right to development, would not be something out of common.

The other Question mark, however, merits a more detailed examination. It has ben observed that in this country a large number of laws governing social issues have been frame and approved but have never really been implemented. Although these laws have been developed to control unwanted social practices, the State has not been able to ensure effective enforcement. Any number of examples ranging from the SITA (Suppression of Immoral Traffic Act) to BLSA (Bonded Labour System Abolition) can be given to illustrate this. Legislation to provide compulsory education, therefore, is likely to meet a similar fortune. Further, it is argued that legislation governing compulsory education may be questioned as an instrument of harassment against the parents. On the other hand, social activities have, long viewed legislation of this nature as a means to compel the State to take action. The BLSA, for example, has proved to be an extremely powerful weapon for NGOs to handle the problem of bonded child labour in situations where the State has not been prepared to take *suo motu* action.

Therefore, though appropriate legislation may not absolutely ensure that the objectives of the legislation will be achieved, its very existence creates an enabling environment where by the State can be compelled to take action. At the very least such legislation shows the commitment of the State to promote an ideal and progressive values system. Moreover, such legislation provides for others working in the field a legitimacy which otherwise wouldn't come to being. The importance of this aspect can be approved with respect to all those activists who have utilized the BLSA to release bonded child labourers.

Thus, while administrators and academicians may question the ability to implement social legislation, the fact remains that the BSLA has extended enormous strength to many of the activists working in the area of child labour in bondage. Legislation to provide for compulsory education, therefore, would be of great value in situations where the efforts of the State are checked in responding to the requirements of the people. We have already found that the government response to the problem of illiteracy and child labour has been quite equivocal. On the other hand, our experience in the field has reflected that there exists a great unrecognized demand for formal education and that parents are prepared to make sacrifices to utilize educational opportunities. As long as the existing set up can meet the demand there is no crisis but the fact is that, more often than not, the infrastructure is faulty. For instance in the limited area wherein at organization alone is functioning it would require educational facilities for more students. Taking the existing facilities into account this would mean a rise in classrooms and teachers. Under the present circumstances there is absolutely no way in the which it can compel the State to provide facilities. There a situation where the same parents and children who have been written off as victims of the "harsh reality" of socio-economic circumstances are asking for educational facilities and the State itself is either unable or unwilling to respond. It is in this context that we feel there is a need for suitable legislation for the State itself to provide compulsory education. No Government can increase opportunities for adult employment without curbing child labour. This is so because the maximum job opportunities created every years are preferentially offered to children as their physical and mental vulnerability makes them easy to be exploited. In addition, children provide the cheapest sources of human labour. Our logical apprehension is that if we do not eradicate child servitude today, we will be responsible for increasing the poverty, object misery and ill health of 55 million adult in the country.

Another fact is that the growth rate of the population is much higher among those communities in which unemployment is prevalent. Obviously, if child labour is not controlled, impoverished parents will continue to succumb to the 'necessity' of adding to the number of earning members the family. Moreover, there exists a correlation between illiteracy and child servitude. In areas where there more employment for children, the drop-out rate in schools is extremely high. If we do not liberate children from their labour today, we will be responsible for keeping them illiterate for their entire lives. Thus, the natural corollary is that the level of illiteracy cannot be checked without eradicating child servitude.

Sometime back, an aggressive anti-carpet campaign was launched; the premises of manufactures were raided, children were released and their rehabilitation started. In addition, the issue has been publicised widely and political will has been created for the total eradication of this menace. SACCS's partner in Bangladesh has taken up the issue of child workers in their garment industry. SACCS has launched some credible moves to combat child servitude. It under took a 2000 kms. marathon march in February 1993. The march generated a considerable amount of awareness among adults and children. Second novel measure adopted in 1993 by this organisation was to generate political will among candidates for seats in the State legislative Assembly of

Uttar Pradesh under the banner of Save Childhood. It was the first time in parliamentary history that a written sought from candidates pledging that they would make efforts to abolish child labour and get a law passed for the free and compulsory primary education of children below the age of 14. Those who were averse to this campaign were blacklisted and their names were published in the local newspapers along with an appeal not to vote for them.

It is heartening to note that foreign NGOs, especially those in Germany, Britain, the United States, Sweden and the Netherlands, have taken up the cause of child servitude seriously and put pressure on their governments and parliaments for the enactment of suitable legislation banning the import of products manufactured by children. As a result of this movement, the Tom Harkin Bills was introduced in the U.S. Senate Seeking a ban on the entry of products who made children party to the production process.

Why should we accept the pro child labour attitude of the Government when our demands are in consonance with Constitutional provisions of the prohibitive laws of the land. Let the conscience of our country men also revolt against the abomination of child abuse in work and force the powers that be to act - now. Let children in the workforce be replaced by adults and let children be prouded free and compulsory schooling with all necessary incentives.

It has been noted, that the exploitation of children is the product of crime. Although child labour has been with us from time immemorial, criminal gangs and individuals are manipulating children to sell drugs, to steal and to commit other crimes is probably an apt example of this situation. Much of it is linked to corruption within national systems and some law implementation authorities colliding with criminal elements. This is compounded by the fact that although various countries have laws to protect children, there is a big gap between the theoretical protection and existing practices; many country suffer from poor law enforcement. The exploitation of child labour is often the product of such deficiencies and concerned vested interests.

Meanever a Point C.L. at International Level

At the international level, various instruments provide an umbrella of protection for child worker. Under the auspices of the ILO, a series of convention and recommendations on the exploitation of child labour has been developed. One important convention is Convention Number 138 which establishes 15 as the basic minimum age of employment, though reduction to 14 may be possible in developing countries. The ILO conventions and recommendations have been supported by the advent of the Convention on the Rights of the Child. The CRC emphasises a new the issue of sale linked with child, labour. Article 32 says that "children should be protected from economic exploitation and from performing any work that is likely to be hazardous or to interfere with the child's education or to be harmful to the child's health or physical, mental, spiritual, moral or social development." The convention brought forward the used or stipulation of pluridisciplinary measures, for example, legislative, administrative, social and educational measures to:

(a) Fix a minimum age/ages offer for entry to employment;

(b) Fix up appropriate hours of work and conditions of employment;

(c) To make provisions for appropriate penalties or other sanction to ensure the effective enforcement of the present article.

As far as migrant workers are concerned, the International Convention on the protection of the Rights of All Migrant Workers and Members of their Families, 1990 also provides security to those in irregular situation, for instance those employed without required papers in another country; they retain their rights vis-a-vis their employers, even in such a context. Although various legal measures have been decided, the issues of implementation and programme planning to realise specific targets remain.

Enforcement: The World Declaration on the Survival, Development and Protection of Children, 1990 highlighted the need for specific programmes of action at the national level. Along with this, UN Commission on Human Rights adopted the Programe of Action for the Elimination of the Exploitation of Child Labour in 1993. This programme of Action put fourth number of measures which should be implemented, particularly at the national and local levels. These measures are as follow:

(a) Campaign movement to raise awareness about the problem;

(b) Training in educational and vocational to prevent child labour exploitations;

(c) To undertake social action to help families and their children;

(d) To provide development aid;

(e) To provide stipulation and enforcement of labour standards;

(f) The adoption by States of appropriate policies and programmes, for example, provision of primary education for all.

In addition, in terms of programming, in Islamabad in November 1992, the International Labour Office, within its interdepartmental project on the Elimination of Child Labour supported to organise the Asian regional seminar on bonded Children,, which developed and adopted a programme of Action Against child Bondage. The Programme of Action suggests the review of the adequacy of existing ligislation.

In particular, the following aspects should be included:

(a) Definition (the various forms of bondage)

(b) Goal (its total abolition)

(c) Description of sanctions

(d) Relief for of victims

(e) Relaxation of debts and other obligations

(f) Enforcement systems, for example measures for quick trial

(g) Provisions for the establishment of special courts

(h) Defamation of violators

(i) Introduction of rehabilitation schemes

Implementation Machinery would involve:

Establish mechanisms to promote and, regulate enforcement, e.g., vigilance committees, task forces:

(a) Strengthen the judicial system.

(b) penalisation of violatots.

(c) General dissemination of violations

(d) Awareness through campaigns and the dissemination of information generation

(e) Sensitisation and training for targeted groups, e.g. officials of implementing authorities, the judiciary trade unions, religious groups

(f) Conduct undertake research and studies for defect problems & rehabilitation package.

Regarding laws prohibiting or regulating child labours, it appears that these vary in aspects such as the age of employment and the type of work found. The enforcement of such legislation of often weak, and taughts only at the formal sector. In 1993, instances or rampant child labour exploitation were found in both developing and developed countries, though the extent varied according to the region. The issue of child marriage in South Asia was raised several times in 1993, particularly concerning purchase of young brides. The nuiseries of child domestic workers and transactional trafficking of children emerged throughout the year. There is also a demand factor abuse children of South Asian, both local and transactional, particularly with customers from the Arbian countries. In addition, numerous concerns were expressed in relation to children trafficked for camel jokies in these countries. In this respect, however, there has been a positive initiative: the United Arab Emirates recently prohibited the use of child jockeys and ordered that they be returned home. In the same way, in East Asia, the sale and trafficking of children for labour exploitation is still existent both locally and across borders. The issue is closely linked with the sex mark.

In unorganised and informal sector, the exploitation of child labour in the reported in various countries of Africans in continent in 1993. In particular, the girl child is a victim of exploitative household work. At times, there is a connection with the remanants of slavery, such as the sale of children for forced labour, particularly from certain ethnic groups. In same parts of Central and South America, the number of children at work is large, especially as there is a huge population of street children. There were disturbing incidents murders of street children during the past years. In this geographical area, too, the problems of child domestic workers and the use of children in the informal sector are rampant. At the other end, children are at time employed to sell objectionable drugs. The problem of child labour in Europe exploitation poses a challenges to many countries. This includes a specific linkage between children used a instruments of crime and as domestic workers.

To clarify, general observation made is that while there are national and international laws, including various Plans and Programmes of Action which cover most of the situations, law implementation leaves much to be desired.

In addition, the existing laws in nature are more remedial rather than preventive.

Suggestions in relation to the sale of children for child labour exploitation, are as offered:

(i) In general states, national and international organisations are invited to keep in mind strategies of prevention protection and rehabilitation in suppressing the exploitation of child labour. All strategies involve short- and long-term planning, implementation and monitoring. Achievable goals depend upon close coordination, adequate budgetary allocation and willingness to cooperate between the national and local agencies including federal and state links.

(ii) Regarding precautionary measures, states along with national and international organisations should initial antipoverty strategies, improved discrimination of information universal primary education, community awakening mobilisation, the satisfaction of basic needs, occupational opportunities and alternative forms of employment for adults.

(iii) Protection of children from exploitation through labour depends upon a adequate and effective laws and policies together with their effective enforcement at the national and local levels. All countries already have laws which can be brought in to use to protect children, for instance, the criminal law. These should be implemented in a more committed manner. The services of the law enforcement authorities, namely police force, immigration authorities, judges, inspectors and others, needs also to be improved. Regarding transnational child labour exploitation, improved links between INTERPOL and national police are required to identify transnational chains. Moreover, extradition arrangements should be enhanced so as to facilitate the transfer of alleged criminals to face charges in the country where the abuse has taken place.

For Rehabilitation, States and national and international organisations should take remedial steps to help children who are exploited. This may include juridical remedies, such as prosecution of guilty and the provision of legal aid and assistance, and/or socio-medical measures such as the provision of hospices, counselling and other support facilities. On the other side appropriate spiritual remedies, for example, religion, should also be considered a tool to counter problems.

Medical and community facilities to help children and their families, as well as measures of protect them against discrimination and other harm should be provided Emphasis should be placed upon family-based and community-based rehabilitation rather than State than through state run institutes. Particular attention should be paid to child trafficking. This requires proper safeguards, including independent monitoring and follow-up, for children to be returned to their country of origin. Pending their return to the native country, they should not be treated a illegal immigrants by the receiving countries but dealt with humanely as special cases of humanitarian concern. When children return home the countries of origin should treat them with respect in accordance with international human rights principles.

As far as child labour is concerned, the whole range of measure suggested by the UN Commission on Human Rights' Programme of Action for the Elimination of the Exploitation of Child Labour 1993 should be implemented. There should be hard and fast law enforcement in the case of child labour, with more incentives for committed law enforcement personnel. All vestiges of bondage should be eradicated, and attention should be paid to the given of the girl child. The Programme of Action against Child Bondage, 1992 should also be considered a priority for all parties concerned. Special emphasis should also be placed on the plight of domestic labour, particularly in regard to children; laws may be required to check abuse in this field. Again, their basic human rights should be protected.

Child labourers who are illegal, or undocumented, should get greater protection. They should be sent back to their country of origin only if their safety and basic human rights are ensured & then themselves want to go back. This should be seen in the context of the International Convention on the Protection of the Rights of all Migrant Workers and Member of their Families, 1990.

For hazardarn sector also, similar descriptions of children at work in can be gathered from countries across the world. In Malaysia, children may work up to 17-hours days a day at rubber plantations risked to insect and snake bites. In Portugal, children as young as 12 subject to the heavy labour and myriad dangers of the construction sites' work. In Morocco, they hunch at looms for long hours and little pay, knotting the strands of luxury carpets for export. In the United State, children are abused in garment industry, sweatshops. In the Philippines, young boys dive in dangerous conditions to help set nets for deep-sea fishing. This is high time the world should, have outgrown the many forms of abuse labouring children endure. But it hasn't although not for absence of effort. Child labour was one of the first and most important issues addressed by the international community, resulting in the emergence of International Labour Organization's (ILO) 1919 Minimum Age Convention.

Some early efforts had been made though partial, because campaigners struggling to end child labour appealed to morality and ethics, values easily ignored by the drive for profit and the hard realities or commercial life. Child labourers were object is of pitty of humanitarian concern but they enjoyed no legal right.

But, now the picture is different at least in this respect. Children have rights granted through international laws, not least in the Convention on the Rights of the Child, which has now been ratified by all but all few countries. Ratification specifically binds governments—in article 32 - to protect children "from economic exploitation and from performing any work that is likely to be hazardous or to interfere with the child's education, or to be harmful to the child's health or physical, mental, spiritual, moral or social development". But beyond that article, children abuse in work contravenes many more of the rights enshrined in the Convention, which includes, children's rights to care by their parents, to compulsory and free primary education, to the maximum attainable standard of health, to social security, and to provisions for rest and recreation. The rights of those children whose primary activity is work are, without question, in danger viewing at children's work through the lens of children's rights and the Convention on the Rights of the Child, as this State of the World's Children report aims at, offers not only new ways of understanding the problem of child labour but also provides new impetus and direction to the at child labour movement.

Our prime interest must always be the best interests of the child. It can never being the best interests of a child to be exploited or to perform heavy and hazardous forms of work. No child should labour in dangerous and exploitative conditions, just as no child should die of preventable illness. On this aspect, there can be no second opinion. Work that endangers children's physical, mental, spiritual, moral or social development must be done away with. Hazardous child labour is a betrayal of every child's rights as a human being and is an offence against our civilization.

Now after a long journey of ratification of convention, at the heights level, governments have begun to move on the issue, to fulfil the commitments they assumed in ratifying the Convention on the Rights of the Child. In New Delhi in 1996, for example, labour ministers of the Non-Aligned Movement said that "exploitative child labour wherever it is practised is a moral outrage and an affront to human dignity." They agreed to give "immediate priority for total and de facto elimination of child labour in hazardous employments." At the local level, activists' groups and NGOs are finding out ways tore pull children out of dangerous work situations and provide alternatives for them. And in August 1996, the third SAARC Ministerial Conference on the Children of South Asia committed member States of ending bonded labour by the year 2000 and to "eliminate the evil of child labour" by 2010.

Another important example is the ILO International Programme on the Elimination of Child Labour. Launched in 1991 to help children in six countries, it now works with NGO and government partners in 20 countries approximately. To cite just two others, in a UNICEF-assisted programme in the Philippines, teams consisted of government inspectors, social workers, police, NGOs, prosecutors and the media regularly those in danger. And in Bangladesh, where primary education is the first priority, a joint NGO/government non-formal education programme for 1.4 million poor urban children was designed in late 1995.

At last for better, structural adjustment programmes have been modified in an attempt to mitigate their effects on the vulnerable. In new agreements being made between governments and the international financial institutions, public expenditure on primary education and other basic social services is increasingly being incurred from budget cuts. But most developing countries are still living with the policies of the recent past: unmodified adjustment packages still burden heavily their poorest citizens. And it is in this state that they must now face the implications of the worldwide fight for competitiveness associated with 'globalization.

Conclusions

Complete analysis of all the various cultural factors that lead children into work is essential. But deference to tradition is often put as a reason for not acting against intolerable forms of child labour. Children have an absolute, unnegotiable right to freedom from hazardous—a right now provided in international law and accepted by every country that has ratified the Convention on the Rights of the Child. Identify & acceptance for diverse cultures should not deflects us from using all the means at our disposal to make every society, every economy, every corporation, regard the exploitation of children as unthinkable.

7

TERMS AND CONDITIONS FOR CHILDREN AT WORK

Though it is an organised or organised sector, may it be adult or child labour employed, most important is the terms of employment and working conditions which determine the employee-employer relationship at work places. In the same may, the Industrial relations at large, their importance in the worker's happiness and productivity can not be under-estimated. The former makes the way for personal satisfaction of the workers in term of remuneration and other conditions of employment whereas the latter emphasises the availability of humane and healthy conditions at work places. The terms of employment indicates various elements such as workers earnings in the form of wages, overtime, other perks like bonus, gratuity, working hours, leave, holidays, medical benefits, housing, etc. It also points out other welfare and social security components linked with the employment. While the terms of work helps the workers to fulfil their personal and family needs, better working conditions help them to work effectively, efficiently and productively with work satisfactions.

The work place equipped with proper and adequate facilities not only helps in shaping the social behaviour of workers but also in deciding on the working norms as well as employee-employer relationships of late, it has been realised that conducive working conditions have a greater influence on various aspects of the workers life like commitment to organise a harmonious interpersonal relationship. Moreover, it has been found that a large chunk of industrial disputes arise due to the unsatisfactory working conditions. Uncongenial, undesirable and poor working conditions coerce the workers to keep away from the work places and result in disenchantment with work giving birth to problems like absenteeism, boredom, monotony, fatigue, accidents, disobedience, occupational health hazards, poor quality of work, unhealthy employer-employee relations and disturbances at the work place. It includes a wide variety of things and can be categorised into two parts i.e., physical conditions and social conditions. Physical working conditions can be seen as (1) nature of work itself in terms of fatigue, monotony and burden, (2) safety measures, (3) lighting, (4) temperature and ventilation and other aspects for industrial health and hygiene. Supervision, communication, bargaining trade unionism etc. are determining factors of industrial relations or employee-employer relationship which may be called as social conditions.

Various items enlisted above as terms of work and working conditions have been regulated through the legal provisions under different state and central legislations, but the scope of these acts are confined to the organised sectors only. It is a matter of grave concern that conditions of work in the unorganised sectors like carpet industry and other small scale industry, conditions are still decided by the employers in an arbitrary manner and these are so horrible and shocking that it becomes difficult to believe that workers can work in such tingy conditions.

In this chapter we shall deal with the term of employment and working conditions of the child workers in the carpet weaving industry. Employers' consideration to employ child labour, place from where child workers are recruited, surety for employment after apprenticeship (training) are also being discussed. In addition to the terms of work like monthly wages, overtime, hours of work, rest period, provisions of leave, holidays, night work etc. The figures on the working conditions and the impact of work on health, social behaviours of child labour, physical and welfare facilities, employer and child labour relationship have also been dealt with in this chapter. An attempt has been made to highlight the nature of supervision, disciplinary action, grievance handling, job satisfaction and other allied aspects related with the work life of the child workers.

Important Reasons for Employing Children

During a survey, the employers (100) were asked to mention their considerations that made them to employ children. A variety of multiple responses were obtained. Maximum of two responses from each respondent were taken for analysis purposes which are presented in the table 7.1 below:

Table 7.1

Reasons Motivating Employers to Employ Child Labour

N = 100

Sl. No.	*Reasons*	*No.*	*Percentage*
1.	Cheaper labour	37	18.5
2.	Hard work	67	33.5
3.	Less troublesome	10	5.0
4.	Longer hours of work	22	11.0
5.	Not trade unions	7	3.5
6.	Easily controllable	14	7.0
7.	They can be put to any job	30	15.0
8.	Any other	12	6.0
9.	No Response	1	0.5
	Total	200	100.0

As is evident from the above table, a majority of respondents, i.e., 67 (33.5 per cent) said that they found the child labour more hard working, 37 (18.5 per cent) expressed that they fond them less expensive than adult workers, 30 (15.0 per cent) found that it was easy to put them in any job, 14 (7.0 per cent) liked them because they were more disciplined and easy to handle, 22 (11.0 per cent) preferred them because of their capacity to labour harder, 10 (5.0 per cent) said that they created less trouble, 7 (3.5 per cent) preferred them because they do not form trade unions, whereas 12 (6.0 per cent) employed them because they were easily available and could be put to any work including domestic chores. This clearly shows that the child labour is cheaper, easily disciplinable and can be put to work beyond the prescribe working hours. This further confirms the opinion that the poor are exploited more by the rich.

Child Labour Specific Communities

As far as recruitment in the big factories and organisation is concerned, is made either through advertisements or scouting methods. When the employers of the carpet weaving units were asked to speak out their preferences, if they had for any community, 19 employers said that they preferred the child workers from the lower communities and castes, 16 wanted from their own community, another 10 preferred from both the lower as well as their own communities whereas a majority of them had no preference for any child worker.

The reasons for preferring workers of their own or socio-economically backward communities may be the lack of social relationship between various communities in rural area. It is a well documented fact that dominance is closely associated with the caste structure of the rural communities. It is only because of this reason that employers prefer the child worker from the lower or from the same community. This pattern was not followed in the cases of 55 employers and this might be due to the recent changes and developments in social relationships between the rural communities.

The table 7.2 present the modalities of recruitment of the child workers by employers. From the above, obvious that 92 (46.0 per cent) employers said that unemployed children and their parents approached them for work, 75 (37.5 per cent), said employer themselves went to hire child worker whereas 33 (16.5 per cent) that workers approached them for employment with the help of co-workers. This shows, that in this occupation the mode of recruitment of children is direct. The data presented here show that in cottage industries like carpet weaving, scouting is the only method adopted by the employers to recruit child workers. This fact also reflects the informal adhoc recruitment method in village industries because of non-urbanised social relationship prevailing in the villages.

Table 7.2

Modalities of Child Recruitment

Sl. No.	*Mode*	*Number*	*Percentage*
1.	Both parents are their child	92	46.0
2.	Employers themselves try for them	75	37.5
3.	Through Co-workers	33	16.5
	Total	200	100

Characteristics of Employers

As already mentioned, the present study has encompassed 100 employers for collection of relevant facts on child labour. The general characteristics of 100 employers sample of study are presented in the table that follows.

It is clear that 44 per cent employers were in the age-group of 21-30 years, 39 per cent in the age group of 31 to 40 years, 11 in the age group of 15 to 20 years whereas 6 were 14 and above. More than half of them (60 per cent) belonged to the backward caste, including 6 who came from Muslim community, 31 belonged to the scheduled caste, 8 belonged to the scheduled tribes and one to the upper caste. Education-wise, more than half (52 per cent) were illiterate, 29 were educated upto 5th standard, 4 per cent were upto middle, 12 per cent upto the high school while 3 per cent studied upto the graduate level. Religion-wise, 94 were Hindus and the remaining (6) were Muslims. As regards the position of the carpet weaving industries, 20 units were running since the last two years only, 31 for 8 to 10 years, 17 for 3 to 5 years, 14 for 11 to 15 years, 12 for 16 and above and the remaining (6) for 6 to 7 years. This shows that the carpet weaving work in the area is growing because the educated and the uneducated persons have been carrying on this work in their houses. The data analysis shows that the people belonging to the backward castes were more aware about the gainful occupation.

Table 7.3

Employer's Characteristics

Sl. No.	*(A)* ***Age group*** *(Years)*	*No.*	*Percentage*
1.	Upto 20 years	11	11
2.	21-30 years	44	44
3.	31-40 years	39	39
4.	41 and above	6	6
	Total	100	100

Sl. No.	(B) **Caste**	No.	Percentage
1.	Upper Caste	1	1
2.	Backward Caste	60	60
3.	Scheduled Caste	31	31
4.	Scheduled Caste	8	8
	Total	100	100

Sl. No.	(C) Educational Status	No.	Percentage
1.	Illiterate	52	52
2.	Upto Vth Standard	29	29
3.	Upto VIIIth Standard	4	4
4.	High school	12	12
5.	Graduation above	3	3
	Total	100	100

Sl. No.	(D) Religion	No.	Percentage
1.	Hindu	94	94
2.	Muslim	6	6
	Total	100	100

Strength of Workers in Carpet Units

The strength of workers in different carpet weaving units were gathered through the employers which is presented in the table that follows:

Table 7.4

Number of Labourers Employed in Different Units

Sl. No.	*No. of units*	*Adult workers*	*Child workers*	*Total workers*
1.	50	70	59	129
2.	28	58	85	143
3.	6	21	25	46
4.	5	22	28	50
5.	3	8	16	24
6.	4	24	38	62
7.	4	12	50	62
Total	100	215	301	516

From the above table it becomes evident that 100 establishments had employed around 516 workers inclusive of 301 child workers. It comes to an average of 5.16 inclusive 2.15 adult workers and 3.01 child workers. This table shows that 50 establishments had employed a total of 70 adult workers as against 59 child workers, 28 employed 58 adults against 85 child worker, 28 employed 8 adults against 16 child labouers, 4 carpet units had 24 adults, against 38 child workers, another 4 had 12 adult workers against 50 child workers. In these number all counted all the workers including family members who were engaged in carpet making. Though difficult to indicate any particular trend, 50 per cent establishments in this study employed more children than adults for the reasons stated earlier.

Fitness Certificate from an Authorised Doctor

When the employers were asked whether their child workers were required to submit medical fitness certificate before they joined their jobs, it was found that all the employers (100) were neighter aware of it nor could they understand its requirement because they employed only physically as well as mentally healthy and efficient children for work. In case of accidents and injuries, Kerosene Oil and carpet wool were used as alternative medicines and reportedly it cured their injuries. Similarly, the parents of the child workers were asked whether their children were medically examined before joining work. All the respondents (100) replied in the negative and also said that in case of any physical mishappening, injury, accident and they had to go to private medical practitioners or to primary health centres. It clearly shows that neither parents nor employers of children had felt the importance of medical fitness probably because of their rural background with illiteracy, lack of legal awareness and neglect by the law enforcing agencies.

Banded Labour Inguise

In the unorganised sectors like carpet weaving units, employers behave in accordance with their middle men. They usually seek security money from the apprentices alongwith bonds to serve their establishments. The researcher asked the parents whether they deposited and surety/security to the employers for employment of their children. They replied in the negative and added that most of the employers had provision of a giving advance money for payment to the parents of the child workers for family needs. This advance money was to be repaid in terms of child labour and as such the children were forced to work with a particular employer till the full repayment of the advance money. Usually this advance is interest free and it remains so till they work with the same employer. Interests are charged only when they leave the employer. Security money is not charged from them at any stage so long as the child workers work with that employer. This appears to be in accordance with the local, tradition and informal social relationship among the rural people.

Skill Empowerment of Children

In occupation such as carpet weaving, training is essential for workers before they can be employed. Without having proper skills, a child can not be regarded as an efficient workers. In this connection, employers were asked whether children were taken in as workers or as apprentices. About 98 respondents expressed that they recruited apprentices whereas 2 said that they had put them directly on jobs. But when parents were asked whether their children had been trained 93 said that their children had undergone training whereas only 7 replied that they started working on the carpet units without any training. It appeals that these children were used as helpers by the employers to pick up the techniques and they worked as skilful workers later on higher wages. In this case, children are at loss because it takes years in absence of a formal training for them to pick up the skill of carpet making. Out of 95 parents whose children had received training and 98 employers who had put the child workers on training were asked to describe the length of training which is presented in the table 7.5 below.

Table 7.5

Duration of training course for child workers

Sl. No.	*Duration*	*Parents opinion No.*	*Parents opinion Percentage*	*Employers opinion No.*	*Employers opinion Percentage*
1.	Less than 6 months	18	19.5	19	19.5
2.	6 months to one year	68	73.0	79	80.6
3.	More than one year	7	7.5	-	-
	Total	93	100.0	98	100.0

The table above is self evidence for the duration of course more important is that there are some discrepancies in the informations given by parents and employers regarding the period of training for children before they were employed as carpet weavers. It appears that children were employed put into longer duration of training to avoid payment of due wages to them. The employers had, however, hidden this fact. They have not mentioned a single trainee for more than one year. Ideally, training should be maximums for one year as per norms adopted by the Govt. of India. Training for less than one year also suffices. It is partly clear from the responses of parents and employers (68 per cent - 73 per cent) respectively.

Terms of Apprenticeship

During this period, although children waste raw materials, they help in production after learning the skill. They are assigned to work with adults in carpet weaving. They are paid according their skills and output. This rate of payment varies from unit to unit and from trainee to trainee in the same unit. In this connection, employers as well as parents were asked about the terms of training which are presented in the table 7.6.

Table 7.6

Amount of Stipend Paid to Trainees (in Rs.)

Respondents	*Amount Paid*				*Pocket money*		*Total*	
	Upto No.	*Rs. 50 Percentage*	*51 to 100 No.*	*Percentage*	*No.*	*Percentage*	*No.*	*Pers.*
Employers	92	92.0	4	4.0	2	2.0	100	100.0
Parents	14	14.0	1	1.0	78	78.0	100	100.0

The table presents, that vary between employer and parents. A majority of employers (92) said that they had been paying Rs. 50 to the trainees whereas 4 said they paid Rs. 51 to 100, the remaining (2 respondents) did not pay money to them except in kind such as meal, old clothing and free accommodation for stay. Similarly, when parents were asked about this, 93 of them said that their children were paid nothing in this period except pocket money @ Rs. 10 to 15 per month, another 14 were given stipend upto Rs. 50 per month, and only one was paid Rs. 51 to 100 per month.

The contradiction can be easily understood in term of human wickedness to conceal unfavourable facts and present rosy pictures about their establishments. Whatever be the truth, onething clear that the employers in this industry are more inclined to exploit the helpless condition of children.

Resource for Likings for on giving job

The unemployment rate is usually found more in the rural areas both for the educated and the uneducated population. The well-known factor behind it include small agricultural holding and lack of industries in and around villages. Due to the increasing population, people migrate to cities and many look for some alternative mode of earning. In their search for all alternative sources of income they prefer carpet weaving industry available in the rural areas of that particular belt. The respondents were asked to list first two important reasons for taking up job in the carpet units and these responses are presented in the table 7.7.

Table 7.7

Factors as Reported by the Child Workers for Preferring Present Job

N = 309

S. No.	*Reasons*	*No.*	*Percentage of responses*
1.	No other alternative	165	28.1
2.	It does not require much skills	52	8.8
3.	It is not risky	7	1.2
4.	Work place is closeby	77	13.1
5.	Family members or relatives are in this occupation.	146	24.8

6.	For more income	74	12.6
7.	For self employment	59	10.0
8.	Other Reasons	8	1.4
	Total	588	100.0

The table above shows that 28.1 per cent joined this job because they had nothing available to them and 24.8 per cent joined because of their family members already employed in the same job. Some of them (13.1 per cent) said that they had joined this job because of the proximity of the carpet unit to their residence whereas 12.6 per cent considered better as one of the reason for preferring this unit work. Other important reasons were that 8.8 per cent wanted to start their own unit, whereas 1.4 per cent considered it as an occupation which did not require much skill.

The Parents of the child workers were also asked the reasons for selecting present occupation for their children. About 61 per cent expressed that their children joined it as no other opportunity was open to them, 31 told that their children joined it because their friends had joined the carpet work and 8 said that employers themselves requested them to send their children for the carpet weaving work. In brief, one can infer form this data that the main reason for joining this occupation is non-availability of alternatives sources of income.

Wages Structure

The rate of payment, is dependent upon various factors like nature of job skilled or un-skilled, semi-skilled work, duration of working hours and hazardous environment. It again varies in cases of casual, contract and regular employments and also in the case of children or adult though the law does not support all these variables for determining the rates of wages. Another important factor in determining the wages is the will of employers. This becomes clear when the wage structure of different establishments in organised as well as unorganised sectors are compared. In the case of the carpet weaving industries, the structure of payment of stipends to trainees has already been discussed. Some is the structure of wages in these units. There is no regular employment or monthly pay it is found in the organised sector. They are employed and paid till the employer has work. In case they do not have work the workers are thrown out and payment is made according to the output of each worker. Sometimes children are employed on monthly basis also but in that case they have to do domestic work of their employers.

Earnings in a Month

Finding gathered from them were divided into different groups for this purpose which are presented in the table below. The table tells that 116 (39.9 per cent) of the respondents earned between Rs. 151 and 200 per month, 103 (35.4 per cent) between Rs. 101 and 150, 44 (15.1 per cent) between Rs. 51 and 100, 12 (4.1 per cent) earned Rs. 50 or less while 18 respondents did not earn anything in cash but in kind. The break-up of their earnings in terms of the category of employment shows that the earnings in terms of the category of employment shows that the earning of the self-employed child workers was more as compared to employed worker. In the employed group of the child workers, more than half (55-18.9 per cent) workers could earn between Rs. 101 and 150 while in case of the self employed 66 (22.7 per cent) earned between Rs. 151 and 200. This shows that about half of the workers earned Rs. 150 or less in month which is very little in term of wages. This clearly proves the on going exploitation of the child workers and carelessness of the law enforcing agencies.

Table 7.8

Distribution of the Child Workers by Category of Employment and Monthly Income

S. No.	Nature of employment	Monthly income Rs. Upto Rs. 50/-	51to 100	101 to 150	151 to 200	201 to 300	Total
1.	Employed	3 (1.0)	29 (10.0)	55 (18.9)	50 (17.2)	7 (2.4)	144 (49.5)
2.	Self-employed	- (5.2)	15 (16.5)	48 (22.7)	66 (3.1)	9 (47.4)	138
3.	Trainees	9 (3.1)	-	-	-	-	9 (3.1)
	Total	12 (4.1)	44 (15.1)	103 (35.4)	116 (39.9)	16 (5.5)	291 (100.0)

Note: (1) Figures in bracket indicate percentages.

(2) 18 were getting in kinds which have not been included in this Table.

Monthly Earning of Educated Group

Educated persons are known to have more knowledge, sense of responsibility and understanding rather than illiterates. Therefore, they should be paid better wages. Keeping this point in mind, the respondents from the group of educated ones were asked to describe their monthly earning which is presented in the table 7.9.

Table 7.9

Distribution of the Child Workers on Basis of Education and Monthly Income

N = 309

Sl. No.	Level of education	Amount of monthly income (Rs.) Upto Rs. 50	51 to 100	101 to 150	151 to 200	201 to 300	Nil	Total
1.	Illiterate	10 (3.2)	33 (10.1)	73 (23.6)	64 (20.7)	3 (1.0)	9 (2.9)	192 (62.1)

2. Upto IInd	-	5 (1.6)	16 (5.2)	11 (3.6)	— —	3 (1.0)	35 (11.3)
3. IIIrd to IVth	2 (0.7)	5 (1.6)	13 (4.2)	26 (8.4)	5 (1.6)	4 (1.3)	55 (17.8)
4. VIth to VIIith	-	1 (0.3)	1 (0.3)	9 (2.9)	6 (2.0)	1 (0.3)	18 (5.8)
5 VIIIth and above	-	-	-	6 (2.0)	2 (0.7)	1 (0.3)	9 (2.9)
Total	12 (3.9)	44 (14.2)	103 (33.3)	116 (37.6)	16 (5.2)	18 (5.8)	309 (100.0)

Note: Figures in the brackets indicate percentages.

As per the table mentioned above the educated child workers earned better than illiterate ones. Out of 55 child workers who were educated upto 3rd to 5th standard earning of was 2 Rs. 50 or loss per month, 5 between Rs. 51 and Rs. 100, 13 between Rs. 101 and 150 another 26 between Rs. 151 and 200 whereas 5 made their earnings between Rs. 201 and 300 per month. Again, out of 27 respondents who were educated beyond the primary school, 15 earned between Rs. 151 and 200 every month, 8 between Rs. 201 and 300, 2 (0.6 per cent) between Rs. 51 and 151 and earning were paid only in kind. Out of all the illiterates (192), only 3 earned between Rs. 201 and 300 in month, 9 did not earn anything except in kind and the rest (180) earned Rs. 200 or less per month. This reveals that the monthly earning of the child workers was less than the prescribed minimum wages. One can than say that education does help in earning better wages. These findings can be explained on the basis of the fact that not the implementation of the legal provisions is to but many other factors like social, political and personality factors are related to education.

Similarly, the information regarding the regularity in payment was also gathered through the child respondents. When wage earners (child workers) were asked whether their salaries were paid in time and in one instalment, 161 (55.3 per cent) answered (44.7 per cent) said that they got it irregularly and in broken instalments.

Response of the Child Workers in Respect of their Income

Out of 291 child workers, 125 (42.5 per cent) were not happy with their income, whereas 86 (29.6 per cent) were satisfied and the remaining 80 (27.5 per cent) were unable to respond categorically. To know the income satisfaction level among the different categories of the child workers. The status is clear from the table 7.10.

Table 7.10

Distribution of the Child Workers based on Caste and Income Satisfaction

N = 309

Sl. No.	*Status of Satisfaction*	*Upper caste*	*B.C*	*Caste* *S.C*	*S.T.*	*Total*
1.	Satisfied	4 (1.3)	61 (19.8)	18 (5.8)	3 (1.0)	86 (27.8)
2.	So-So	4 (1.3)	64 (20.7)	10 (3.2)	2 (0.6)	80 (25.9)
3.	Not-Satisfied	8 (2.6)	89 (28.8)	26 (8.4)	2 (0.6)	125 (40.5)
4.	Did not Receive payment	1 (0.3)	10 (3.2)	5 (1.6)	2 (0.6)	18 (5.8)
		17	224	59	9	309
	Total	(5.5)	(72.6)	(19.0)	(2.9)	(100.0)

The table 7.10 shows that out of 86 (27.8 per cent) satisfied child workers, 4 (1.3 per cent) belonged to the high caste, 3 (1.0 per cent) to Scheduled tribe, another 18 (5.8 per cent) to the Scheduled Caste, while 61 (19.8 per cent) to the Backward Caste. Further, out of 125 (40.5

per cent) dissatisfied children, 2 (0.6 per cent) belonged to the Scheduled Tribe, 8 (2.6 per cent) to the upper caste, 26 (8.4 per cent) to the Scheduled Caste and the remaining 89 (28.8 per cent) to the Backward Caste.

Similarly to know the satisfaction level in different categories of the child workers a distribution the basis of category of employment and income satisfaction level is presented in the table 7.11.

Table 7.11

Distribution of the Child Workers as per the Category of Employment and Income Satisfaction

N = 291

Sl. No.	Category of work	Level of Satisfaction			
		Satisfied	So-So	Dissatisfied	Total
1.	Employed	35 (12.0)	40 (13.7)	79 (27.2)	154 (52.9)
2.	Self-employed	50 (17.2)	38 (13.1)	40 (13.7)	128 (44.0)
3.	Trainees did not receive wages	1 (0.4)	2 (0.6)	6 (2.1)	9 (3.1)
	Total	86 (29.6)	80 (27.4)	125 (43.0)	291 (1.00)

The above table shown that 50 (17.2 per cent) of the self-employed children were satisfied while in the case of the employed children only 35 (12.0 per cent) per cent were happy with their salaries. Similarly, dissatisfaction in the case of the self-employed was 13.7 per cent whereas in the case of the employed it was 27.2 per cent. It seems that the self-employed are more satisfied with the income than the employed ones. One may say here that satisfaction of the self-employed though apparently related to their salaries may be due to many other factors like freedom of action and movement and feeling of ownership, etc.

Duration of work

The number of hours of work in carpet weaving depends upon a many factors such as (i) demand of carpets at a particular time, (ii) availability of labour force, (iii) the time schedule for delivery of carpets. We were told that the working hours of children are long, adequate rest intervals are missing, and weekly and other holidays are not given. The working hours of the child workers have been from 4 to 16 hours per day. While collecting data, it was found that most of the child workers, reach their work place at around 6 AM and finish their work at around 6 PM.

Rest at Work

In the taugh work situation, it becomes necessary to make provision for intervals so that the harmful effects of work on health caused by non-step work for long hours may be avoided and workers' efficiency may be restored and maintained. So far, as the rest period of the working children is concerned, the team could not obtain precise statistical information but during the survey it was found that the self-employed children in their family units, in most of the cases, had not fixed periods for rest. These children were at liberty to attend their family members working on carpets. In the cases, had no fixed periods for rest. These children were at liberty to attend their personal or family needs with due permission from their family members working on carpets. In the case of the employed child workers their period of rest differed from season to season. During the summer season they were given rest for two hours (from 12 to 2) while in the rainy season as well as in the winter season, it was generally for one and a half hours. In some of the carpet weaving units, workers began work after taking breakfast but in most of the cases, especially in the summer season they began work even earlier and were given half an hour for their breakfast, but in case of the migrant child workers who were residing with their employers, were given much less time to have breakfast as well as lunch. Other child workers from the neighbouring villages brought their meals with them or brought these during the lunch time.

Leave and Holidays for the Child Workers

On enquiry from the child workers and their employers, it was known that there was no thing like paid holidays and leave of any kind. It was based on the principle that the wages would be paid according to the number of days they had really worked. If they remained absent, their wages were accordingly deducted. They could get leave for any number of days without pay on one condition that they would inform their employers before hand. Leave without pay was also refused to them if there was more pressure of work. In this respect, the self-employed children were much better as they enjoyed leave and holidays as and when required.

Night work

According to the factory Act, 1948 work during nights by children is prohibited this is quite in common in the carpet industries. During the interview of child respondents (309), a majority of them, i.e., 264 (85.4 per cent) said that they had to work at nights whereas 42 (13.6 per cent) did not work and the rest, i.e., 3 (1.6 per cent) did not disclose anything. The child workers (264) who worked at nights were asked to described their working hours which are presented in he table 7.12.

Table 7.12

Working Hours of Children at Night

S. No.	*Hours*	*No.*	*Percentage*
1.	One hour	76	28.8
2.	Two hours	111	42.1
3.	Three hours	74	28.0
4.	Four hours	3	1.1
	Total	264	100.0

The table 7.12 shows that 76 (28.8 per cent) of 264 child workers accepted that they worked daily during nights. In addition, 111 (42 per cent) worked for two hours, 74 (28.0 per cent) for 3 hours while 3 (1.1 per cent) worked for fours hours daily during night. This further shows the exploitation level of the child workers by their employers.

Facilities Provided to Children at Work

When asked about the provision of facilities for the child workers at work such as rest place, medical aid, drinking water, canteen, toilet, recreation, etc. the employers replied in the negative and most of them were not aware of it.

Employers and Employees Relations

The significance of industrial peace for production and better social life has been realised. The relationship between the employer and the employees along is not sufficient, relationship between workers and workers is also important. In order to know the pattern of relationship in these units the child workers were interviewed. The two tables that follows shows the relationship between the workers.

Table 7.13

Adult Workers Behaviour with the Child Workers

N = 309

S. No.	*Behavioural type*	*No.*	*Percentage*
1.	Supportive	93	30.0
2.	So-so	133	43.1
3.	Non-supportive	83	26.9
	Total	309	100.0

It may be seen from the table 7.13 that only 93 (30.0 per cent) spoke of their supportive relationship with their co-adult workers whereas 83 (26.9 per cent) had not good relationship with them. The rest 133 (43.1 per cent) could not mention their relationship with their co-workers accurately.

Table 7.14

Employer's Behaviour with the Child Workers

N = 309

S. No.	*Behaviour*	*No.*	*Percentage*
1.	Supportive	75	24.3
2.	SO-so	211	68.3
3.	Non-supportive	23	7.4
Total		309	100.0

The table 7.14 shows that 75 (24.3 per cent) and cordial relationship with their employers whereas 23 (7.4 per cent) workers did not have cordial relationship with their employers and 211 (68.3 per cent) could not clearly say about their relationship.

Demands and Grievances

The employers were asked to list the common grievances and demand put forward by the working children and their parents. Each employers was asked to mention important grievances out of which first two are presented in the table 7.15.

Table 7.15

Grievances and Demands by Children and Parents to Employers

N = 100

Sl. No.	*Type of demand and Grievances*	*No.*	*Percentage of responses*
1.	Low wages	56	36.0
2.	Irregular payment	12	6.5
3.	Poor learning of skill	9	4.8
4.	Long duration of work	9	4.8
5.	Threat of adult workers	4	2.2
6.	Advance payment	47	25.3
7.	Pocket money	20	10.8
8.	Any other	29	15.6
	Total	186	100.0

Has been shown that 56 (30 per cent) respondent's grievances were received by the employers for payment of low wages to the child workers, 47 (25.3 per cent) were received for non-payment of cash in advance, 20 (10.8 per cent) demanded pocket money, 12 (6.5 per cent) grievances were for irregular payment, 9 (4.8 per cent) were for long period of work, another 9 (4.8 per cent) were poor learning of carpet skills by the child workers, 4 (2.2 per cent) were regarding bad behaviour by employers or co-workers, 29 (15.6 per cent) for other reasons such as leave with pay and welfare facilities. These facts give the impression that children are subjected of exploitation more after because of the lack of any organised attempt through (trade unions) to solve their problem. This is quite common with the unorganised sector where there is no regular union to approach the employers for redressal to their grievances.

Handling of Grievance

Next table containing information on the agents who put up grievances and demands of the child workers to their employers is given.

Table 7.16

List of Grievances in Terms of Agents

Sl. No.	Grievances came through	No.	Percentage
1.	Children themselves	168	54.4
2.	Co-Workers	44	14.2
3.	Parents	90	29.1
4.	Don't' know	7	2.3
	Total	309	100.0

The table 7.16 shows that out of 309 child workers 168 (54.4 per cent) said that it was mentioned personally by them, 90 (29.1 per cent) through their parents whereas 44 (14.2 per cent) told that they put it through their co-worker and the remaining 7 (23.3 per cent) did not specify the agent.

Similarly, next table contains information on grievance redressal. This table reveals that when children were asked about their grievances redressal and their satisfaction, out of 309, 146 said that these were always listened to by their concerns, another 113 said there were listened to less often and 50 told that their grievances were never attended to by their employers. Another 50 child workers said that their grievance were redressed properly, 113 said that there were handled sometimes whereas 146 expressed that their grievances were never taken up.

Table 7.17

Handling of Grievance

Sl. No.	*Listens*	*No.*	*Solves*
1.	Every time	146	50
2.	Sometimes	113	113
3.	Never	50	146
	Total	309	309

Disciplinary Action Against the Child Workers

Childhood is a period of socialization. This period is marked by immaturity, high sensitivity, plasticity and impulsiveness. It is only through guidance and loving care that the child learns the normal behaviour which is expected from an adult. It is natural for him to commit more mistakes because of his physical and mental immaturity. The table that follows tries to present the reactions of employers to mistakes, misbehaviour and damages made by children. The responses of the child workers about the disciplinary action taken against them by their employers have also been included in this table. It can be seen that 35.8 per cent children said that they received threats form their employers and them. Similarly, 27.7 per cent workers received beating whereas only 2.7 per cent employers accepted using physical punishment against children. There were same cases (4.3 per cent) when the employers terminated the services of the child workers. It seems that the punishments were given to as per the nature of mistakes.

Table 7.18

Action taken by Employers Against the Child Workers

Sl. No.	Nature of Action	Employers No.	Employers Percentage	Child workers No.	Child workers Percentage
1.	Counselling	38	20.5	126	24.7
2.	Threat	43	23.3	185	35.8
3.	Complaints to parents	44	23.8	41	8.0
4.	Battering	42	22.7	143	27.7
5.	Termination from services	8	4.3	10	1.9
6.	Recovery of money for damages	2	1.1	10	1.9
7.	Controlling them any how	6	3.2	-	-
8.	Any other	2	1.1	-	-
	Total	185	100.0	515	100.0

Conclusion

The impression formed from the findings and analysis made in the various tables is that the children in work at the victims of a child of organised in office. There is nothing like registered terms and condition for them. All depends upon the discretion of employer and main of the time, they send from the selfish interest & profit motives of there employer. Time and again, it is being repeated that more make legal provision is not sufficient the need is to enforce them effectively to same there tiny human creatures from even lasting exploitation.

Section— III

CHILD SEXUAL ABUSE

8

CHILD PROSTITUTION

Absues of children go beyond labour. Young girls are beaten, raped and starved, and thus forced into receiving customers. A 14-years-old girl in Mumbai brothel opposed all pressure for three weeks. Consequently, she was put in a small room with a live cobra. She sat there numb, unable to move or sleep for two days, and eventually bouned before here captors.

Forced children prostitution is found in male children also. Rohan first sold sex at the age of 15 when he met an Englishman on a beach in Sri Lanka. The men offered Rohan to come to his room and he was paid US$3. Since then Rohan has been with more men than he cannot remember. He uses condoms only if he is asked to. His friend, Sampath, is 12 but looks barely seven. Sampath's father is handicapped and his mother chronically ill. He left primary school to feed his younger brother and parents. He was earning less than US$0.50 as a casual labourer. Rohan introduced Sampath to a foreigner who was willing to pay Sampath US$2.75 if he went with him to a sub-standard guest house. Rohan received US$4 for the introduction. Rosario only at twelve,was brought to Olongapo City General Hospital in the Philippines, in extreme pain. The doctors found in her uterus parts of a broken sex toy, many inches long, and with a rusty screw at one end. They guessed that the object may have been inside Rosario's uterus for as long as five months. Despite the removal of the object, she could not survive. An

Austrain tourist, Heinrich Ritter, was convicted, but later released on request to be deported.

It is not only physically painful to them, children involved in the sex industry usually experience guilt and low self respected. Abused children in Thailand are quoted as saying, "I am no good", "god cannot forgive me", or "we are the scum of society". The question of rehabilitation of there children in difficult circumstances came up several times during the discussions. Mr. O'Grady experienced that the expertise to deal with the problems of such children could not be found easily. In most Asian countries, one can not even talk about the issue of child prostitution. "A lot of work has been done in the West in the area of sexual abuse of children within the family. We are trying to draw from that expertise in our work. Obviously it is an important area, care for such children should go on even after hey are released from that environment of exploitation." He said that the would happily accept partnerships with NGOs equipped with these skills.

Sexually exploited children have had such traumatic experiences at an early stage in their lives that they suffered from deep emotional scars. In most of the cases, normalcy is not restored by merely sending them back of their families. A point was made that many times, children of prostitutes were initiated into prostitution by their own mothers. The desire of the prostitute mothers was to send their boys to school, but induct their girls into the professin as early as possible. It was argued that often the prostitute mothers were helpless as they were themselves in the strong holds of the pimps and brothel keepers. In such a situation, girls found it impossible to escape having grown up in that violent and exploitative atmosphere and knowing little else, though the mothers had always expressed the desire to educate their children and keep them out of the business.

At a Seminar, a social workers, Lalita remarked that when she started her work among the prostitutes in Delhi's G.B. Road their main concern was for their children. "Do something for our children," the request made to her. But finding space for a centre and resources to run the centre was the biggest problem. In 1990, JWP initiated a day care centre for the children of the prostitutes, where they could be taught. After five years of formal education, the children were admitted to government or boarding schools. Femal children of prostitutes had to be considered as highly vulnerable to becoming prostitutes. She said that when the mothers came to lake back their children in the evening from the centre people in the neighborhood objected. When the children were to put the boardng school's their parental background was often not disclosed as that led to further stigmatization.

From the Ministry of Welfare, D.K. Manvalar talked about the government funding for programme for the children of prostitutes in big cities. He remarked that very few NGOs working in this area. "Voluntary action is called for," he said, "especially in psychological rehabilitation of children in such explotiative situations. The government could fund any sepcial training required for the NGOs." Returning the children to the parents is a debatable issue, as activists argue that the parents have under gone no counselling and rehabilitation programmes, and there were prostitution the children would end up in some or other from of exploitative situation. NGOs need to come forward in setting up more rehabilitation centres for such children.

Another participant, Dr. Mukhopadhyay said that working on the rehabilitation aspect was the softer and the easier way out for NGOs. To be based in the villages which were the sources areas could be quite risking as the NGOs would have to confront the trafficking netwroks, which is more difficult option. He also said that rehabilitation programmes should be designed only for those wanting to come out of the profession. Target should be both social and economic rehabilitation of the prostitues and also at providing them a dignified life free of stigma and isolation. He added that success could be achieved with regard to rehabilitation of the child prostitutes or the children of prostitues unless society's attitude towards this group of children improved.

A number of programmes with the problem of child prostitution focus on children from communities at danger who have not yet entered the sex trade.

A project called Daughters' Education Northern Thailand provides sponsorship and self-esteem workshops to help female children from poor families to stay in school. The Centre for Protection of Children's Rights, in Thailand, provides information to the villagers about the risks of physical and psychological damage, and HIV and AIDS, that the children face in the fresh trade. The centre provides a home for up to 15 girls freed from brothers. One more centre, d'Estudiosy Rehabilitation Psico-social in Chile, contacted 360 children above six years. With help of skilled staff including teachers, a psychologist and as social worker, 280 girls were able to avoid a return to prostitution.

In the wards of Mr. O 'Grady, "The wisdom of trying to check the prostitution of children rather than attempting to assist the victims has been confirmed. We have seen no evidence that children who have been systematically prostitution for more than a short period of time can ever be successfully rehabilitated. When a child is being forced to receive several sexual partners seven nights a week, the traumatic effect appears to be impossible to over-come. The experience of social workers in Asia is that extremely few children rescued from brothels have been able to begin living anything like a full and healthy life again." Mr. Grady also expressed his anxiety about telling people "to go do something for the children", as this required sensitive handling . He related the example of a sincere and sensitive European woman who took it upon herself to rescure a Nepali girl from a Bombay brothel. She managed her escape but could not obtain enough documents to get her out of the country to send her back home. Finally fed up with the situation, the girl went to the brothel, as she had no community support to restart her life. The following day she was killed, and her body parts were thrown on the streets to serve as a warning for all those girls who might attempt to escape.

As per law, sexual inter-course with a child is rape, and the police prosecutes such cases regularly. The number of prosecutions that have taken place are few due to many reasons. Deputy Commissioner of Police, Delhi, Maxwell Pereira, in his presentation, however, demanded that more powers be given to the police in dealing with interstate ganges involved in trafficking children for prostitution. He talked about the regular raids the police department has conducted at one of Delhi's red-light areas and said he had found most of the girls joined this he had found that most of the girls this profession out of sheer poverty. He continued that the police did not always find children or minors in this profession. When the police raids, they rescue the young girls and send them to Nari Niketans. As far as he was infromed, none of those rescued in Delhi had returned to the same trade. "The police continuously keeps the pressure on the red-light areas by maintaining vigil". Though child prostitution, he admitted, was existing , he did not believe that it had expanded or reached alarming proportions in Delhi.

Social activist Lalitha charged that the police officials often used the Prevention of Immoral Traffice Act (PITA), and the Juvenile Justice Act (JJA), to harass the prostitutes and their children.They often call their children as neglected children and pick them up. The women are arrested and examined for HIV. The young girls are put in vigilance homes or remand homes. "How safe are these homes run by the government?" she questioned. Research has shown that children in these observation homes often express a feeling of emptiness and isolation, and that the police officials were also insensitive while enquiring about the parental address of the girls. Representative from police side, Mr. Pereria admitted that there were some problems, but also that there were differences in the role expectations on one hand, and the officially assigned roles of the police on the other. Gerry Pinto of UNICEF, disclosing another fact said that in most of the cases it were the children who were penalized and not the adults. "Can we mobiles opinion to make the laws more child-friendly and ensure they are implemented in the right spirit?" he asked. According to Naina Kapur of SAKSHI, there is everthing faulty with the legislation regarding prostitution and rape. "Prostitution is not the issue, it is the people who use the women and children. That is what is wrong. The definition of sexual assault in our laws is very narrow. Not enough is being done to arrest the clients, who are the exploiters," she asserted.

Mr. Manvalan responded to her by words that unless and until intervention went to the apex Court level, the government does not take the pains to change the faulty provisions of the law. In his book, Rape of the Innocent, Mr. O'Grady, narrating his experience in Thailand, writes: "In many Asian countries, the police are paid shockingly low wages. In such a situation, those who control the sex industry know that they will always be able to find police who can be bribed into closing their eyes to the abuse of children and to those who are the abusers. In metro Manial alone, the National Police Commission has listed 93 cases of policemen providing protection to sex centres."

The point of common agreement was that there was a need for gender sensitization programmes for the police.

Dr. Singh alleged that all the training was being given to the upper level officials and not the constables who gave protection, and were in many cases, running this profession. Both the organisations, JWP and SAKSHI have been involved in training programmes in Delhi for police constables towards a more sensitive understanding of the problem of sexual and family violence and women's rights.

Recommendation by Dr. Mukkhopadhyay was that the law-enforcing mechanism should consider the phenomenon of child prostitution as a socio-legal and human problem. They need be strict, on one hand, with the persons involved in the procurement of girls and, on the other, be sensitive to the girls who become vicitims of fategue circumstances.

At the end of his preesentation, Mr. Pereria expressed some of the problems that the police faced: "The impact of police action is often negated as most accused are released on bail, and change their name and address and indulge in the trade again. It is not unusual that they jump bail, or the lawayers secure long term postponement on flimsy grounds. The courts ask for independent witness to give credibility to the police version. And the police cannot disclose the identity of the informer. How much social backing is there for police action against prostitution?"

NGOs' Plan of Action

India is one of these 178 countries who have ratified the convention on rights of the Child . It gives the NGOs, lawyers, government officials, and police officers, no option except to take all possible steps in ensuring protection of the rights of children. We do not need laws any more. We already have enough enactment which are not being implemented.

Role of NGOs has almost become a pattern of speech. The chosen rhetoric is that the NGOs are the closest to the target groups, that the role of an NGO is the critical one. It is a way of transferring responsibility from one sector to another. The government and NGOs however, cannot escape the responsibilty. There is a need to generate public sensitivity to these problems that confront us in our work. The time has come to rethink of the definition of NGOs. It has to include sections of media, legal agencies, women's groups, and academicians. We have to broaden the network. We need to form new aliances. There are number of young lawyers who are committed and sensitive to this problem. Why child prostitution has not figured out in the mandates of feminist organisation is a question worth asking.

Generally, NGos have to face a lot of problem in dealing with the police. Recently some street children were picked up by the police and harassed. The street educator was by matter of chance present there and he protested to the police officials against the behavior of the police. The police caught him and beat him up badly for interfering while the police was performing its duty in this case beating the children. There are, however, some sensible officials in the police force, and we need to build a positive relationship with them and use them as a catalyst in the processing change.

The issue of prostitution among children has to be addressed not merely through rehabilitation, but with greater stress on prevention. There are backward villages and districts that are the birth makes for the trafficking. That is where the real problem is the brothels in the cities are a symptom of the problem. NGOs working in rural areas should target such poor families that are forced to send their children to earn. The proverty alleviation and development programmes should help such families that are at risk.

More importantly, both NGOs and the police should work in partnership, and not watch helplessly when a child is being bailed out by pimps and taken back to the same environment.

Emphasis in discussion was on the non-legal ways of dealing with the offenders. "We do not have the skills to search the underworld mafia. It is dangerous. There are people who are making a lot of money in trafficking. NGOs, need to approach it with firmness. If the police won't act, put pressure on the offender by mobilishing public support, media support, lawyers' help, and sympathetic leaders. We have seen the strength of community action in Manila where the parents of the children went on a march and asked for justice; and in Goa where protests are going on; on the beach areas of Sri Lanka, where small community groups are determined to monitor the problem in order to protect their own children. The community has to be awakened and it is not something that is going to be easy. Like the drug trade, there is a lot of crime and a lot of money in child prostitution too. NGOs have to be very very careful."

It was pointed out by Dr. Singh that in a village in south India, a 12 year old girl was sent to Mumbai to work as a labourer because her parents could not afford feeding her. They did not know anything about Bombay or the nature of job she would be doing over there. A main who had lent some money to the family would talk her to Mumbai. It such for people who are sending their children away that needed to be indentified, he said. NGOs should task the village panchayats which now have women heads, to put this issue on their agenda, to support these vulnerable families and help intensify community action in these areas. Mr. Pinto warned against looking at problems in isolation. When the struggle to withdraw working children from the garment industry in Bangladesh was on, it was served that a number of children displaced from the work went to the flesh trades. We have to took at the totality of the problem and not just one particular aspect and need to pursue approaches which are holistic, he added. This however should not take us away from our commitment to eliminate any kind of child labour-including child prostitution.

Another NGO, JWP, who had taken up the task of obtaining identity cards for the prostitutes of Delhi, found that it had to face problems from the government officials who said that many of them were not citizens of India. "With these cards, we can prevent child prostitution or new entries, and give them basic rights to a ration card and access to health," said Lalitha. She also said that the first phase of their day-care centre project funded by the Social Welfare Department, had been stopped since. The officials at the Delhi Administration asked to be yellow handed to send a report to the department. She lamented about the amount of time they had to spend in establishing rappor with local police officials and sensitizing them, only to find that they were transferred within months.

Towards the and of the seminor it was also pointed out that if social action groups worked in the red light areas, and worked towards making education a must for children especially for girls they would not be sent to work at all. Primary education for every child should be made mandatery. Dr. Mukhopadhya warned the NGOs that in their initiatives to rehabilitate these children, care should be taken that they did not suffer any social stigma or disrespect in the process.

It was felt that the problem of child prostitution could be effectively dealt with only if these agencies worked in coordivation with each other rather than in isolation because the problem of child prostitution itself encompasses many factors in itself. Unless and until each one of there factor in handled by an NGOs the problem cannot be rooted out in fatality. Above all, the committment and sensitivity of all those governmental and non-governmental units involved in the process has to be ensured.

9

CHILD SEXUAL ABUSE : SOME NOTEWORTHY FACTORS

The cases of CSA bring to notice various vulnerable conditions of victims . But that is not all there are various care taken of sexual abuse children which need to be discussed. First among these in the search for greater understanding of how and why child sexual abuse occurs. It leads to an examination of characteristic of children themselves.The aim is to recognise factors that contribute to children's vulnerability. *Vulnerability* is defined as physical and psychological characteristic of children associated with risking their safety or protection. The definition excludes risk factors, which are situations and circumstances that increase the likelihood of victimisation, (e.g., presence of a step father in the home). Rather, vulnerability refers to those features, specific to children, that may make them victims of sexually abusive advances. Theories of childhood vulnerability to sexual abuse have included intrapsychinc, biological, social, and familial contributions. Therories, mostly unexamined, regarding victim variables have flourished, and positions on the victim's possible role in victimization cover the gamut. The child has been depicted as everyone from instigator and solicitor of the adult perpetrator, to the hapless target of men's misguided rage at women (Rush, 1980).

Some Definition of Child Sexual Abuse

In 1978, child sexual abuse man defined the national Center on Child Abuse and Neglect (NCCAN) as follows:

"Contacts or interactions betwen a child and an adult when the child is being used for the sexual stimulation of the perpetrator or another person. Sexual abuse may also be commited by a person under the age of 18 when that person is either significantly older than the victim or when the perpetrator is in a position of power or control over another's child"

The above definition of childhood sexual abuse includes a variety of activities perpetrated by relatives (intrafamilial abuse) or unrelated adults (extrafamilial abuse), such as strangers, neighbours, community supporters, or friends.

Another defination by the NCCAN notes that a child "is being used." Wurtele and Miller-Perrin (1992) define that "... sexual abuse involves the exploitation of children's ignorance, trust, and obedience". Thus, one would expect to find children's reactions to victimisers filled with confusion, mislaid layalty, and automatic compliance with authority figures. If, as Wurtele and Miller-Perrin maintained, definitions of childhood sexual abuse are "culture bound" and "direct reflections of the values and orientations of communities and societies at large", one would take children's views of sexual abuse to reflect a "subculture of childhood" characterized by knowledge, beliefs, actions, values, and hopes shared by most children.

The most important question one asks is, how children develop an understanding of sexual abuse? For example, sexual abuse is frequently referred to as "bad touch", with little or no emphasis on the sexual nature of sexual abuse. Children may ignorant of the fact that the physical contact associated with "bad touch" is considered 'bad' because it is stimulating to the perpetrator. They may be unaware of any difference between the 'good' feeling of sexual excitment and the supposed 'bad' feeling of sexual abuse. Adding to this confusion is the possibility that, as in the case of intrafamlial abuse, the perpetrator is a known and, often, loved care provider. An illustration of some form of intrafamilial sexual abuse tells why both children and adults have difficulty understanding childhood sexual abuse. Lawson (1993) described five different types of domestic sexual abuse, including mother-son incest.

The first type is *subtle abuse,* which is identified as behavior that is not intended to be sexual or harmful to the child, yet in some way gratifies the perpetrator's sexual needs "at the expense of the child, yet in some way gratifies the perpetrator's sexual needs "at the expense of the child's emotional or developmental needs. " This kind of abuse does not involve force and it may or may not involve genital contact. Instead, some parents may believe that their child needs special attention, or that their behavior is simply as expression of parent-child love.

Seductive abuse, is nest type defined as sexual stimulation that is inappropriate for the child's age and is motivated by the perpetrator's sexual needs or desires. This type of abuse involves seductive posing or gestures, allowing a child to see nude and/or sexual displays, or verbal excitment.

Perverse abuse is the third type defined as behavior that is targetted to sexually humiliate the child. This abuse may include taunting a child about his or her development during puberty, implanting fears about sexual preference in the child, or forcing the child to wear or do thing typically associated with the opposite sex.

The fourth type of abuse is *overt sexual abuse,* known as direct sexual contact between the abuser and abused. This abuse includes intercourse,digital penetration or fondling, and it involves some types of coercion.

The fifth type and last is *sadistic sexual abuse,* defined as any sexual behavior that is also intended to physically harm the child. Lawson gave an example of this type of abuse: a boy whose mother sodomized him with a broomstick. He later became a serial killer of women.

There are difference of opinion regarding should children be prepared for all the difficult, confusing, perverted realities that childhood sexual abuse encompasses? Limited understanding of sexual abuse can leave children unprepared to an abuser, yet too much information may deprive them of the safe and secure feelings that they deserve during childhood. Alerting children to the existence of "bad touch" may seem a reasonable compromise between disastrous lack of awareness and brutal overexposure to concept that alarm adults.

Cases of Childhood Sexual Abuse

For sexual abuse involving contact between the victim and perpetrator, reported prevalence rates for children under the age of 18 range from 7 per cent to 45 per cent for females and 3 per cent to 5 per cent for males. Other noncontact of body estimates rage from 10 per cent to 62 per cent for females and 3 per cent to 16 per cent for males, depending on the sample population and definition of abuse.

Occurrence and Vulnerability

Melton reported that sexually abused children and their families have some features in common. To distinguish between individual traits and environmental forces that contribute to the occurrence of childhood sexual abuse, a difference is made between vulnerability and risk factors. *Vulnerability* is defined as a feature of the child, such as small stature, naivety in social reasoning, or feeling lonely, that increases the likelihood that the child will become a victim. *Risk factors* are identified as situations in the environment that increase the likelihood that the child will be exposed to a perpetrator, such as living in a single-parent home or having a parent who was molested as a child.

Four preconditions necessary for the occurrence of childhood sexual abuse are: factors within the perpetrator, the child, the family, and society. Factors within the abused child include lack of knowledge regarding sexual behaviour, lust for attention, low self-esteem, emotional neediness, and insecurity. Other risk factors include membership in a discordant family, lack proper care, of emotional estrangement from parents, marital conflict involving uneven power distribution between the spouses, the sexual milieu of the family, isolation of the family, and characteristics of the mother, such as being busy, physically sick, mentally ill, or working outside the home.

Most vulnerable characters for children are particularly vulnerable incest. Survivors' reports of incest include references to the trickery, deception, coercion, persuasion, and betrayal experienced by children at the hands of a parent or relatives. Survivors frequently report feelings of powerlessness in response to a related abuses and confusion about whether the sexual activity is some sort of special attention, punishment, or game. Incest is more likely to exist in households in which the mother was a victim of childhood sexual abuse risk factor is alcohol abuse by the perpetrator. Risk of mother-son incest increases for a boy in a single-mother or lower income household. For male children, risk factors associated with being molested outside the home include: low-income houselhold, divorced parents, neglectful parents history of runaway, and drug or alcohol use.

Risk factors for male children have been identified by research resulting from the increased reporting of male victims of child sexual abuse. For example, Banning (1989) and Vander Mey (1988) determined that, in terms of recognizing and resisting female abusers, boys may be vulnerable because early sexual activity for males is viewed as "good experience." In terms of reporting the abuse, boys' vulnerability may go up due to socialization: to be macho and not show pain, referred to as the "I' am fine" syndrome. Moreover, boys face negative social consequences for reporting same-sex and incestuous activities, which violate existing taboos.

Prevalence of childhood sexual abuse exposes children's vulnerability in interactions with adults. Melton argued for interpretation of children's vulnerability based awareness of normal child development. For example, one area or research related to child development focuses on how children develop trust. *Interpersonal trust* has been defined as "a child's confidence that a person's verbal and non verbal communications precisely represent, or correspond to, internal states and external events," and includes the child's "sensitivity to lying, deception, and promise violation" Bugental, Kopeikin, and Lazowski (1992) saved that children under the age of 7 averted their eyes from the faces of strangers displaying deceptive smiles while continuing to gaze at authentic smiles. By age 10, children ignored deceptive smiles and showed greater interest in authentic smiles. The authors observed that the older children understood the false, "polite" smile to be a common, minor social deception, whereas the younger children were confused by a "polite" smile and acted with social avoidance. The authors concluded that the older children's responses reflected "increased understanding of the significance of these two types of smiles". Girls proved the ability to make this distinction earlier than boys.

These observations suggest that a child's understanding of social interactions with adults experiences changes throughout childhood, and that the quality of the adult child interaction may have a profound effect on a child's chances for normal development. At least two implications of the observations related to social development are relevant to a discussion of childhood sexual abuse. One child may be an easy prey for perpetrator's deception due to children's undeveloped interpersonal capabilities. Two, abuse, including sexual abuse, may be associated with negative impact for victims, not only in terms of emotional development, but also in the realm of cognitive development, including social reasoning, interpersonal trust, and social inference.

Age and the Abuse

Age of a child plays an unclear role in terms of vulnerability to sexual abuse. Childhood sexual abuse has been perpetrated on infants as young as 40 days, and has been reported for individuals reaching age of majority i.e. 18, at which time they are no longer considered children. The modal age of sexual abuse onset is reportedly around 10 (Peters, Wyatt, and Finkelhor, 1986); the mean age for reporting sexual abuse is also found to be between 9 and 11 (Gomes-Schwartz et al., 1990). Reports of prevention education efforts suggest that children become less vulnerable to sexual abuse as they grow older (Wurtele and Miller-Perrin, 1992). Daro (1991) wrote that perpetrators may target younger children because these children more readily maintain secrecy. Adding lack of surity about risks and vulnerability associated with age is the necessary distinction between when abuse occurs and when a child discloses that abuse, or when the abuse is detected. Because many instances of sexual abuse, particularly incest, involve on going and escalating activity.

The age effect of on childhood sexual abuse is exercised in at least two ways. First, increasing age for children is likely to bring decreasing supervision, with oder children unsupervised more often than younger children and younger children more likely to be under regular adult care. Thus, younger children may risk being sexually abused by caregivers, such as parents, babvsitters, and relatives. Older children may be at increased risk for abuse by strangers and acquaintances, such as neighbours, teachers, group leaders, and so on. Second, age is correlated with growing knowledge and awareness of sexual abuse (Wurtele and Miller-Perrin, 1992. Younger children may be abused, but be unaware of the implications of abuse, report:

Non disclosure is a prevalent feature of childhood sexual abuse. Victims do not report their abusers, families do not report the occurrence of incest, and abuse is hidden from family, friends, and the society. Only a small per centage of victims may reveal sexual abuse during childhood. The reasons for children's reluctance to report remain largely unexplained. Perpetrators report their dependence on children's silence. In comparison with younger children, larger numbers of older children may report abuse or have abuse detected due to an awareness that reporting is a means to stop the abuser. Thus, age and associated factors, such as supervision and social reasoning, are likely to affect children's vulnerability to sexual abuse. This is yet to be researched, however, regarding who is most vulnerable at what age.

Gender Factor in Child Sexual Abuse

There is no doubt that females are more likely to experience sexual abuse than males. However, there is little agreement as to why or how this is the case. Males may underreport sexual abuse due to socialization factors that show that boys be self-reliant, that sexual involvement is normal for boys, that homophobia is masculine, and that being vulnerable is feminie, weak, or socially unrecognised. Still, males' failure to report cannot be used as proof that the sexual abuse of boys does not occur. Indeed, it has been reported that sex offenders sexually molest young boys at five times ware than young girls.

Along with the males under repoting the occurrence of sexual abuse, the subject of boys being victims of sexual abuse has not been historically examined. The neglect of male child victims may by due, in part, to the issue of childhood sexual abuse first being raised by the women's movement. Similarly, the possibility of females beings abusers of sexual abuse was not seriously considered, with some believe females incapable of pedophilia, or sexual attraction to children. However latest investigations of women as perpetrators and males as victims have come to light.

Gender based differences and their role in vulnerability to child sexual abuse are important characteristies of a child-generated model. Are girls and boys equally, and simultaneously vulenerable throughout childhood evalution? For example, one aspect of children's vulnerability to sexual abuse is their naivety and some what abvious adherence to authority. It can neither be assumed nor proved that these tendencies are found only in girls. Similarly, child sexual abuse is associated with certain risk situation such as lower socio-economic status (SES) and single-parent homes. These risk factors are present with both the genders. Finally, incarcerated molesters have confessed sexually abusing both boys and girls, or solely boys. Means of sexual arousal confirm molesters' attraction to children, including both boys and girls, which demonstrates abuser's preferences for the type of child they abuse. The information makes it believable that boys are more likely to be sexually abused and exploited than previously believed.

Recent reseach has evaluated gender growing differences in the occurrence and the effects of childhood sexual abuse. A study by is commendably thorough, including as much informatin about each victim and his or her perpetrator as possible, and demonstrating that children of each gender are vulnerable in varying ways. Provious reports found boys to be molested at younger ages than girls, suggesting that boys are more vulnerable at earlier ages and girls are more vulnerable at older ages. However, Faller strdied a clinical smaple of 87 male and 226 female children who were victims of sexual abuse, interviewing not only the children but, whenever possible, the abuser and a nonoffending parent or parent figure. Faller found an older age of initiation of abuse for boy victims (6.3 years) compared with the girl victims (5.5 years). In flow with earlier findings, boys may first become victimized at an older age than girls because boys are more likely than girls to be victimized outside home.

One more point of difference between the girls and boys in Faller's study was that boys abused in the home were more likely than girls to be abused along with other siblings. Of the 13 cases in which boys were only victims of related abusers, 9 of them came from households in which each boy was the only child and, therefore, the main target available to the abuser. Boys and girls who were the solitary victims of related perpetrators were the youngest in this study, i.e., 3.6 years. The next youngest group i.e., 6.2 years involved boys from families in which several children were victimised. Regarding girls, who are more likely than boys to be sexually abused in the home, may be more accessible to their abusers at an earlier age. Boys, who are more likely to be abused away from home than at home, may not become accessible to their potential victimisers until they are old enough to be out of the house. In one way or the other, all children may share some degree of vulnerability to sexual abuse simply by virtue of being young and innocent. Specific risks and vulnerabilities for boys and girls, at different ages throughout childhood and in the company of different types of potential perpetrators, have been suggested, but not reliably determined.

Opinions of Adults About Childhood Sexual Abuse

According to the findings of a survey of college students, Wellman determined a difference in views between males and females about childhood sexual abouse. The respondent for this research were students at an urban New England college, whose average age was 20 years. Of the 824 participants, 167 were male and 657 were female; minorities students were, 4 per cent African American, 9 per cent Hispanic or Latino American, and 1 per cent Asian American. Ninety students refused to participate in the study. The subjects were given a 59-item questionnaire, and were instructed to answere each with strongly agree, disagree, or strongly disagree. A sample opinion is: Most abusers were abused themselves as children. The findings of this survey indicate attitude differences about sexual across gender:

(i) Males were more likely than females to report "sexually aroused when sexual abuse is discussed.

(ii) Females were more likely than males to report feeling "threatened when sexual abuse is discussed.

(iii) Males were more likely than females to report believing that child sexual abuse victims should bnot receive treatment for their abuse because it would remind them over and over of the things that happened.

(iv) Males were more likely than females to report believing that fathers do not absuse daughters until the girls reach adolescence.

(v) Males were less likely than females to report agreeing that abused should receive long prison sentence.

(vi) Males were more likely than females to report believing that the children who act "sexy" are more likely to be victimised.

(vii) Males were more likely than females to report believing that the recent publicity of childhood sexual abuse is blowing things way out of proportion.

(viii) Females were more likely than males to report believing that boy's are victims of childhood sexual abuse.

(ix) Female were more likely than males to report believing that incest is sexual abuse.

Various observations of the Wellman study raise the possibility that male and female victims of sexual abuse may report and express different reactions from sexual abuse as a functin of a larger, stable set of gender differences in attitudes about sexual abuse.

Understanding child sexual abuse means understanding the common and uncommon circumstances under which children may encounter perpetrators, and the possible and necessary responses that children should be prepared to effectiively thwart their perpetrators. Given the complexity of social situations that children may encounter, including related victimisees within the home, deceptive strangers outside the home, and confusing physical and psychological manipulations that children are unable to handle, it is little wonder that children may be unprepared to effectively respond to an abuser.

Preventive Education Against Child Sexual Abuse

Along with prevention as childhood sexual abuse rapidly emerged in response to increased reports of victimization, so, too, have questions and concerns about the effectiveness of prevention programmes . Studies of children's responses to abusive adults and situations have provided both promising and challenging findings for concerned caregivers. Simplistic or optimistic adult certainly about the efficacy of preparing children to recognize, resist, and report perpetrators has been tempered with research findings that indicate modest immediate rise in knowledge, diminishing long-term retention of prevention measures, and unknown changes in acutal safety behaviour by children after prevention education. Children have proved less effective to inoculate against sexual abuse than some adults than some adults expected-a finding that undoubtedly does not surpirse parents, who are well aware that children do not always do as they are told.

Melton warned against putting the primary responsibility for the prevention of childhood sexual abuse on children.

"Neither evaluation research nor knowledge about cognitive and social develoment gives any reason to believe that sexual abuse education programmes are effective in preventing abuse. Moreover, on the basis of research on the epidemiology and process of sexual abuse, I have expressed doubt that prevention of sexual abuse is possible, and if it is possible, whether prevention can be achieved without substantial negative side effects."

While fears that children might be traumatized by prevention education have not been substantiated a more subtle concern may came into existence: Perhapschildren, due to normal limitations in thinking and reasoning abilities, are "weak" candidates for protecting themselves from perpetrators, who deliberately exploit children's vulnerability. Preventive education research, including long-term and follow-up research is likely to continue. School and home-based programmes for prevention education remain the best established ways to limit fresh victimization and identify abusers. Questions remain, however, regarding how children should be taught to respond to perpetrators.

On the issue of educating them to handle childhood sexual abuse it has become a priority as the negative consequences of victimization have come to light. Prevention efforts have primarily targeted children, placing the responsibility (or burden) of prevention on the potential victim. Both parents and teachers have displayed the ability to effectively educate children (even preschoolers) to recognize, resist, and report perpetrators, with few report of negative effects associated with the training. An emphasis on "age appropriate" programmes merely hints at what may be a key feature of successful intervention: knowing what normal boys and girls of various ages are capable of understanding in order to avoid childhood sexual abuse.

Undaubtedly, prevention education depends on a definition of what constitutes protection. Is a child who knows facts about sexual abuse protected from a victimiser? Is being told what to do if a victimiser approaches sufficient to gurantee performance of the safety behavior? What concepts can be taught that are compatible not only with what children should know, but also with what they are able to learn?

Though a survey or teachers by Abrahams, Casey, and Daro, (1992) it was found teachers may feet unprepared to detect and report child abuse, including sexual abuse, among their students, although there was support for prevention education among subject of the study. Wurtele and Miller-perrin (1992) indicated:

"We advocate an expansion from a primary focus on classroom-based approaches toward broader and more system-wide reforms. Our thesis is that child-centered aproaches can be most effective when augmented by school, family-, and community-based efforts, each of which should be viewed as contributing toward the prevention of CSA."

A nated, researcher, Daro warwed against reliance on or abandonment of child-focused prevention efforts "in the absence of clear scientific proof regarding the efficacy of these programme," and asked all parents and teachers to provide safer environments for children, in additon to preparing them to protect themselves. Anther finding mass children's difficulty with generalization of recognition and resistance skills acquired in personal safety programmes, and suggested behaviuoral remedies to increase generalization. Although older children have been indentified as faster learners of facts about sexual exploitation in comparison with younger children, the former's advantage has been neither regular nor long-lived. No consistent gender differences in prevention education outcomes have came to forefrant though the research.

Some Features of the Abusers

Hardly much is known for certain about perpetrators of child sexual abuse, except that "an overwhelimng number are men" and a majority of sex offenders themselves report being victims of childhood sexual abuse (Green, 1993). This suggests that sexual abuse of males is, indeed, more prevalent than believed. That male victims of childhood sexual abuse become sexualized by the experience and are excited by reenacting abuse in which they are the agressor may be a distrubing characterstic of sexual abuse, which is seldom considered outside clinical treatment settings. Some perpetrators report abusing children who remind them of themselves. Despite guess of underlying motivations for perpetrator behavior, it is likley that many perpetrators enjoy the act of abusing children.

More often than not offenders are related to or acquainted with their victims, thus it is reasonable to assume that, like victims, perpetrators are found in all aspects of society. Some abusers repeatedly abuse the same child-a circumstance that is more likely to result in pathology in the vcictim. Perpetrators seldom came farward for treatment.

Regarding female perpetrators, it was found boys 10 times more likely than girls to be sexually abused by their mother or other figure. However, boys were mostly exploited by men, making them more likely than girls to have experienced same-sex abuse. Boys were also more likley than girls to be abused by multiple victims, and to be abused by professionals outside home.

To a large extent, perpetrators, are opportunists. As stated by Wurtele and Miller-Perrin (1992), "potential perpetrators must have access to potential victimes.

Situations in which offenders are alone with children, especially if they are in positions of authority, increase the likehood of abuse". Perpetrators are known to be individuals who fail to inhibit their sexual impulses with children. Wurtele and Miller-perrin (1992) proposed that the "child's initial reluctance to decline the (sexual) activity or willingness to participate" may be a "powerful disinhibitor" for the perpetrator. Thus, a tragic exploitation of children's inability to protect themselves is put is motion: Perpetrators abuse children because children do not know how to stop them and children are unable to stop them because they are children. Thus, children's lack of resistance may be perceived by the perpetrator as permission or green signal.

Support Structure for the Victims of Childhood Sexual Abuse

In the history of support efforts, for the first time, the *Diagnostic and Stattstical Manual of Mental Disorders;* American Psychiatric Association, 1994) iuncludes sexual exploitation of children within the category *Other Conditions That May be a Focus of Clinical Attention.* This is response to public and professional concerns about both victimisers and victims. Other psychological and behavioural disorder, including dissociative identity disorder (previously multiple personality disorder), posttraumatic stress disorder, depression, eating disturbance disorders, sleep sexual dysfunction, and substance abuse are associated with childhood sexual abuse in both clinical studies and survey based repots. Individuals diagnosed with borderline personality disorder often report childhood sexual abuse (American Psychiatric Association, 1987). However, child sexual abuse has not been detected to be a necessary and sufficient cause of any specific psychiartric disorder, despite rigorous assumption and dramatic claims among treating professionals about the role it is assumed to paly in the etiology of psychopathology. The American

Psychiatric Association shows continuing uncertainty regarding the role of childhood trauma in the development of multiple personality disorder, now called dissociative identity disorder.

Eight variables that influence the severity of a victim's symptoms are as follow:

1. the preexisting personality and resiliency of abused child
2. age and developmental level of the abused child.
3. onset, duration, and frequency of exploitation
4. degree of coercion and physical trauma
5. the closeness of the relationship betwen the child and perpetrator
6. the degree of supportiveness of the family reactions to disclosure
7. the nature of the institutional response to the abuse, and
8. the availability and quality of clinical intervention.

Through research, it was found that the poor psychological adjustment of some sexually abused children may be a result of both pre and postabuse factors, as well as "the trauma of the abusive experience itself". Even noncoercive sexual exploitation may produce psychological disturbance suggested that negative effects of sexual 'abuse can be minimized or reversed by treatment. As noted by Green (1993), "there are no specific behaviour markers for sexual abuse," and sexual abuse is best considered "an event" rather than psychiatric disorder. To illustrate, comparison was done of a group of sexually abused children from a child sexual abuse clinic to a group of children being treated for routine well-child care, matched for age, gender, and race. The children were ages 4-8, and 75 per cent were girls. The researchers used the Child Behaviours Checklist (CBCL) and the Sexual Behaviour Scale to assess differences in behaviours, possibly showing immediate effects of the abuse. The researchers law no significant differences in some of the behavioural symptoms popularly thought to indicate sexual abuse, including: headaches and stomachaches, temper tantrums, thumbsucking, nightmares, enuresis, and withdrawal. Behaviours that were found significantly more often in the sexually abused sample were: demands for attention, attacks on people, too much sex play, secrecy, sexual troubles, strange behaviour, sudden mood changes, sleep problems, unhappiness/depression, and excessive worry.

As far as age and gender interactions are concerned, the only significant findings involved girl victims between the ages of 4-5 years having high scores on the Schizoid subscale, and boy victims ages 4-5 years having higher scores on the Sex Problems subscale. These findings recommended that males and females may differ in the ways in which they respond to sexual abuse. Studies involving long-term effects have indicated differences between male and female victims. It is been seen that female victims are more likely than male victims to display internalizing symptoms such as depression or anxiety. Several reviews indicate that male victims of child sexual explotation are more prone than female victims to identify with the victimiser and later sexually victimize others, Female victims are more likely than male victims to take on a victim role that pervades their later half of life, with subsequent revictimization at the hands of wife batterers or other molesters. Furthermore, male victims as adults are more likely than female victims to report the sexually exploiting experience as neutral or even positive.

Such gender based variations pertaining to sexual abuse may also be present in the professionals who treat the sexually abused victims. Adams and Betz (1993) assessed gender differences in counselors' attitudes toward incest. The subjects of the study were 67 female and 44 male counselors. Their opinions about incest and sexual abuse were scaled. Regardless of counselor gender, the victims of the abuse were not blamed for their abuse. The researchers found that counselors were less likely than noncounseling samples to blame the victims. Some significant gender differences for counselors were observed. Female counselors were more likely than male counselors to be optimistic about the prognosis for the abused to get over their abuse. Male counselors tended to define incest more narrowly than female counselors, and were more likely than female counselors to believe that charges of incest could be fabricated or just fantasy. These findings suggest that, even among the ranks of the most unprejudiced and well-educated adults involved with the treatment sexual abuse, gender differences may affect attitudes toward victims and perpetrators.

Conclusion

The Need for a Child-generated Model: It is believed that the children accommodate perpetrators' requests. Wurtele and Miller-Perrin (1992) identified guilt, lack of vocabulary, and socialization toward not discussing sex as contributors to children's failure to report abuses. Melton (1992a) believed the prevention of sexual abuse is unlikely because children are limited in their self-protection abilities. Despite growing knowledge and awareness about sexual abuse, both on the parts of children and their caregivers, sexual abuse carries on and prevention efforts stumble. A fundamental question is: Why so? Finkelhor and Strapko (1992) asserted the need for research studies that "get a large sample of young children to talk candidly about abuse and attempted abuse" incorporating "intensive investigation-type interviews with children".

More important is to see that number of research studies does not matter much. What matters the most is child sensitive research studies which unprejudiced analysis so that the problems can be attacked from the why root and of possible rooted out before it starts.

Section— IV

CHILD BATTERING

10

THE CONCEPT OF CHILD BATTERING

Amongst all the forms of child abuse and atrocities against children, the most shocking form is battering of children by family members and parents themselves. Even worse is the perpetration by mother of a baby whom is considers an inseparable part of her ownself. In this chapter, let's see what is child battering and why it is exercised. For most people it is less easy to accept that a mother can burn a loved child than to accept that she could hit it. Several doctors and psychologists have tried to define a personality difference between parents who hit and those who burn, but the general feeling is that the actual form of injury is purely a question of the parent's own specific fears or inhibitions, and is not relevant beyond that. To one mother screaming uncontrollably and flinging a child against a wall is the ultimate, while for another, burning incorporates so. So we must look beyond our own personal reactions to the particular *kind* of punishment a parent actually gives, to consider instead the *degree* to which he/she inflicts it on the child.

Undoubtedly, there is a world of difference between a father who occasionally loses his temper to the point where he hits his son hard enough to knock him down, and another father who repeatedly beats his child until the boy receives a mass of bruises and half-healed fractures. The first father might more or less accidentaly cause a fracture; the second one might eventually kill his child. In the light of really violent cases, the mental suffering that is caused probably proves more harmful in the long run as pointed out by the psychiatrists.

The question arises is, what is the precise meaning of battering if it does not simply mean that a baby has been picked up and battered? If it can only be a parent figure who is involved, how are we to differentiate between an excess of parental strictness and the first stages of battering? At the other extreme, what is the difference between an insane psychotic who violently murders his child in an unctrollable attack, and a parent who repeatedly abuses his child until eventually it dies? There can be no simple answer, because we are not dealing with an inert substance which can be sceintifically measured, but with live people who rarely fit neatly into any precise slot.

The phrase 'battered child' itself did into existence in 1960s. The phrase was Dr. Henry Kempe's, an eminent American paediatrician, who had developed concern at the large numbers of children who were brought to his clinic suffering from injuries which were clearly not accidental. There was no satisfactory method of explaining these injuries unless the possibility that their own parents had caused them was taken into account. But there was still a great deal of resistance to this idea of child battering of course, is no new phenomenon. Children have always been abused by their parents, but because such medical aids as scans and X-rays were not available until comparatively recently, many symptoms were not recognized as having been caused by physical voalume. Rickets, syphilis, malnutrition, scurvy, fragile bones: many explanations were given to describe swellings caused by fractures. Several children in one family suffering from such problems only confirmed the diagnosis and treatment instead of causing suspicion. The discovery of X-rays in 1895 opened the way to greatly improved diagnoses, altough the newly-revealed injuries to the bones of babies thoroughly confused doctors, who at first could find no clinical reason for them.

Research findings in medical papers suggesting various diagnoses began to be published and slowly further pieces of the jigsaw began to fit together. In 1946 the real break through came when John Caffey, an American radiologist, described six cases where fractures bone of young infants were associated by subdural haematoma (blood clots under the skull). He suggested that these injuries had a violent origin and were not caused due to weakness or ordinary illness. In 1953 Dr. Silverman, another eminent American radiologist, insisted that such children had definitely been attacked, and this view was at last confirmed by Drs. Woolley and Evans in 1955 after an eight-year research on injured children and their parents. However, most people still found difficulty in accepting the possibility that parents could be held responsible for battering their own children. It was not until 1961 when Dr. Kempe, speaking at a symposium conducted by the American Academy of Pediatrics, used the deliberately emotive phrase 'battered child syndrome' that the issue of child battering became really widely discussed. The resultant publicity revolutionized attitudes everywhere: many doctors and social workers throughout the world followed Dr. Kempe's lead and began to look more minutely and carefully at the young children coming to them with injuries which were somehow confusing through observations, one important fact to emerge was that the newly-defined battered children were rarely found to be neglected; indeed, it is generally admitted that one easily recognizable symptoms of a battering mentality is an excessive concern with neatness or cleanliness. The child must at all costs be a credit to his parents.

Let us see what are the differences between neglect, abuse and battering? A neglected child might be malnourished, insufficiently clothed, perhaps left unattended for hours at a time or even all night. He may never be physically attacked in any way but he is likely to suffer many accidents because nobody realises to remove dangers out of his way. There may be real love between him and his family, or there may be extreme indifference on the part of the parents—either way, the child's welfare is ignored. The physical *abuse* of children has been defined by Dr. D. Gil (in Helfer and Kempe (ed.) *The Battered Child,* 1968) as 'non-accidental physical attack or physical injury, including minimal as well as fatal injury, inflicted upon children by persons caring for them'. Further the quality of the parents' affection for their child is not linked with the diagnosis of 'abuse'. A *battered* baby is a baby who is also physically abused by his parents or guardians, and whose injuries are frequently repeated. Nevertheless, his parents, who appear to love him, are generally over-fussy, over-anxious and over-possessive or over-ambitions.

In traditional concept of child love, one psychiatric theory is that battering one's child is only another way of punishing one's own flesh. To examplify a case, a mother punishes her child she is punishing herself, not only for her guilt over the pain she knows she has caused her husband but also for what she sometimes finds as her own inability in not walking out on him to go to the man she really loved. Child's unfortunate facial similarity to his real father only increased her ambivalence between love and hate for him: he is a thorn in her side reminding her all the time of the lover she has lost. Again, although she is affectionate to him by the very fact of this resemblance, her upbringing has taught her to distrust and dislike boys. She can never quite put out of her mind her ever lasting jealousy of her brothers.

These days, the term 'battered baby' is becoming more common than 'battered child' probably because most infants are battered at a surprisingly early age. In the NSPCC's *Study of Suspected Child Abuse* (1972) 19 per cent of the babies were not more than 5 months old, 18 per cent were between 6 and 11 months, 14 per cent were between 12 and 17 months and 11 per cent between 18 and 23 months, making a total of 62 per cent being battered under 2 years of age. The figures in their earlier 1969 *Retrospective Study* were even more shocking 56 per cent of the babies were under 12 months and 22 per cent between 1 and 2 years of age. After about four years of age the pattern generally changes for various reasons then the child is able to hold off parental attacks by threatening to tell the matron of his nursery school. Also, at the hospital, the older child can conradict his parents' explanations.

To put problem at ease, the discrepancies between the parents' explanation of the child's injuries and the actual injuries is one of the ways that battering is now identified. The sister in charge of the children's ward of a large London hospital defined battering to as a case of abuse where the injuries are inconsistent with the description of the accident given by the parent. She added, 'Children bounce. In the case of a child who'd fallen nearly fifty feet from a building and it hadn't even fractured its skull. But another mother brought in her baby with a severe injury which can only have been caused by physical abuse and do you know what her explanation was? It had fallen off the table!' This particular sister was worried that publicity about battered babies might make parents hesitant to bring in children suffering from genuine accidents, in case they were suspected of having injured the child themselves. She emphasized that an experienced staff could nearly always tell immediately whether or not an explanation was the true one.

After having looked at several definitions of baby battering—battered children are normally under four years of age, and most frequently are under two; they are very hardly neglected but are rather the victims of over-anxious, over-possesive parents; they have been attacked by those who are responsible to be caring for them, (i.e.

an intruder burgling a house and assaulting a child is by definition not a baby batterer); often the batterer punishes the child because he were punishing himself and finally, after some delay the parents usually take the child for medical treatment but betray themselves by giving unlikely explanations for the injuries.

The whole explanation is bit confusing and to clarify the situation even further here are some descriptions of battering by three people who have been highly concerned with the problem. First is Joan Court, the original Head of the NSPCC Battered Child Research Department. She said: 'Battering is a potentially lethal disease and a significant cause of infant deaths and morbidity in many countries.' Viewing it as a disease it becomes considerably easier to see the parents not as sadists to be shunned but as sick people suffering from a literally killing illness. Victimised themselves in their infancy, they pass on their sickness to their surviving children, who in turn perpetuate this terrible disease unless at some point the chain is broken. The next two comments come from people with very different views. The first was given by a consultant paediatrician: 'The fact of the matter is, this is not a crime like others: it's not like hitting someone over the head to take their purse. No standard criminal gets a three months old baby and bashes its head then takes the evidence to show what they'd done to authority. If you bash someone on the head you run away and leave them to die on the street, you don't pick up the victim and take him to the nearest hospital, which is exactly what these parents do.'

We find on the other end, Detective Superintendent Roy of North-ampton, one of the founders of an excellent scheme for over coming the problems of liaison between the various authorities who handle battering parent, sees battering as essentially a crime. He says, 'You mustn't divorce this from other sorts of crime—when you talk about battered babies, by definition you're talking about children against whom criminal offences have been committed. Battering is an offence under Section 47 of the Offences against the Person Act, actual bodily harm.... Let's be sensible about this: is there any difference between a distraught young mother who batters her child, and a distraught daughter looking after an aged mother who batters that aged mother?'

Lastly, we are giving a brief passage taken from Juliet Berry's *Social Work with Children.* She writes: 'I have an image of a battering mother combing her child's hair with harsh thoroughness, whereas a neglecting mother may not even bother to comb her own hair'. It does not take much imagination to find how short a step it is from tugging a brush through the tangled hair of a resisting child to clouting that child round the head with the brush when she attempts to escape once too often: what parent's fingers have not itched to do just that in similar circumstances? Battering often takes place while the infant is being attended to or being cared: a resisting child can be particularly irritating, especially if the mother has been deprived of sleep, as is generally the case. Time and time again battering parents report sleeping problems, and no one consistently deprived of their proper quota of sleep can be said to be completely themselves. Add this to their other problems, and their actions begin to seem more comprehensible and therefore less horrifying.

After comprehensive research on the issue, there are still people who deny that defining a battered baby as such has any value. An abused child is an abused child, and that's all there is to it, they say. Others think that battering is receiving far too much attention: only a small fraction of children being cared have been battered, and they do not want to see scarce resources concentrated on one small field of child care to the possible exclusion of the rest. Most important of all is the fact that even today, there are many people—doctors, lawyers and social workers among them—who deny that battering, as it has been defined, exists at all. They cannot convince themselves to accept that 'ordinary' people could ever attack their own children 'Pathological', 'insane monster', are the kinds of words used by people who ought to know better, as though battering parents can be brushed out of existence by denying their customary normality. Certainly they are ill but they are not psychic nor are they monsters. But these extreme cases must not be allowed to deviate care and sympathy away from the more common type of battering parent who can nearly always be successfully helped.

Even more difficult is for a family doctor to bring himself to suspect that a patient, whom he may have known for many years has attacked her own child. Some doctors generally accept explanations which are patently untrue without making any further inquiries. For example, one paediatrician talked about a little girl he had been treating. 'She had already been treated earlier by another hospital—not this one—for a head injury, but they'd done nothing formal about it. We wonder if anyone at all realized at that time what had actually happened. When she was admitted with this second head injury some investigating was done and naturally got suspicion when it was discovered that the mother had been attending a psychiatrist for some time. It turned out she was very depressed, a completely immature and incompetent personality with three children under five. She couldn't handle this, it was beyond her. It was a professional family, quite well off, in their late twenties. Now what is important here is that their doctor, a personal friend of theirs by the way, simply did not realize what had been happening. He *wouldn't* realize it, absolutely refused to. When he was suggested that there was a possibility the child had been battered he nearly jumped down our throats....'

Had that family doctor been able to accept the possibility earlier that a pleasant, middle-class woman whom he had known for years could have intentionally attacked her own daughter, the child might have been spared a further injury. As it was, the paediatrician at the second hospital kept the girl in hospital under various excuses while the mother continued psychiatric treatment, untill eventually it was felt safe for the girl to return home.

Is not it shocking the extent to which experienced doctors can delude themselves on this subject. If it is difficult for doctors to doubt patients whom they have known for some time, it must be even more so for social workers. Many families who batter have already had good contact with the social services for various reasons. Some may have been incapable of organizing their dialy life, needing advice on how to handle the weekly rent and hire purchase matters, others may have been without a regular income due to the father's unemployment or imprisonment. Perhaps an older child has already had a contact with the law and is under probation. Social workers may meet their clients two or three times a week for several years on end; in such circumstances they become personally attached to them and so much involved in their success in one aspect of their life that they may not observe danger signs elsewhere.

In a retrospective study in 1969, Ray Castle (the present head of the NSPCC Battered Child Research Department) and Angela Skinner wrote that 'The need for very skilled social work with these families was apparent.... There was sufficient evidence to suggest agency pressure, together with the emotive nature of the problem, created anxiousness in the workers which resricted their ability to offer help. *Many social workers found difficulty in accepting that child battering is a reality.* In the example below the social worker encouraged the parents to find an acceptable explanation for their child's injuries, and the interview thus turned out to be worker focused, instead of client focused. "I pressed with all the questions I could think of, I even suggested the dog, but she assured me she had no idea how the child received the injuries." In another interview the worker read to the father the statement that the mother had made. He said it was true and strongly maintained that if there had been an accident he would have said so. "I again suggested all kinds of accidents, but he would have none. I felt he was on the verge of tears".

The question that after bothers is why is it that so many people are unable to accept the possibility that comparatively ordinary people might batter their own children? The most common suggestion made here is that they cannot face up to the violence within themselves. We have all been taught that vilence is bad unless it is officially licensed, as in war. Confirmed forms of violence retain their popularity—some people are still calling for the return of flogging and capital punishment. Since we are forced from early infancy to control our own violence to the point where we may no longer accept that we possess any aggressive instincts at all, we may be especially hard on those who carry out unpermitted violent acts. For once you recognize that ordinary people, people not very unlike yourselves, can in certain ininhibited circumstances do terrible things to their own children, then you have no choice but to accept the possibility that a similar violence might lie within you too. It may be that doctors are particularly used to this negligence as they have devoted their lives to healing: it may not be possible for some of them to accept that they themselves might also have strong destructive instincts. Certainly it seems strange that, even now, there are many examples of doctors not identifying cases which ought to have been obvious to them.

What else, even people, such as lawyers, who are professionally involved with crime may feel emotional reactions clouding their normally cool judgement when they study the details of the severe injuring of a child. Carolyn Okell writes (Law Society's Gazette, September 1969): 'Social workers and doctors, for example, may be so affected by the emotive nature of the subject that their ability to offer therapeutic help is diminished, and lawyers may find excuses for refusing Instructions in these cases.' In the case of a four-month-old infant with black eye, bruising on buttocks, bilateral fractured ribs, four long bone fractures, fracture of skull, incomplete amputation of right great toe and laceration of left ear with partial loss of lobe' in order to illustrate the kind of case a that come to a lawyer on certain situations, solicitors practising in the criminal courts sometimes give their clients the impression of being callous. Even the most hardened practitioner, however, must shudder at the list above mentioned.

While going through the incidents of baby battering it is easy to lull oneself into a sort of woolly-minded kindness; easy, as one imagines oneself in their place, to feel pity for stressed parents who have given way to their impulses. But quite often one comes across the kind of case quoted above and instantly one's whole attitude changes. Everyone dealing with such families experiences this revulsion—nurses, doctors, policemen, social workers—but fortunately extreme cases are becoming rarer as more knowledge is gained. The NSPCC have found that although more cases of battering are coming to them, the main increase lies with the number of moderately injured children: the proportion of these to seriously hurt children has grown considerably. The assumption is therefore that parents under depression are beginning to be picked up early enough to prevent the worst kind of 'accidents' from happening.

Another lacunacmists system it self is that me do not have much knowledge of the parents themselves. Who are these people? What has made them act as they do?

The answer seems to be that you cannot accuse one particular type of personality, but they all have a good deal in common. First it must be borne in mind that those parents who injure and kill are at the far end of a continuum: at the opposite end are those who have never actually physically battered their children at all. We can assume here of the kind of mother who sits weeping as she looks hopelessly at the child she feels inadequate to cope with, or of the ineffective father who secretly finds himself a failure in everything he has ever done. Parents like this give their children no enthusiasm for life, no confidence in themselves. Often marrying people like themselves they spend their days in a more or less permanent state of depression, ill-organized and only just coping with the demands life puts on them. If they are lucky and their circumstances do not deteriorate, they will probably do no worse than raise vaguely unhappy, confidenceless children much like themselves. It is, however, from such a background that many batterers come. This does not mean that all battering backgrounds are necessarily stressful, but almost invariably, however apparently successful and confident the family appears for one reason or another the abusing parent suffers from a severe lack of self-esteem. It is as though he has one skin less when you compare him with a more successful personality: he lacks the resilience which self-confidence brings.

The question the is, why is this so? What has caused battering parents, so disparate in upbringing, standard and intelligence, to be so alike in this one vital aspect? The answer offered by most people studying the problem is that most importantly, a battering parent has been deprived of the one thing almost universally acknowledged to be the necessary foundation for the formation of a fully mature and balanced personality—a centented 'mothering' experience in his infancy. No one suggests that a absence of good mothering is the sole cause for the eventual breakdown of a parent's care of his child, but there are few who would not place it at the top of the list of the causes due to which battering parents labour.

To explain mothering, it may be carried out by either a mother or a father or by a substitute parent. It means far more than merely being looked after by a natural mother. Irene Josselyn has summed up motherliness as being the qualify to show tenderness, gentleness, and empathy, and to value a love object more than oneself. Joan Court writes, "It seems that battering parents have not enjoyed an empathetic, caring relationship with a mother or mothering figure and go through life constantly yearning for such a relationship in spite of their disbelief in the probability of ever finding it. As a result of never finding the loving reassurances they are still searching for, this burden of unfulfilled dependency needs often results in a chronic low-grade depression. The parents complain of loneliness and are usually very socially isolated. Frequently they are apathetic and disorganized in their social relationships although the latter may not be apparent initially.'

Renowed authorities on the subject, Steele and Pollock, looking at the personality of battering parents from a psychiatric point of view, found that they could not but the parents in their study into any single one of their usual categories. 'On the contrary, they present the lot of emotional disorders seen in any clinic population—hysteria, hysterical psychosis, obsessive-compulsive neurosis, anxiety state, depression, schizoid personality traits, schizophrenia, character neurosis, and so on....' Despite all this, one common trait they did find was that 'all of our parents were deprived as infants and children. We are not concerned here with material deprivation. Some were brought up in poverty with great material deprivation, others in average circumstances, and a few in the midst of material abundance and wealth. We are talking about deprivation of basic mothering—a lack of the deep sense of being cared for and cared about from the beginning of one's life... This does not imply at then patients had lacked maternal attention...their mothers have hovered over them, involving themselves in all areas of the patient's life throughout the years. But...this became a pattern of demand, criticism, and disregard, designed to suit the mother and leave the patient out.'

It is this drawn that the mother is trying to produce a child whose excellence will shower credit on her; the actual needs of the child's own personality are neglected. The child, recognizing quite clearly that her mother is uninterested in her as she really is gains no confidence in her own natural abilities: instead she exhausts all her energy trying to please her mother by attempting to become the kind of person she imagines is wanted. This desire to please those in authority may later prevent her from obtaining the help she really needs; and she cannot help showing only her best side when she visits people in authrotiy whom she sees as potential blamers. Often she will manage to convince her doctor that she is a conscientious person capable of looking after her child successfully, thus denying herself the very support and counselling she went to him for in the first place. The distraught person underneath will be completely camouflaged: only the immediate family gets to see both sides of her face.

There are people who will object that almost every human fault nowadays is blamed on inadequate mothering. Yet battering parents are caring parents: they undoubtedly want to have a happy home with happy children. Of all the disturbed families social workers have to deal with, these are the ones who are most clearly motivated to improve themselves. I am not suggesting they are the easiest to deal with, but there is better chance of helping them successfully than there is, say, of trying to persuade a not very bright lad fresh out of Borstal to become an honest sober citizen when till today he has spent his life in a low intelligence family with a long tradition of criminal activities.

We can, this may say that it is not a question of *blaming* parents because they are failing to be one hundered per cent perfect, but of looking squarely at whatever facts have already been detected and saying, this is what we know, and this is where we must begin to tackle the problem. Today's parents are in the process of shaping the next generation, and if these future parents are to be prevented from passing on the disease in their turn, we must stop allocating blame and tackle immediately with every scrap of assistance the State can be persuaded or bullied into providing.

To support the observations above, let us look at one or two example of the memories battering paretns have of their home and their parents. Mrs. Jones said: "I'd never had a good relationship with my own mother, I never remember kissing her: ours was not that sort of a family. Even when I got married I didn't kiss her or anything like that"; and later 'My father always worshipped boys, and my brothers always enjoyed preference at home... they've got several photos on the sideboard of my two brothers, but there aren't any of me and my sisters not one. My eldest sister, I think *she* could have been identified as a battered child, though you didn't have them then.

Researchers mentioned above, Steele and Pollock believe battering parents have ambivalent feelings about the mother image, seeing it as potentially good and bad, with stress on the bad side. They reported a dream of one of their patients, Penny. 'I was with mother. There was the usual feeling of tension. The situation was like we were in a motel and we had gone to bed in twin beds. I woke up. Something in white was standing over my head very threatening. It was terrifying. I called to my mother for help. She answered, "I am your mother," and it turned out that she, herself, was the horrifying creature in white who was threatening me. I woke up screaming!' Steele and Pollock go on to explain that battering parents typically feel that people they approach help are untrustworthy and may attack instead of helping. This patient had bad problems with her punitive feelings towards her five month male child, and she feared she was no better a parent than her own mother had been, and that no help would ever be forthcoming. They further comment that although motherliness may appear oriented towards women,. it applies equally to men. There is no essential difference in the origin of motherliness in men and women. In both genders it involves a pre-gender identification in the infant's early life with the mother's behaviour. In males later masculine strivings and identifications may permit persistence of motherliness or suppress. In females the early motherly identification becomes woven into the normal psycho-sexual development leading to motherhood and identification with the child-bearing woman. Without doubt, we believe child-caring and child-bearing behaviours have separate and distinct origins.

There is no definite answer as to whether more males or females attack, there is no clear-cut answer. Different studies show diametrically opposed results. Everything seems to depend upon where and how the studies are conducted, and who is organizing them. For example, in their *Retrospective Study of 78 Battered Children* (1969) the NSPCC found that in 42 cases it was the mother who had battered, in 33 cases the father and in 3 cases the two were in very close collusion. Other reports (mostly American) show as many men as women battering, and a few even showed a predominance of men. But the study undertaken by steele and Pollock found that in 50 instances it was the mother who was the attacker and in only 7 cases the father.

An important factor is the financial position of the parents. A middle-or upper-class man in a satisfactory job has several strong incentives to keep on working, whereas an unskilled labourer will like to be unemployed occasionally. Bearing in mind that battering parents have basic problems of stability and self-esteem which could lead to a higher than normal mobility of work, fathers in the lower income groups are likely to be around the house more than the businessman reaching home after the the children are in bed. The consequent interactions between father and child in the first case will thus the more provocative towards battering.

Other family problems also play equal role. In 1969 the NSPCC reported problems with housing in 35 per cent of the families, though many apparently left their district to escape from the criticism of their neighbours and also from the various social agencies hot on their heels. A later report published by the NSPCC in September 1972 observed similarly high figures of families moving from their homes during and after the time they came to the attention of the NSPCC. Flight may also mean escape from debts, such as hire purchase promises, television rentals, or rent arrears, the last a common problem. For many it is also a flight from reality, a belief that a change of environment will ensure better times. Frequently immature mentally, the battering parents often cling almost kiddishly to the hope that everything will be alright in near future.

The fear of investigation can be enough to make a family leave a district, even when they have not yet battered a child severely enough for the police to be able to place a Care Order on them and arrange for regular supervision. This means, of course, that the children are still at risk but are now in an area where batterers is unknown and unsupervised. Since such families rarely leave forwarding addresses, tragedy may be the outcame if the new situation does not work out as successfully as the parents had expected.

Data of NSPCC seems to confirm the suggestion that batterers are frequently nomadic, but the bias of the NSPCC's case-load towards the working classes must be kept in mind. Dr. A. Jackson, Consultant Paediatrician at the london Hospital in the heart of the East End, finds the nomadic habits of many of his working class patients difficult to hands, irrespective of what they have come to see him about. Medical records needed to check up on previous vaccinations or details about old illnesses are generally impossible to trace because the patient has moved several times over the last few years and no longer remembers his doctor's whereabouts if he was ever officially registered at all. We can also say that the breakup of the old working class structure where several generations lived permanently within access of each other is no doubt responsible for much of the growing stress on younger people today.

During the probing of who battering parents are in this chapter, we discovered that the one thing which is firmly established is that they have been deprived of *'good mothering'*, owing to which they lack self-esteem, frequently to a crippling extent. Additional observations such as that batterers may be of either sex, that they are often nomadic and therefore without local roots, are important factors and facts about child battering, but time and time again we keep coming back to this severe lack of self-esteem. We shall therefore devote the last part of this chapter to looking at the origins and results of their lack of self-esteem, for it is here that the whole root of the problem seems to lie.

Without doubt, it is difficult for naturally confident people to put themselves in the place of a person who is not only sure that he can never do anything right, but also that no one will ever really like him, and that therefore no one will be ready to help him in times of trouble. A child needs to be convinced from earliest babyhood that he is cared and is loved, no matter what he does; smiles with no warmth behind them cannot impress him. As with animals, it is the wordless communication which counts. If the certainty that one is wanted and loved is ingrained, most problems can be dealt with a confidence which in itself is often enough to solve many difficulties, especially where dealings with other people are concerned. But the unconfident mother or father with lack of confidence and faced with a stressful situation, has no inner certainty to fall back on.

Moreover, in agreement placed can be that most unconfident people do not batter their children. Perhaps the most important characteristic of 'extra' motivating battering parents is that their own parents had unrealistic expectations of them, and now they are making similar demands of their own children. These high hopes can take many forms: each parent will have his own list of needs and ideas of the perfect child. The one demand that all battering parents seem to have in common, however, is that their children should be absolutely obedient. To cite example, one twenty-three-year-old father said when he was questioned by the NSPCC after he had gone angry with his child: "I love my children and I wouldn't want them to grow up disobedient... when I say jump, I want them to jump." He accepted that he was 'beyond control' himself when he was a child (though this may well have been his parents' view of his behaviour rather than the actual reality) and he was determined that his own baby son should not move on the similar lines.

It has been found that high expectations do not necessarily bring about a lack of self-esteem, of course–many a person has attained to success through the prodding of ambitious parents—but it must be possible for these expectations to be fulfilled. This is the centre of the problem. The demands these parents but forward cannot be fulfilled because they are unrealistic. The child is therefore predoomed to failure and a growing certainty of his total inability ever to do anything useful. Together with this insistence on absolute obedience usually goes a pathetic demand for clearly expressed love. The parents think of what they never had in their own infancy—uncritical love—and who better than their own children to give it to them? Unfortunately they do not realize that small children are very self-occupied creatures: infants need to cross many stages of development before they are ready to offer selfless love to anybody. Sadly, some parents do nevertheless manage to win some precocious sympathy from their babies at an age when no child should have to face such situation. Small children hardly capable of talking can sometimes be seen running to comfort a clearly distressed parent after a family queue such children often develop an anxious air as they watch to see what is going to be needed of them.

In most of the cases, this demand may begin from birth. One 19 year old mother threw her 10-week-old son causing severe injury to his skull, because he didn't love her. When probed why she thought that, she replied that he wouldn't stop crying no matter what she did for him and that proved he couldn't love her, because had he loved her, he would have smiled at her instead of crying all the time.

On the basis of various observations discussed above, Steele and Pollock came to the conclusion that all the parents they had been studying had been brought up in the manner in which they were now rearing their own children. The excessive demands made on the parents when they were young, which they were incapable of fulfilling, had made them think that all they did was 'erroneous, inadequate, and ineffectual. No matter what the parent as a child tried to do, it was not enough, it was not right, it was at the wrong time, it hunt the parents, it would disgrace the parents in the eyes of the world or it failed to enhance the parents' image in society. Undoubtedly, the growing child felt, with much reason, that he was unloved that his own needs, desires and capabilities were disrespected unheard, unfulfilled, and even wrong.

These factors appear to be essential determinants in the early life of the abusing parent; the excessive demand for performance with the criticism of inadequate performance and no regard of the child as an individual with his own needs and desires. Everything was oriented toward the parent; the child was less important'. In addition to these factors, Steele and Pollock realise that suppressed aggression also helps to increase the parents' lack of self-esteem: 'at the (same) time the parent is making demands and attacks upon the infant, he is also disappointing some of the infant's most basic needs for comfort and empathy. Such disappointments are repetitive stimulations to the basic aggressive drive. Stimulation of the aggressive drive with its associated anger toward the frustrating caretaker (i.e. the mother or father) coupled with the parallel development of strict superego rudiments, obviously leads to a strong sense of guilt. This guilt, largely unconscious, predominantly in relation to the mother, through the patient's life, and leads to turning much of the aggression inward toward the self. It accounts in the adult for the frequent period of depression and contributes to the pervasive sense of inferiority and low self-esteem'.

Thus, through this kind of behaviour, by the age of three or four, the small child has already been moulded into the shape of a future battering parent. His aggressions are well on the way to being fully developed, he has formed the impressions that adults are strict people who punish severely if they are not instantly obeyed, who demand love and don't give it, who are never satisfied and always super-critical. As a parent he will also contain the feelings of guilt, hopelessness, even uselessness, but he will probably not be able to avoid acting as he has been taught adults should do even though he wants sincerely to make his children happier than he was when he was young. He will not inevitably batter; he may be fortunate and have a succession of kindly understanding teachers, gaining some faith in self from doing well at school, he might even find the right marriage partner and have good luck in his employment—but if none of these things happen, at best his life will be a difficult one; at worst, he might end up battering his children in the way he had been taught at his mother's knee.

If we imagine ourselves in the place of a woman brought up in this manner, all of us who are parents have probably spent some hours in the middle of the night trying to persuade an unwilling baby to fall asleep. Depressed parents babies seem to wake more often than others: whether this is because the parents' nervousness is passed on to them or whether parents are nervous because they do not have enough sleep, who can say? Imagine then that night after night, sometimes many times every single night, you are not allowed to sleep by a crying baby. It lies there snug and warm in its blankets while you rock it backwards and forwards, backwards and forwards, half-frozen. Can you not feel how obviously such a mother's control might crumble, how she might find irresistible the desire to fling the baby down, to fling it anywhere as long as she can get rid of it? A child psychiatrist discussing this kind of situation, said more than half seriously, 'It's not the fact that some parents bash their babies which surprises me, but the fact that most parents don't!'

The next doubt raised can be that if these parents feel so bad about their child and themselves, why don't they get help, tell someone about their troubles? One answer is that from their childhood they have learned that asking is not the same as getting. They are convinced they are not the kind of people whom others thinks highly enough of to bother about.

For a moment, let's imagine a child who tries screaming when its lip trembling is unsuccessful, but only receives a hard slap for his pains? His lesson is a simple one and quickly learnt that it is not use expecting a comforting answer to his signals for help. In later life, faced with exactly the same situation but reversed, the now grown-up uncomforted child stares at its own infant, and is momentarily paralysed by a turmoil of emotions. If the child was a female and is now the mother, her guilt is added to by the universal hope that she will instincively know *how* to 'mother'. She stands there wanting to do so many different things, only some of which are conscious. She wants to pick up the distressed child and but it at ease because she loves it. But she also sees in the crying child herself as an infant and automatically feels guilt because her own mother hated her crying and made it quite clear she did so moreover, she is angry with the child because she had expected it to give her the love she feels she never had when she was a child and now the little brat is bawling its head off at her instead of smiling and showing its love. Obviously it doesn't love her any more than her own mother did. She both sympathizes with the disappointment the child must be feeling at being neglected but also feels frustrated herself that yet once more she has failed, has produced an unloving snivelling little thing which must be punished or it will never grow up in correct manner.

At this early stage such ambivalence of feelings might result in little more than the mother screaming at the child, or perhpas slapping its hand. Quite likely she will take her baby to her doctor with some trivial excuse, perhaps about a non-existent rash on its arm or her concern that it has not started sitting up yet; she might even complain it doesn't sleep. Unfortunately, because she does not really expect help and because she learned as a child to appease authority at all costs, she does not disclose with the one vital fact which is eating her away—

that sometimes she wants to hurt her baby to an extent which terrifies her. The doctor sees a clean, tidy mother and a clean tidy baby with nothing physically wrong with it, and reaches the conclusion the mother is one of those irritating women who fuss over every detail, wasting a great deal of his time. Outside waiting in his surgery is probably a woman suffering from breast cancer, a man with angina, a young unmarried girl who wants an abortion, and a couple of fresh patients—is it any wonder he gets rid of the fussing mother with a few words of reassurance that the baby will grow out of whatever it is she has complained about, prescribing perhaps a dose of something or other, intended to shut up the mother rahter than the baby?

In that situation, the mother returns home, perhaps not knowing why she is so unhappy when the doctor has just reassured her that nothing is wrong, or possibly she knows perfectly alright why. She is not too badly stressed—her husband, though inadequate in many ways, means well and she is fond of him—but debts are accumulating and she has a doubt she may be pregnant again already. Two or three days later she smacks the baby much harder than she meant to when it wouldn't stop struggling while she changed its nappy, and she is terrified at the red mark that stays on its skin. Again she goes to the doctor with some excuse, and again he dismisses her this time rather more brusquely. Generally, she will make two or three more of these 'cries for help' as they are called, but she is unlucky: either her doctor hasn't studied the subject of battered babies or he thinks it's all exaggerated—what such parents need is control over their ownselves. Either way he doesn't connect it with this particular mother. The day her baby is six months old the sun is shining and she suddenly feels extremely happy. She spends most of the morning preparing a special lunch for the baby to celebrate its first half year. Unfortunately the baby doesn't like changes in its diet and vomits it out. The mother's mood switches disastrously: once more she is rejected, her efforts are despised and flung back at her unwanted. She pulls the baby out of its high-chair and throws it on the floor.

When the next day, she takes it to her doctor's surgery and explains away the cut on its forehead and the surrounding bruising by saying it fell out of its cot, he trusts the explanation.

The next time she loses her temper she takes the baby to the outpatients' clinic at a hospital several miles away: this time it has a heavy bruise round its mouth where she threw the bottle at it so hard it cut the skin of the lips. Again she is unlucky: it has been a bad day and the casualty officer is tired because he was up half the night deputizing for a colleague ill with flu. He knows a litle about battered babies: he went to a lecture on them a couple of years ago when he was a studying medical. He sees the nearly healed scar on this one's forehead and, as he examines the cut lip and bruised mouth, at the back of his mind a warning bell is ringing. But the mother is so naturally concerned, a pleasant anxious woman, half in tears about her baby; there are a dozen people in the row out side to see him; he is so sleepy himself he can hardly keep his eyes open and anyway, it is only theory he has learned—he has never actually met a case of battering but surely this isn't the type of woman who would.... He tells the nurse to apply a plaster. Now it might have been the last time. The mother, now over three months pregnant, has threw her baby so hard against the wall she has fractured its skull. This time she runs to the local hospital with it, doesn't wait, because she knows it is an emergency. Here the casualty officer is more alert, he calls the sister, a very experienced woman, who instantly senses the situation. The baby is X-rayed, taken into hospital and the mother is seen by the paediatrician who by matter of chance, is sympathetic. No charges are preferred, and after several months the baby is allowed home to the mother who is now under supervision from a very supportive social worker. She will need help for many days to come, but the baby is safe now; the family has been lucky.

All this situation produced above is only a simplified imaginary case, but the pattern of injury and cries for help is typical. So many children are injured at first in places that can be easily identified small cigarette burns on the hand, bruising on the face, especially around the mouth—that we must assume that the parents are placing a kind of mark on the child as an overt cry for help. Sadistic parents cover up their crimes; what is done, is done in secret. Battering parents nearly always start by hitting where it is visible and then taking the child to a doctor. Often when a coroner makes investigations about a dead child he finds it has been taken a numbers of times to several hospitals, but since there is no co-ordination between hospitals no one is conscious of the steady progression of the severity of the battering, except the parent doing all this. The pity is that most of these parents cannot bring themselves to communicate their distress overtly because it means accepting their failure once again. Their self-esteem is so low they *cannot* reveal themselves. 'It soon becomes evident that this sort of person is a very self-defeating person. Therefore, if the patient defeats you in the process of defeating himself remember he has had lots of practice doing himself in.' Producing the fact Ray said that often these parents will not admit their feelings even to themselves, writes: 'The fact that the child battering adult was often ignorant of the basis of the problem and unable to be explicit, was one reason why it received so little attention from social workers. A clean and tidy home and outward concern for the child's welfare has often hidden the problem.'

The illustrated little story above reveals several of the points we have been talking about, particularly the excessive demand for excellence which is the background to many battering parents' own childhood. A middle-class mother who had battered her child talked about her own childhood. My mother would have made a marvellous foster mother to small babies. She wanted a perpetual baby. She loved me when I was small and helpless, but she rejected me from the day I first said "No"....

The question arise is for all this who was to blame? Certainly not the baby son, who was clearly blameless. The mother? But perhaps she could not do otherwise, because of her own childhood and her present circumstances. Researchers are now finding the likelihood of a long chain of many generations' growth. It is true that the members of each new generation get a fresh opportunity to break their own links, but they start heavily handicapped in comparison to most of us.

Quite often, we get to hear the comment that this is a terrible century which allows such things to happen. But is not the opposite the truth? The reality is that we are the first century to take it for granted that such things should *not* be allowed to happen. From the beginning of history children have suffered their share of man's cruelty to man. Many early societies—Babylonian, Egyptian, Greek, Roman—did not even consider newly-born children as full members of the human community until they had been purified by special rites, unwanted children being exposed or disposed of in other ways. Infanticide has always been practiced for solving the embarrassing problem of illegitimate babies or of babies born to overcrowded families in times of war, famine or deep poverty. As for child abuse, right from the early Egyptians onwards to the present day, children have been whipped, beaten and humiliated in order to make them learn, most parents asking teachers to be ruthless in the treatment of their charges.

In one shape or the other, purposeless cruelty to children has also always existed: old records report children being deliberately burned, stuck with pins, left unclad in winter, starved, and hit badly and only when treatment became so gross that neighbours could no longer ignore it was action taken. The appalling system of baby-farming which attained its height in the last century was responsible for the slow death, usually by starvation or poisoning, of many thousands of babies. The ruling classes, many of whom knew quite well what was happening, made no efforts at all to check the practice, possibly because they themselves were partly responsible for the system by their purchase of wet nurses, who were thus forced to farm out their own babies. Child labour, i.e., setting small children to work was another cruelty which frequently inflicted worse torture than most baby batterers commit today. Heavy industrialization resulted in many children of six or seven years old working in the mills from 6 a.m. to 7 or 8 in the evening. But it was not only at work that last century's children suffered. Victorian fathers of all social classes most of the times, chastized teir children so severely and expected such perfection of manners and behaviour from them that much of their treatment would today be identified as battering. Yet in their epoch they were seen as admirable men.

To sum up, it should be borne in mind that child abuse has been a continuing factor in nearly all societies throughout history in one form of the other. Today we look at the world with very different eyes from those of our ancestors, but man cannot change his brutal nature overnight, but it is not pointless to expect him to do so. Because accepting brutality as part of invitable human nature will only result in more and more child abuse—a strong justification against child abuse. This is high time we should mend our whays and to admit the hardest fact of human nature, we need to have 'strong' machanism of purity to stop child battering from now onwards.

11

SOME CONTRIBUTORY FACTORS

After having gone through this concept of child battering and its various dimension in the previous chapter, the present chapter specifically deals with the battering by parents until a scientific experiment has been successfully repeated several times by different researchers, its results are not considered to be established. Few investigations into the pattern of baby battering have also been submitted to such rigorous retesting. Nevertheless one grasps eagerly at the results of any properly based research, particularly those stemming from the work done over the last ten years at the University of Colorado. Of especial interest were the results obtained when Kempe and his fellow-researchers made a predictive study of a thousand normal mothers who came to their Obstretrics Clinic as part of a perfectly ordinary post-natal routine. If battering parents can be identified at an early stage much suffering can be avoided.

Problems of Mothering

Working on their hypothesis that 20 per cent of women experience some difficulty in mastering the art of mothering, their investigation took note of the 200 or so mothers who appeared to them to fall in this category. They narrowed this group of 20 per cent down to a hundred mothers, about whom they felt fairly serious concern. They then divided this further sample into two, using one group of fifty as a control group. To the remaining fifty they gave consistent help, arranging for weekly visits in their homes by mothering aids and so on. The result was that none of the mothers who were being helped assaulted their children, whereas of the control group, three children were battered and one was even killed.

One would question in what queries were made, to identify the potential batterers? The questions were fairly simple, obvious enough when you consider their implications; nevertheless few people would think of putting them of a young mother. They asked things like: 'Do you get angry at the new baby? Do you feel people are critical of the way you take care of the baby? Are you scared of being alone with a baby? Many ordinary young mothers are going to answer yes to least one or two of these questions, and it takes the right answers to various different groups of questions before one can feel fairly be certain that one is dealing with a mother who is going to have more than the normal difficulty in handling new motherhood. Other revealing questions might be: 'Do your older children understand your problems? Do they help you? Or, 'How does your mother feel about her new grandchild? Does she feel you are handling motherhood well?' When questions such as these are followed by the ones about discipline, attitudes become clearer. If a mother feels that it is possible to slap a three or four week-old baby in order to make it behave properly then you are dealing with an abnormal situation. Parents who believe discipline at such an early age is not only but possible, and who consider an eight week old baby is capable of being deliberately this mischievous, are in danger of battering their child and they need supportive care. Not all doctors or social workers, however, are capable of asking the right questions in the right manner and of arriving at the right. Conclusion by getting right answers.

To avoid these obstacles, three American doctors (Schneider, Helfer and Pollock) have been trying to develop foolproof questionnaire which will discover parents with a battering potential, but it is not an easy project. Parents tend to give the answers they believe are safe, or they many reply with what they genuinely imagine to be the truth. How to get them to delve into their deeply-buried feelings is the real problem. The answer seems to lie in a highly sensitive questionnaire with various cluster of statements which the parent marks on a 7 point scale ranging form 'strongly agree' to 'strongly disagree', to make sure that a normal parent might respond to some of the questions as would a potential batterer, he would not respond to all questions which would reveal his child to be in danger. The work done so far on the formation of such a questionnaire is highly promising, and it is hoped that soon it will cross the developmental stage. The one involved into second research can feel that one of the difficulties in attempting to arrive at a useful state of communication with these parents is that in the past worlds have not been very helpful to them, and as a result, they continue to mistrust them in their adulthood. It has been suggested that their personalities have been shaped at a very early stage of their development than verbal communication. Proof that someone really does care what happens to them needs to be visualised physically by workers visiting them in their own houses, by aiding them with their own hands, showing by touch and look that they actually mean what they report. No matter how often the worker is rebuffed she must persevere until the client begins to have trust in her. A person who has no regular sense of his own identity needs to gain an image of himself from the way other people see him. Having been faced all his life by his parent's under evaluation of him, he may be thoroughly confused by the good picture a social worker will be trying to present, and will sometimes be able to function as affectionate wise father. But this concept of himself is very shaky, and he can change only too swiftly to the role of punitive parent (learnt from his own and who he wants to be, but no one clear image of himself as a mature men, so that he is very easily shattered by some mildly stressful even that would not cause a more stable personality the slightest disturbance.

This is not wrong to say that these parents have no confidence in their own ability to do anything successfully when one considers that their own parents continuously scolded them for their inadequacy as children, never giving them a sense of pleasure or pride in themselves. Frequently they were not even allowed to make friends on their own choosing since their parents were jealous and wanted to keep them close. New friends would be denigrated or prohibited outright, so how could they develop any from of social ease or confidence in others? It may seem over-simple to keep harking back to their childhood, but it must be kept in mind that many of these battering parents have only recently left it behind. The NSPCC found that 73 out of 286 battering mothers were aged between sixteen and twenty, while a further 140 were as twenty-one and twenty-five, making a total of 74 per cent under twenty-five aged between sixteen and twenty, and 97 were above twenty-one and below twenty-five. The average ages of the total sample was 23.59 years for the mother, and 26.7 for the fathers. Astonishingly Selwyn Smith and his colleagues, researching on battering parents at the Queen Elizabeth Hospital in Birmingham, reached at an identical figure for theirs mothers, who averaged 23.5 years also. They also point out that these mothers on average had given birth to their first child at 19½, whereas the national average age is even over 23 for a first birth.

Is not it tragic to find that for the younger mothers at least, many of their old school mates will still be buying unlimited garments, make-up pop magazines and the latest top-of-the-pops disc, and probably more important will be going out dancing and to the cinema with a variety of boy-friends who have plenty of money in their pockets. The young mother instead is imprisoned in some small flat or in the in-law's house with a squalling baby and a young husband who is every bit as discontented as she is. Is it any surprising that some of the more immature snap under the strain?

An effective solution for such mothers is to go out to work as soon as possible, not only to earn extra money but also to get out of the house, but in fact it has been seen that few battering mothers do so. The NSPCC found that only three out of seventy-seven mothers in their 1969 sample went out to work, and these findings agree with those of other studies, both in England and in America. It seems that these mothers have such an emotional dependency on their children they will not but them to custody of anyone else so that they may go out working; indeed, this refusal to be parted from their babies is one of the problems doctors have to face if they attempt to keep a child in hospital.

Next obvious issue of curiosity is what sort of personalities to these parent have? Are they usually intelligent or stupid? Questions such as these are being examined through research and the general picture is becoming clearer, although there is still much to learn. Sometimes they are stressed passive people, overtly seeking the support and affection of their children, perhaps competing with their spouses for their children's love, or vice versa. Others are indifferent and make extreme demands which are impossible to fulfil; often they show compulsive traits such as fanatical tidiness or cleanliness. Both these types show signs to many similarities: they are unbalanced personalities who have been deprived of mothering and wish to make up this deficiency in their own families but are incapable of doing so.

Aggressive Anti Social Behaviour

This type consists of those whose aggressiveness is the Retrospective Study 1969 that forty-seven per cent of the sample consisting of 25 men and 10 women were characterised by essentially anti-social behaviour of the predominantly aggressive type. There were indications that these parents were habitually aggressive and that their behaviour tended to be released against any source of in convenience. Many of them had criminal records and were prone to violent outbursts of temper in the home. They displayed a readiness to enter into conflict with authority and all their personal relationships were disturbed.

While looking for solutions, it has been found that many of these people can be helped successfully, although it is not possible to remove entirely their ingrained aggressiveness. Selwyn Smith and his fellow researchers have been exploring the organic condition of parents, as they considered that very little attention had been paid to this side of the problem. On examining the electroence phalograms of thirty self-admitted baby batterers they found that eight had abnormal EEG patterns, and they accepted that they persistently hit one or more of their children. They therefore conclude that some parents batter because they are organically exposed to violence regardless of whether or not stress exists. Of their sample as a whole (214 parents of battered children) they found that one third of the fathers had a gross personality problems and that nearly half of the mother has mental disorders. However they classified only a minority as being obviously mentally ill and felt that since the injuries these parents under study inflicted were so clearly of highly bizarre nature they should to be considered quite separately from the rest.

Criminal Background

Third factor discovered out of Birmingham research was that nearly one third of the fathers in the sample had a criminal record, while Skinner and Caste found in their 9 per cent of the women had known criminal records. They point out that in the country as a whole the expected rate of the cases of indictable crimes for the age groups of twenty-one to thirty years during the same period was 1.9 per cent for fathers and 0.2 per cent for mothers. However, the NSPCC deals in the main with a socially restricted class of poorer people, and their figures would probably not correct for a sample taken from the community as a whole. Nevertheless there seems so doubt that the criminal record of battering parents is higher than the national average.

Law Intelligence Levels

After the subject drew attention, the intelligence of these parents is the subject of much debate. Selwyn Smith found that the subjects with abnormal EEGs had low intelligence; indeed he found that almost half of the mothers in his sample were of subnormal intelligence. It is frequently suggested that it is the less bright who physically abuse, while the more intelligent inflict mental battering, which may in the long run be more disastraus. At present there simply not enough data to prove anything, but there is no question that number of very intelligent people do physically batter their children. It may be that they are caught less often, however, being capable of finding their way out of a situation more easily. This is yet another side of battering which needs more research, for the American findings show very different results from the English ones, probably because of the wider class coverage of parents studied by the researchers. Steele and Pollock write in The Battered Child (1968), 'There is no evidence of a significant relationship between intelligence as measured by intelligence tests and abuse. The IQs obtained by the patients seen for testing range between 73 and 130, with most of the patients falling into the average range (90-110).' The question of class and intelligence has been hotly, discussed, and any new books by Eysenck or Herrnstein, for example, are certain to initiate fresh controversy. What ever stance one takes on this subject, however, no one is going to deny that there are plenty of stupid ones in the upper classes. The intelligent, regardless of their class, will probably be better at hiding the situation if they are attacking their children. Not only will they be able to offer more convincing excuses, but in many more cases they may see their requirements more clearly and be able to obtain outside aid more easily. If they are rich enough they may send their children to boarding school or get paid nannies if they do not have them already, they can go to restful health firms or manage an extra holiday abroad, they will take frequent weekly off with their spouses and will without much problems be able to opt out of the situation.

The stupid rich have the same advantages, and can here advisers to arrange for them what they are unable to do for themselves. The NSPCC will not be called in, the Health Visitor will not approach their door, and not a soul except their doctor, their psychiatrist and perhaps and intimate friend or two will ever know about all that is going on. The stupid poor will enter the statistics, however, and it is mostly this group about whom we all read in reports. But let us not be misled into impression that this is purely a lower class problem arising among the mentally subnormal, whatever the statistics seem to establish.

It is assumed that of every single case of mild battering were to be followed up throughout the entire country (though this could never happen as much of it would never be suspected by anyone) it might seen that a higher per centage of poor people eventually progress to severe battering than do rich people. There are still many who live in miserable conditions, deprived of physical comforts taken for granted by most of us; for thousands more, a minor crisis such as a lost overcoat, which would hardly matter to a well-off family, can assume disastrous proportions when money is really short. The rich can not only afford to buy their alternatives of a dangerous situation, they never even begin to experience the stress under which some people pass their entire lives. Nevertheless, mental anguish is not the prerogative of the poor, and well-off children can still be maimed emotionally even if they do not experience severe battering more frequently than poorer children. Several people suggested that these are the children who when they are a little older come up before the Juvenile Court for stealing, for instance, and everybody asks, how can this nice middle-class boy have done such a thing-he must have got in with a bad set. Again, the upper class boy will probably avoid even this disgrace: I am not for a moment suggesting corruption, but a boy at a famous public school who is caught filching from a local shop might end up in front of his headmaster instead of a magistrate. He will be punished, but it is likely to be a less public punishment than a less well-off lad might receive.

It simply means that although money, together with the know-how that membership of the middle and upper classes brings, may lead an actual or potential battering parent to avoid serious assaults, nevertheless the preliminary stages of battering are thought to be as severe in these classes as in the poorer classes. There are many known cases of actual severe assault among the wealthy, although I such a case has never been publicly discussed. Aristocratic families of famous title, highly respectable families living at 'excellent' addresses, good bourgeois parents whose lives appear to be ideals on the surface, behind all these facades there occasionally occur scenes as brutal and horrific as in any slum.

High Hoper from Children

Battering parents wish to have a child who will bring them credit and who will shine above all others: in the upper classes where most children anyway enter in to the polishing process at an early age this demand can quickly amount to cruelty where a potential battering situation already exists. One such mother in her thirties disclosed how from four years onwards she was given French lessons, bridge lessons, dancing and social mannerism lesson, her progress being checked each afternoon by her mother. If she was less than perfect she would be beaten. If she refused to apologize for not having learned her lessons properly she would continue to be battered more and more severely all afternoon if necessary. A stubborn child, she took a certain perverse pleasure in defying her mother; the protest continued for years until her parent's marriage broke up and she was sent away to school. At the time several other people knew what was happening-her father, her nanny and other staff-but she was generally considered a difficult child and no one chose to interfere. She later said that when her own son was small she hated him when he cried, and sometimes she had an intense desire to kill him. Now that the child is older the family seems pleasant enough, but she willingly admits that if she had not been able to buy help and occasional freedom away from her baby when she needed it she almost probably would have severely assaulted him when he was a baby.

One cannot deny that there are many such cases, but mostly they remain unreported in the media. Their own doctors usually cannot bring themselves to suspect patients such as these, there exist many case histories by hospital doctors and others to who their appeared by the refusal of some medical practitioners to believe in the guilt of such people. It is difficult to believe that battering is exercised in a comfortably off, educated household, when the parents, on the surface at least, are obviously self-controlled and self-aware people.

Pollock and Steele (in Helping the Battered Child and his Family, 1972) observed that parents who physically attack their children come from all social levels. In considering the treatment and prevention of battering, therefore, it must remembered that this problem is spread throughout all society, and that propaganda must reach every level. A child suffers no less because he happens to be financially rich but unhappy.

The Problem of Unemployment

It is enough to add here that in the NSPCC's Retrospective Study of 1969 over 38 per cent of the fathers were jobless, while the 1972 study showed that 22 per cent were. They add that both figures were far higher than the then current national unemployment figures. In number of American studies a per centage above the national average of families were shown to be receiving financial help, i.e., from public welfare departments. These facts imply that there is generally a high degree of unemployment among battering families. However, it must be keep in mind that these parents have a reputation for being nomadic, they have difficulty in relating to other people, they lack faith in themselves and their ability to carry out a job properly, and if they are of the aggressive nature, they are liable to argue or fight their way out of a job. With that sort of background it should not be surprising at if the best work the majority can find for themselves, when they are working, some labour work this particular statistic does not prove that they are ineducable morons who (as one incensed reader recently wrote to a newspaper) should to be sterilized before they bring any more unfortunate children into this world.

Disturbed Marital Relations

Let us look more closely at the kind of martial relationships battering parents have. Statistics can be wrong: Selwyn Smith found among his sample (1973) that almost one-third were unmarried and three-quarters of all the mothers had fallen pregnant before they married. However, the fact that a child is labelled illegitimate does not always mean that the mother is not living with the father or with another man in a fairly stable relationship. The NSPCC Retrospective Study found that out of their sample of 78 families, the majority (77 per cent) of the abused children were at the time of injury living with their natural parents, of whom fifty-four were married and only six were in live in relationship. Another 18 per cent lived with their natural mother but with a substitute father (half of these couples were married to each other). Out of rest four battered children there were only two living in single parent families, and in both these cases the parent was married but living apart from the spouse. A survey carried out by the National Opinion Research Center of the University of Chicago in 1965 found that over 80 per cent of the abused children understudy lived with married parents or parent substitutes, and only 15 per cent were living with a single parent. Another survey undertaken New York City in 1966 by Simon and Down found that only 2.4 per cent were one-parent families. They found, however, that 32 per cent of the children were out of illicit relations, as against the normal New York City average of 12 per cent. From all these figures it shows that a higher than average number of battered children are conceived out of wedlock, but that a large majority live in a two-parent family, most often with both their natural parents. Nevertheless, marriage or cohabitation does not necessarily control loneliness. Nowadays there is hardly much inter-family support, however large the family unit is: couples are expected to manage on their own without popping round to Mum every few minutes, and in some cases only spinster aunts to support in this modern world. Marriages are supposed to be self-sufficient in a way that has never happened before, and for some the strain is too great.

Tragedy with this modern set up is that these parents tend to pick each other out with unerring aim. Although many of these marriages follow on premarital conception and might therefore be considered unplanned, it takes two negligent stupid adults to make a baby: thoughtful responsible young men and women are not very likely to conceive an unwanted child. Experts on marriage sometimes remark how extraordinarily calculative most people are at picking out either opposites or their twins: they either marry someone they want to quarrel with (perhaps continuing battles unsolved in their childhood)) or they choose someone just like themselves. There are those who even manage to find a combination of the two, selecting a partner with similar emotional hang-ups to their own but with the basic characteristics of which ever parent they struggled most violently. While such a situation can be therapeutic, the main danger is that when the battle is over, one spouse may emerge a changed character with no further need of the old partner.

Another characteristic of battering of parents is that they marry for the same reasons as everybody else, but the demands they make on marriage are excessive. They have a great need for reassurance deep love, tenderness, strength: but neither side is prepared to give the other such gifts. Since they rarely believe in the value of words they cannot communicate with each other. Their demand is mute, and doomed to dissatisfaction. They want to union love, but can only offer in exchange criticism and complaint. The birth of a child complicates matters for such marriage partners even further. The love they did not succeed in wresting from their suppose they now expect from their infant, but the new baby, instead of releasing in the mother the instant maternal love she had hoped to experience merely produces exasperation and anger. Further, if the father gives the baby the love and concern his wife feels he has denied her she will then be intolerably jealous, thinking not only that the baby hates her (mistaking its cries of hunger or boredom for disapproval) but that it is also stealing her mate's love. The father, who a few hours earlier may have been feeling exactly the same way himself, may now take advantage of his temporary primacy and taunt the mother, suggesting that the baby prefers him, or that she doesn't know how to take care of it and had better leave it to him. The situation is liable to see-saw, each parent changing position, until the sense of tension in the home grows to a dangerous intensity.

It has been seen that such parents do not support each other, though support is what they desperately need. They each sense the other's lacks and ignore them because they are their own lacks: at good times they would reach out to the other, but they cannot express themselves, and worst of all, they hardly trust. However, their very needs and fears bind them together in a hopeless struggle.

In the situation where one of the parents is of the aggressive type, the other may be frightened to protect a child who is being attacked for fear of drawing the violence to herself, though generally such people seem to invite the voilence in subtle ways. Indeed, it is often impossible for investigators to decide who was responsible for any particular incident: collusion between the two parents can sometimes be so involved that many feel it is useless trying to discover who is the 'guilty' partner. Of course this pattern is not invariable; there are marriages where one persons is genuinely uninvolved, for instance through absence, but where two people are living together it is virtually impossible for one of them not to bother at all of how the other is treating their child.

To discover the marriage patterns of battering parents, some research is being done on the kind of marriages battering parents have, but there are few facts available till today.

An important guideline to the recognition of a potentially dangerous marriage has been outlined by Schneider, Pollock and Helfer (1972) who suggest that there are basically three possibilities where an individual has had the kind of upbringing which could result in his battering a child: the first is that if his potential to batter is weak and marries someone with a normal upbringing there are ten possibilities of abusing his child; the second is that if his potential is strong and the spouse has a passive character, then almost certainly there will be battering lastly, if two adults with weak or moderate potential marry, then battering is likely to occur. Obviously if two people with strong potential marry, then battering is almost invitable to take place. The lives of a married couple are so interwoven that disentangling the truth of it may be impossible in an ordinary social welfare situation continues to be explosive then the child should be removed until matters are mended; insisting on trying to discover which of the two partners actually committed a particular assault, or whether the partner who goaded the other into the attack was more to blame than the attacker, is not only pointless but actually disastrous. The parents will be feeling guilty enough as it is without outsiders stirring up further rounds of accusations and arguments. Of course if the abuse is a serious one and legalities are involved then a social workers may have no choice in the matter. Either way, both parents must be heard: taking the word of one parent only may lead to a misunderstanding of the reality of the marital situation.

Perception of Battering Parents

Do battering parents see their children differently from the rest of us? How do they react to their babies, and why if they love them so much, do they also attack them so brutally? These vital questions are only just beginning to be answered, and various clues are emerging. Finding out the parent's genuine attitude to his child is complicated by the fact that most of the time, he does not know it himself. A child psychiatrist said that the early period of motherhood is universally accompanied by feelings of rage and anger. One's faced with a situation in life where one has made a balance, one has one's pleasure, one's difficulties, but it's all organized, under control. Then suddenly there's this new life, everything's turned upside down, and it lead to anger, however much the parents they want the child. You aren't allow these rejecting feelings near the surface, so you cope with them by being over-protective. One feels like saying to such parents, for God's sake let him fall, let him scratch himself, he'll never learn otherwise. It's normal, it's the way most people are. Then most parents suddenly experience that children are tougher than they think and if they leave the for ten minutes nothing terrible will happen. A lot of parents don't discover this, however: they won't give in. It's the reverse of battering, you see, in a way, and yet it's the same process at work. It can end in battering, of undoubtedly.

Physical Disliking for the Child

Not only the over-cautious attitude, there may also be a physical distaste for the child resulting from the extreme disappointment the mother feels in it; although actually cuddling the child because she knows intellectually it requires such attention, the mother may nevertheless be hating the physical contact. One mother said, 'I have to force myself to touch him; I'll pull him on to my lap by his clothes so that I don't actually have to get hold of him.' Imagine the turmoil in the mind of this mother who all through pregnancy longed to love and hold her own baby, only to find the reality repulsive and entirely unrewarding.

Through the finding of experiments with monkeys which had been reared by various surrogate mothers, it has been found that proper mothering of the future parent is essential if its eventual offspring are themselves to be successfully mothered. How much one can make of these experiments in case of human beings is a subject of debate; also one must bear in mind that these monkeys had to endure other unusual conditions besides unnatural mothering, such as a non-availability of their peers to play with, and these factors must also have had a bearing on the eventual sociability of the mother-to-be. However, commonsense would indicate that the results bear some similarities for human mother, especially when the findings are so identical to those reported by many researchers in the baby battering field. When the time came for the monkey mothers who had been deprived of normal mothering in their childhood to rear their own babies they threw them aside, assaulted them, and even occasionally killed them. Aggression towards infants is not limited to the human species.

On the basis of her experiences, a psychiatrist suggested that it is not the fact that battering parents have these aggressive feeling which is important— all parents have them, he says—what matters is what they do with these aggressive emotions. It they have not learned to cope with them during childhood then of course, difficulties will be experienced. The psychiatrists Anthony Storr, who regards it as a natural drive and considers its proper understanding to be root necessity to mankind, writes that if we are to control aggression, it is important to determine whether there is ... an internal accumulation of aggressive stress which needs periodic out set, or whether' the aggressive response is simply a potential which need never be brought into use. If the first supposition is true, what is needed to control aggression is the arrangement of suitable outlets for aggression. If the latter is true, what is required is the avoidance of all stimuli which might arouse the aggressive response.

Of the various alternatives suggested by various authorities, whichever is true, the outcome for many battering mothers is the same: the only outlet in such a housebound mother's life may be her family, and unfortunately the response is normally such that the aggression is intensified, and not controlled. As to avoiding all stimuli, few situations could be more stimulating for a potential aggressor than an unresponsive, demanding baby lying shout for attention while the spouse is out at a football match or sitting with hands over ears reading a newspapers or a journal. The attack, when it does come, may well pass right out of the attacker's mind immediately afterwards, so that he or she will be unable to recall what had taken place. Cameron writes that 'guiltamnesia is a well-recognized condition in most of the abusive parent': certainly the parents is likely to be severely hazy about what actually happened, owing to the emotional turmoil taking place in his mind at the time. The child may be for the time-being seen as the attacker's parent, or as himself as a child, or as some hateful amalgam of everything the attacker detests about himself and others. The memories left in the attackers's mind after the assault may be so confused and unreal he is genuinely not in a position to make any sense of it or to relate the thing he attacked to his own familiar child. Some parents, however, are able to recall clearly enough what happened, but will not speak the truth because of fear of the consequences, or from straight forward guilt. It is a rare parent who can bring himself to openly admit what has happened.

Post-Natal Depression of Mothers

Lastly, what makes some parents attack their own children, while others are able to control their impulses? That some mothers suffering from puerperal or post-natal depression 'lose their minds' and kill their young babies has been proven for some time now with understanding. Such a mother usually receives sympathy and will not be imprisoned. The emotive term 'battering' is not generally used in such cases of infanticide, although it may well be that some of these babies had earlier also suffered undetected abuse. Why should the young mother suffering from post-natal depression, who is found to have tortured her child, not be treated with the same sympathy as one who actually kills it? I cannot help feeling that there may be an artificial difference between these two categories based on the abhorrence of the idea that a mother could kill her own child and the intense need of everyone concerned to find a justful explanation. Puerperal depression is a perfect excuse, can be seen as an illness and is therefore forgivable. One imagines the mother in a sudden access of anger cleanly killing her baby. But in fact children die by atrocities like stabbing, strangling, smothering, drowning and bashing: where then is the difference? If hormonal imbalances are at the bottom of the mother's depression, this will affect million of mothers. Might one therefore not expect there to be large numbers of mild cases of battering where the disturbance is comparatively mild? Does a severe hormonal disturbance normally result in one sudden violent assault causing immediate death, or is the murder perhaps the result of progressive bashing which has remained unrecognized, as in many ordinary cases of baby battering?

Through their research, Kempe and Helfer (1972) suggest that one of the causes of postnatal depression may be that some mothers are depressed because they find they cannot love their babies, the more usual theory being the reverse that they could not love their babies, the more usual theory being the reverse, that they could not love their babies because they were undergoing depression brought on by the pregnancy and birth itself. Whatever the cause for puerperal workers in contact with young mothers known of its effect, and several saying that they were sure it was behind many of the attacks their mothers had made.

Skinner and Castle (1969) state that of the forty adult mothers in their sample seventeen were expecting at the time of the battering incident and another four had battered an older child within two months of giving birth to a new baby: that is, 52 per cent were either recently confined or were pregnant at the time they made their assaults. Similarly-based figures are not given for the 1972 report, but out of 292 children 56 were under five months old and a further 54 were aged between six to eleven months, that is to say, over a third of the children were under eleven months of age when they were attacked, falling within the age limit for infanticide. How many mothers were pregnant again at the time of the attack is not known, but a certain number were, bound to have been. Here is another field where further research is immediately needed.

Along with the above, premature birth brings problems of its own. For a start, the mother is completely separated from the child at birth, affecting the normal process of imprinting where permanent impressions of the other are made on each partner. If this process is most effective immediately afterbirth, a separation perhaps lasting two or three months may find it impossible to feel any physical or emotional connection with the tiny tender baby lying sealed away from her in its hygienic cot, side by side with a number of other such babies. She may be upset by its appearance, even revolted by it, and by the time the child is returned to her she may find it to be a total stranger.

In their 1969 and 1972 samples the NSPCC found that 13 to 14 per cent of the abused children were classified as premature, a classification which includes those children who are born in the normal time span but are underweight at the time of birth and therefore need special attention. This figure is double that of the national average. The question to be solved here is how interlinked are these facts? Were the babies are premature or underweight because of stresses in the expectant mother, or was in the failure to have a normal birth and the problem arising from prematurity which disturbed the mother after birth,' causing the stress which later resulted in battering? The 1969 Retrospective Study reports that the premature babies, along with a further category of failure-to-thrive babies, were infact more severely injured than other normal babies. Certainly a weak baby needing additional care is not the best kind of infant for a mother with a battering potential to rear. It appears that some babies are more likely to be pattered than others. Premature and underweight babies are automatically in danger. Not only does their care demand special patience on the part of both parents, but the mere fact that they are 'difficult', with its implication that the parents are not capable of handling a normal baby, will be enough to rouse antagonism in anyone with a battering potential. A baby who dies not eat well, or who wakes up full of energy at mid night will also cause much stress due to sleeplessness of mothers.

Many babies have different body rhythms from their parents, or have body clocks functioning outside the twenty-four cycle so that it is unusually difficult to train them to fit into a standard routine pattern. Even well-adjusted parents can find this situation almost intolerable. If the parent has only a weak impulse to assault and he is blessed with a contented baby which sleeps most of the day and all the night, which unprotestingly eats all it is given and puts on the right amount of weight, all is likely to be well. If, however, the baby is not quite perfect in some respect, perhaps has a small birth mark or some other defect, or if he suffers from three-month colic or is very fussy with his food, then he is in some danger especially with a parent whose potential is undoubtedly high.

It is indisputable that when the mother was pregnant she fantasized about her future child. Perhaps she desperately wanted a girl and feared having a boy. If when the child is born it turns out to be a male, then the chances are already stacked against him. Equally many men desire for a son, and will be bitterly disappointed if a girl is born. If the baby reminds a potentially dangerous parent of some member of the family (including him or herself) about whom he has strongly unpleasant feelings then doctors to ask such parents is whether the baby looks like or behaves like anyone else in the family. If the reply is 'Yes, he's got my husband's temper', or 'She's got all my faults, I'm scased' then they should sit up and observe.

One more not worthy symptom is that the child is often found by the parents to be different from other children, although the worker may be incaple of spotting any such difference. The idea that one particular child may be chosen as a scapegoat was popular for some time, and while this situation certainly does exist, it is probably a different problem from the battered baby syndrome. A true scapegoated child may be locked away, starved, beaten, denied light and fresh air while all the other children in the family are scared quite normally and comfortably. With battered children the distinction between the children is rarely so clear-cut. There may be one particular child which is being beaten at the moment, and because such parents are often highly fussy about clothing and general caretaking the other children may appear to have escaped all abuse. However, in many such cases on looking up old medical records it has been found that the siblings have also suffered a series of 'accidents' in their days.

Despite a lot of research, few statistics are available at present to prove how likely a parent is to abuse all of his children or only one of them, but some were put forward in the NSPCC's 1969 Retrospective Study. The sample of 78 families was too small to be totally inclusive: for example there was only one family with as many as four children in it (most of the families in the study were still young and therefore not yet very prolific). However, 68 per cent of the families for whom full details were acquired had battered their first-born child. More may have done so, but no hospitalization was recorded for the rest. In the 22 families where the first-born was assaulted and further children had been born 26 out of the 28 siblings were also meted out the same fate. The authors tentatively estimate that any second children born in the eighteen families which up to them had only had one child, stood a 13 to 1 chance of being attacked. These figures are based on a small number of cases, and incomplete data were available.

A much wider survey including some bigger families with older supposedly-unbattered children who could be X-rayed for healed fractures, etc., would be invaluable. For the time being one may perhaps assume that if a parent's attacking potential is not very strong and if circumstances do not go too severely against him or her, then it may be that only one child will receive any battering severe enough to require some form of the medical treatment. But if unfortunate crises occur, or if the battering potential, is strong, then all the children in the family will be at risk. Certainly where the first child has been battered every subsequent child should be considered as being.

In danger too the power of a child's cry is phenomenal. Watch what happens in any shopping street full of housewives if a child shouts 'Mum!' Heads of young mothers, middle-aged women and even grandmothers turn instinctively, immediately, looking for crier. Once you have been a mother your child may be grown up and in another country; but if such a cry sounds urgent, perhaps noticeable danger, for a moment the old feelings are awoken and adrenaline starts pumping through you before you have chance to laugh at your mistake. Persistently weeping child can break down concentration or peace of mind quicker than any other noise known to man. There was a post-war story that tapes of screaming babies used to be played outside the bunkers of stubborn Japanese soldiers who refused to capitulate. Within a short time they invariable came running out, requesting for the tapes to be stopped. It could have been true: it almost certainly would have worked.

To conclude, various agreements and factors have been placed to prove child battering. In some cases, one also sympathises with the batterer who in turn is a sufferer at the hands of a tough child. But this can neither be used as an excuse nor a justification to let the child battering carry on. At whatever cast, the evil needs to be checked to what the tiny raw-looking babies are allowed to grow into fully developed balanced human beings.

12

CHILD BATTERING: THE ROLE OF POLICE

When we talk of redresal of problems of child abuse, it is police which deserves first mention because the process of justice start with them. In an address to the Royal Society of Health in 1972 a doctor who has had better experience of the subject, said, few aspect in the management of these children generate such heat as the involvement of police... The two positions are widely polarized; on the one end, there are enthusiasts who maintain that under no circumstances whatsoever should the police ever get involved; at the other extreme there are police forces who insist that since the physical injury of a child is crime against the state, the concealment of these cases is unlawful, and all these injuries to children should be reported to them. Clearly this tough situation and the doctor, in the centre of two such clearly differing views, must give serious thought as to the attitude he must adopt in these circumstance.

"Most of the times, the police in these situations receive the co-operation... they deserve. If a force is determined to prosecute irrespective of whether it be a deliberate assault or whether it be a battered child, then they will receive very little co-operation. If on the other hand they are required to play their part in the management they can expect to receive the co-operation of the personnel engaged in handling the situations." Police on the other hand, would deny that last sentence.

They say that however willing they are, there are still many social workers in the field-who distrust them and will give them no information whatsoever unless the assault is so severe that there is no option. Most doctors may be won trusted more easily, but even there prejudice dies hard.

It may be hard fact for many policemen but the truth is that if they are to receive any worthwhile co-operation they have no option but to agree not to prosecute except in severe cases where everyone agrees prosecution is utmost. That there exist almost diametrically opposite views among policemen is not particularly astonishing-no one imagines every policeman to be identical-but the remarkable variability of action taken in different cases may surprise those who are not aware of the unlimited limit to which country police forces are autonomous. Each force is responsible to itself only: what the Chief Constable of Northampton decides to do on a specific issue may be identical to or the completed against what has counterpart in Dorset does; the decisions are their alone, and till they are clearly behaving in a bizarre or dishonest manner they will not be interfered with by the Home Office. Nevertheless, most of the times, there is probably less difference in certain basic attitudes among policemen than there is in most professions. There can be few, if any, policemen who do not believe at all in law and order and in the value of self control.

Due to this basic similarity in attitude among the police which occasionally wrecks the most well-meaning efforts of some of them to come to a working compromise with workers in other fields. Doctors and social workers on the whole learn to conceal their personal reactions, putting their professional face forward. Policemen, who perhaps more than most have chosen their job as a result of their individual attitudes, seem less adept at keeping up a smooth line of talk without revealing sooner or later their own inner feelings with regard to of law and order.

So that a policeman truly wanting to help a battering mother may almost succeed in gaining the confidence of her social worker, but may then lose that trust totally commenting that he can't help feeling that the woman could have stopped herself from attacking the child if she had really wanted to. At once the social worker counts put him back into the category of 'punitive official' and sets about protecting his client from the spectre of the law.

The present chapter specifically light on what social workers and the medical profession have to say about policemen bearing in mind complaints coming from areas where working pattern of co-operation between all of them has not yet been developed . In the words of the Director of Social Services of a large London borough: "I don't think the police in fact have much contribution to make in a society which gets anguished not only about the injury to the child but also about the pressures on the mother and father which led to that injury. I have talked for hours with the police about the point at which we should tell them we've discovered an injury to a child which might be the result of a battering, but all they seem concerned with is calling the mother into the station and saying, right, this is a chargeable offence. Now that is a largely irrelevant act as far as I am concerned. No, we don't go racing after the police as soon as we hear of an injury because I think British law lives just about a century behind the times. We don't really keep them in the dark, but we try to steer the situation along in such a way that the notion of a police enquiry is the last in the line of sequence of actions rather than the first. This comment was typical; even where I had spoken to policemen and women in an area and knew for a fact that some at least were highly sympathetic, amongst the social workers concerned I would still often come across almost total distrust and a refusal to risk co-operation. It's not like the police tell you, they insist. They'll bring a charge of attempted murder if they've half a chance, and then everything you've done is wrecked. Even if they don't do that, they accuse, and that's unbearable to these mothers."

Consulted psychiatrists, treating the mental health of their patients uppermost in their minds, can be even more outright. One London psychiatrist said, "The police are just acting as agents of vengeance, that's all, they're acting as society's super-ego conscience to attack those who've done wrong: if you've bashed your child than you must be bashed too. "In the time of potential tragedy for the family, and police have absolutely no significant place in this at all. As it stands the law is quite adequate: if a child is in danger it can be taken into care without any need for police intervention.'

The greatest source of referrals to the NSPCC, i.e. hospital, rarely call in the police in the first instance. In a few rare areas the local social services insist on all cases being reported to the police regardless of how minor or unproven the attack—an instance was given in of a paediatrician, asking for a social worker to call on a stressed parent and to uniformed policemen came in instead. But such a policy seems to be unusual: normally quite the opposite is the case. As the same paediatrician pointed out that. In medicine doctors simply not prepared to make a diagnosis until they have all the signs and symptoms and tests in front of them. You can't come to a snap decision as to whether a child has been bashed: it takes time to be certain, and it's pointless bringing in the police until you are clear.

This argument of, psychiatrist about the police acting as our agents of vengeance is of course true to some extent. Few people can be so humane that they will wish no punishment to be meted out to parents who have killed or very severely hurt their children. A psychiatrist spends his day investigating the prominent reasons behind human action: when therefore he considers some terrible act a man or woman has done he looks at it as the with ultimate result and judges it accordingly or, more likely, forbears to judge at all. But most of the time, people see such a crime as an isolated act and are not seriously concerned with its background: an old lady lies battered to death on the floor-beside that fact what does it matter that her assailant were a drunk father and an unjustful mother? A bank manager is shot dead and his young secretary blinded, her face scarred for life-who is keen to know that the murderer grew up in a slum and was self-conscious about his puny stature? Most of us demand punishment in such events, and we employ the police to see the that the criminal is caught. The police as a whole are unlikely ever to be forerunners of reform; the public perhaps gets what it asks for, and if the most committed radicals are disappointed in their desires for penal reform so, fortunately, are the core-hard conservative who would bring back the birch and the scaffold.

While during treatment the doctors fear the effect on the parent and her relations with her child if the police enquiries are accusative: the police answer that they must know about assaults of any kind, it's their job to know. But as a psychiatrist pointed out, if the child is going to live there's absolutely no point in calling in the police, it only complicates matters and makes treatment more difficult. If the child dies, there still would have been reason to police. They would have been too late to protect the child, and if it's only public vengeance they're these, far, then they can get it after the child is dead. After all, if someone is being poisoned they don't expect the murderer to give them evidence while it's going on.

If we put the police's argument-that they are there to protect the child as much as the parent-to the paediatrician mentioned previously, he replied, 'You can't do one without the other. Anyway, it's not true. The police's job is to detect crime and to put it to the court for the courts decision whether to punish or not to punish.

That's the primary objective of the police, to detect crime, not to protect the child or to see that it's rehabilitated with its family-that's the job of the social workers and the doctors.'

For this argument, this the police will reply that very often the families need separating from each other, even if only temporarily while feelings recovered, and that only the police can be sure of succeeding in bringing a case successfully to the Juvenile justice Courts. Magistrates faced with a social worker who is not only uneasy in his mind about separating families even though he is actually wanting from the court for a care order, but who is also untrained in the finer aspects of court proceedings, may well decide to go against that social worker's request and leave a child in the bosom of its family out of misplaced sentiment.

Perhaps, by now quite clear from the general tone of this book that the author sympathize deeply with the parents, but it must be admitted that in some of the cases police are justifiably annoyed that they were not called in earlier. Let us quote one example which comes from an area where the police forces are highly sensitive to the problem of battering, and certainly do not prosecute unless they are sure it is necessary for everybody's sake. The colour slides they showed were of a baby girl a few months old with gaping stab marks around the public area at the top of the thighs, both front and back. 'That kid was brought into hospital on a Friday afternoon the casualty officer noticed that they were knife marks, the consultant knew they were knife marks, but he thought he was doing the right thing in contacting the social services. Unfortunately they are off here on Friday evening so nothing happened until Monday. They went to see the father (who'd done the stabbing) and got the usual sort of yarn from him about a fox terrier having bitten the baby. It was not until Tuesday that they heard about it, and even then it was by accident that there was a four-day-old line to follow which had been fouled up by the previous investigations. Now in fact in that prosecution was brought in-there was never any choice. The whole family had been under the social services for some time—it was a real problem family, subnormal and incapable. The bloke who did the stabbing—he'd already got a record of exploitation,- was not only the child's father, but the mother was his own sister. It wasn't just casual between them-they lived together almost like man and wife in the same house as the rest of the family-and it was going on like this until the girl (she was only 15) took up with a proper boy friend. Most probably, out of jealousy the brother suddenly stabbed the baby and damn nearly killed it. There was no choice but to get him away, and he's in the local mental hospital at the moment, diagnosed as a psychopath.

This incident took place three or four years ago, and the police force involved think it unlikely that now a days they would not be informed immediately if such a case were to occur again. But many area have not yet achieved a successful rapport between the police and other services, and in this kind of a situation could still easily arise. It takes a great deal of experience to decide how threatening a situation is and what sort of action must be taken immediately: whoever makes such a decission must be a senior person capable of looking at the available facts without prejudice.

The biggest difficulty lies less with the dramatic kind of case just discussed than instead those where only mild injuries are involved. Often these are not even definitely recognized as having been made by the parent.

It has been seen that the root of the dissension between the police and almost everybody else involved in the treatment of battering families lies in their varying attitudes to punishment. The situation is further complicated by the fact that many ordinary members of the public are ignorant about the value of punishment intellectually they may think that punishment is ineffective as a treatment, but they themselves have been brought up to except punishment to follow wrong-doing and they are comfortable with a situation where this does not happen.

On the other hand, the police are single-minded on the question of punishment. Although they insist their job is the detection of crime and that their prime objective is not punitive, it is unlikely that someone who doubted the virtues of punishment for wrongdoing would agree with the police force in the first instance, just as one would not expect a vegetarian to become apprenticed to a butcher. It is instructive to see what various policemen and women, all of whom are willing to and sympathetically-minded about baby battering, have to say. The reader should bear in mind that they are speaking of their sincere values and are not merely handling out the official line which they have not considered and thought about. For those to whom such ideas about behaviour appear shocking in the light of today's popular psychology, they should try to understand the attitude behind the words, because it is mostly the attitude of the majority of people in this country. What is best for a society may not necessarily be best for an individual, although this unpalatable fact is very tough to accept in an individualistic society like that of our own.

'Battering parents expect to get punished, we must realize that. They've been brought up that if they've done unjustful, they'll get whacked for it, and if they don't then they feel society is saying, it's O.K., we don't mind what you've done. Then they go and do it again.' From another area, 'Why shouldn't someone who's violated one of society's rules be punished? What's wrong with punishment? As long as it goes hand in hand with treatment, and when the punishment is completed the crime is put away and forgotten. I know that's easy to say but difficult to be done, but it's not the concept of punishment that's at fault, it's society's treatment of the prisoner and his aftercare that's wrong. No, punishment is required in a well-run society, but punishment shouldn't mean looking up someone up in a cell without any treatment, then kicking them around afterwards when they come out.'

Along with this, the undoubted dangers of police intervention are summed up by Joan Court: 'Prosecution, if successful, is unlikely to have a deterrent impact on parents who are not capable of controlling their conduct, and merely confirms them in their negative self image. If they are acquitted then they feel flameless and justified in their conduct, and future therapeutic work with them may prove impossible. Most important of all, perhaps, is that the resultant publicity stops other parents from seeking help in the early stages. The injured child, who could have been adequately protected through the Juvenile Court, is then in bigger danger.' Kempe adds a further thought: 'I see child abuse the way I see failed suicides, with much compassion. We no longer punish people who fail at attempting suicide. Well, I think attacks on small children by their parents by and large are attacks on themselves and I would treat it in exactly the same manner. Not as a police matter, but as a disease. After all, we've shown that punishing does not work. Gaol does not make you love more. In our experience there have been six parents who have gone to gaol; three have bashed again their children, one has not, and two we've lost track of. So three out of four have failed to be reformed in jail. Prison, to these people, is simply reinforcement of what they have always known: that it's a punishing world and you deserve to be awarded that, so they think it's perfectly all right for society to punish them.'

Next significant point is that police surgeons, many of have learned how to present a case properly and to successfully stand by their opinion while searching cross-examination. If a child is in danger and needs, however temporarily, to be separated from its parents, a successful result is essential. Clever lawyers can sometimes make mincemeat of men and women who are normally more than capable of holding their own, with the result that many children are returned to their families inspite of the expressed fears of the doctors or social workers who have been looking after them. Naturally, this is less likely to happen when an experienced police surgeon is presenting the evidence. If a Care Order is being asked for and this is granted, then the child will be put in the care of the local Social Services Department, and it will be the police surgeon who earns the opprobrium of the family for this action, rather than the doctor. It seems hard on the police surgeon that this should happen, but as Dr Davies says, 'My back's broad; what matters to me is the future welfare of the family, not who gets their gratitude.

One more member of the team must be a senior police officer, and since battering is considered a criminal assault it will normally be the CID who will be assigned this function. CID officer with definite proof that some one has assaulted a child must 'put the evidence before those responsible for deciding whether a prosecution should be made, but in our experience, the latter person or persons invariably follow a humane and adequate course, and if it is in the best interests of the child that a prosecution should not be made, then this line is usually taken.' Behind these official phrases lies the fact that the Chief Constable does in fact listen and listen hard to them. There have only been one or two instances of disagreement where police action was taken against the suggestions of some of the other members of the committee, and they claim that much was learned from this. The team, whose primary job is to collate all the information collected by its various members and then decide the best course of action to be taken for the child and its family, is called together as soon as possible after the injury. The meetings are as far as possible kept informal: obviously the scheme would cease to work if each member went to the meeting grimly determined to wrest as much as possible from 'the other side'. There will also be a NSPCC officer if he has been involved; any policeman or woman who has been handling the case—this might be a chief inspector or a sergeant; the social worker for the area, and the family's GP if he wants to join, though most decide not to. When the case has been talked about and looked at from angle, a decision is arrived at, and this will be communicated back to police headquarters. From then on every case is different, by whatever the final decision, team keeps in touch, informally by phone or by occasional meetings.

Regarding the something applies to police representation on hospital case committees; several doctors told me they have assured the local police they would welcome them provided they would agree to take no action except in extreme case, but nearly always the police reply that they would like to come but if they heard of anything they thought might be a crime, however confidentially they were informed about it, they would have to investigate-with the consequence that they are rarely asked on to these committees.

This circular also reads : 'A battered baby case is by definition one in which there is at least a suspicion that a serious offence has been committed. *When a case come to the notice of the police they are bound to investigate it* although a prosecution will not necessarily follow. Once the facts are known to them the police have to decide whether to prosecute'. On the other hand they accept that the : Police representation at the case committee level is reported in very few areas and this is a reflection of a reluctance of doctors and social workers to get police along with them before they have been able to assess the social consequence of such action in situations which are so often complicated. But instead of drawing the obvious conclusion from these two facts, they end up with a first-rate piece of officialese saying precisely nothing. Therefore, this is one important area where greater flexibility may be needed and where attention should be focused on the possibility of improving co-operation between the police, medical persons and social workers. It would be wrong to assume that the measure of co-operation necessary can be easily achieved but the encouragement of a continuing dialogue between all those concerned might inculcate the best hope for the future.'

In cases, a policeman sincerely believes he has no choice but to investigate and possible prosecute on hearing of certain cases, then the first statement above will reassure him he is correct in his stand. The last paragraph will in no way encourage him to co-operate since the first pararaph has just told him he must not. Let us be quite clear about this: to an those involves except the police, police investigation at any level is not 'co-operation' unless it has been requested. Thus saying that 'police representation at the case committee level is reported in very few areas'—will continue to be true until something far more concrete is dare than issue a few woolly statements to the effect they expect that it will probably all work out in the end. The Home Office is the only agency who can make it work out and they can only do so by issuing unequivocal orders which everybody can clearly understand. For example, where a paediatrician suspects a battering but does not consider the child's life to be at present at risk, then the police should be informed so that they may know what is happening. The police in their turn should attempt to keep right out of the picture as far as the parents are concerned until a case committee (on which they would be represented) has thought what action ought to be taken. Where a case committee cannot come to an agreement then the argument will have to be taken to a further high-level committee, on which all professionals are represented, for pondering over the case. If, as at present, a doctor knows that the final decision will be made by a policeman, then he will not give information, and however many pious hopes the Home Office may express in future circulars, they will be doomed to remain unfulflled.

One because of being critical of have office in that of we leave the impression that its influence has been entirely negative it will be unfair. The various communication sent out over the past few years have certainly brought the existence of baby child to the attention of many who might otherwise have preferred to ignore it. The first action was taken in 1970 when the Home Office demanded inter-professional discussions on a local basis. In a memorandum entitled *The Battered Baby* (February 1970) the syndrome was described in some detail. It was a right summing-up owing much to the NSPCC's research, though its tone was not always that used by the NSPCC's Research Department (for example, hospital casualty officers are directed when talking to battering parents that, throughout, the parents must be told repeatedly that the first concern of the doctor is to make their child better and, next to make sure that it does not happen again.

In May 1972 they released out the circular which was the analysis of all the reports submitted to them as a result of the consultations they had requested in 1970. This 1972 report was a broad-based review of what was being done all over the country, and carried various suggestions for improvement. From the analysis it appears that in the majority of countries police were involved in the review committees, but these were merely general committees which were supposed to discuss what could be done locally to deal with baby battering in principle; although some discussions no doubt proved valuable, others resulted in the kind of polite squabble. The Home Office analysis advised that the members these committees should meet regularly, and that their function should be to 'sure that research, education and training programmes are conducted, also that they should co-operate with review committees in other areas to make ensure that management procedures are either uniform or the differences clearly seen and understood'. These are sound ideas, but not a great deal seems to have happened as a outcome, whether through local lethargy, a lack of funds or a lack of time, it is difficult to judge.

Another committee which local authorities were encouraged to set up was the case committee, formed to deal with individual cases; Unfortunately, the Home Office analysis proved that in most areas the police are invited once in while to these case committees, for the reasons already explained. Again and again in the report the importance of what we might call the three 'c's' is emphasised co-ordination, communication and co-operation. But pious hopes are not enough: the Home Office knows what requires to be done-they themselves have made it clear in their own circular-so when will they accept that progress on the popular question of police co-operation must originate from them? It is one of Britain's strengths as a nation that on the whole then police are incorruptible and that they follow the rules they are given. We do not want a police force that can change or adapt the rules as they see adjustable: the dangers are too great. Therefore it is important that they are given a clear lead where issues such as baby battering confuse the normal process of the law.

There is no guarantee that all policeman will agree with the concept of special rules for baby batterers and some will object strongly. As one policewoman said to me, 'Many of the policeman on the beat are young fathers and when they see what some man has done to his poor bloody kid their first instinct is to take their jackets off and have a go. It needs tremendous amount of self-restraint on their part, you know, to keep control under those circumstances'. Whatever the case may be, all policemen dislike the public image they have gained in recent years and feel they are not given sufficient credit for the large amount of social work they do as part of their job responsibilities. The role of the policeman in society needs to be perpetually re-examined. In an age of mass communication some of the opprobrium attached to police in less accommodative societies than ours has brushed off on to our own far milder police: if they are to restore the image of the friendly neighbourhood policeman then they must do more than make revolting noises when they are attacked. They will have to be seen making positive gestures of good will as a body even if it involves them in some sacrifice of their own freedom. After all, no one in the public services is any longer acting as a water tight compartmental unit. Modern social welfare is part of such a complicated structure that it can only function successfully if the interests of the people who are being helped are put before departmental ambitions. The police are not excused and should not be treated as such unless they wish to remain quite apart from other professions and be seen purely as a detecting, punitive force. The choice has to be made, and the sooner it is made the better. Then and only then, the issue of the child battering can be fought with effectiveness.

13

CHILD BATTERING: THE ROLE OF MEDICOS

In the previous chapter we have examined the criticisms of the police and the social services, but there is one important professional body which hardly comes under attack: the medical profession. At present many aspects of medical training are faulty and wrongly centred. If, for example, doctors were trained to treat patients as part of a family unit the cases of battering could drop dramatically.

More important is the fact that medical students are not trained about healthy bodies, healthy families; the emphasis is not on maintaining health but correcting damage. They learn about different parts of the body, are taught what can go wrong with these separate bits, and what they can do to set them right back. They learn about *sick* people, and they are taught to be interested in illness, not in gaining health, just as until recently nearly all psychiatry was founded on the study of mentally sick people, deductions from these studies then being popularly applied to non sick person as though there were no difference between them and the mentally sick. The result of this wrongly-biased training is that for many young casualty officers in hospital emergency wards a man coming in with a broken leg is literally a 'broken leg'. The remainder of the man hardly exists for the doctor-the body which the leg normally supports, the head controlling the body, is of almost no interests, and the home the man comes from, his marital relations, his success or failure in his job, none of these matter in the slightest. Now where an accidentally broken leg is concerned, these details are not especially important (though even here recovery may be delayed if the man is worried about losing his job or keeping up his hire-purchase repayments), but if it is an ulcer the patient is suffering from, or if the he is a child with a fracture arm or a burnt hand, then it is of the prime importance that the examining doctor should have been taught something about people as units a family rather than people as individual collections of different limbs and organs.

This is an unfortunate state that such training is rare. Some teaching hospitals do now try to include a lecture on the subject and another lecture or two on problems specific to children, but not every student attends every lecture. Since an understanding of the patient within his family setting is not yet asked of the qualifying student, a hangover, a heavy cold, or a piece of work waiting to be finished can attract a young student to skip what does not seem to him to be a lecture of particular importance.

Therefore, when, after a year, the brand new casualty officer is faced with a small baby with a nasty bruise and a cut on his head he undoubtedly believes the mother's explanation that the previous day she had walked too quickly through a door while carrying the baby, catching its head on the door jamb. No one has trained him to be suspicious of the twenty-four hours, delay in reporting the accident, typical in cases of battering, no one had warned him that such mothers can be true looking liars; not even bothering therefore to wonder how the rather peculiarly shaped cut could possibly have occurred under such circumstance, he tells the nurse to slap a plaster over the cut, and sends the woman back home together with her baby. After all, she is obviously committed to it and is furious with herself for having been so careless. It would have been insulting to have undressed the baby to see if there were any other cut, even if he had thought of it (which to be honest he didn't, just as he did not think to have the baby weighed to see if it was an accurate weight for its age). As there is no compulsory registration of suspected battering cases there would have been little scope in his trying to find out quickly if the baby had been seen at any other local hospital, and he was too occupied to check in the normal way. He could not know, therefore, that twice in the last three months the mother had brought her baby to another hospital, once with a similar head and leg injuries.

Though this young doctor is not stupid; on the contrary, he is rather an intelligent ambitious young man. His present aim infact is to emulate as closely as possible the chief paediatrician of his hospital, a very impressive man whom he deeply recognises. The paediatrician himself would not have found that particular small baby any more interesting than did his young casualty officer: now could these be treated on similar terms as yesterday's newly-born spina bifida case or the hole-in-the heart baby the consultant was examining at the very moment the plaster was being applied on the doomed baby's head, it would have been another matter. Many hours and much money will be spent on the spina bifida child who will die anyway at six months of age, but the basically sound little battered baby will not live even as long as that unless somebody realizes very quickly what is happening.

It is a myth that doctors are omniscient creatures whose wisdom is above reproach dies hard. General practitioners, whose egos are not bolstered by daily contact with an obsequious staff, have far more opportunity to obtain a proper understanding of the limits of their own capabilities, and a good GP is one of the most valued members of the society. But hospital consultants are encouraged to remain remote, almost divine, creatures.

It is a positive sign that for the progress of medicine there are many men and women of a quite different capabilities, and in such hospitals a different atmosphere rules. However, even where the chief paediatrician himself is concerned with the problem of battered children, it is not always easy for him to ensure that every possibly doubt case arriving at the emergency room is reported to him. There is still a great resistance among doctors just as there is amongst the general masses to the fact of battering, and it will take a fair amount of persuasion on the part of the paediatrician before he can train some of his juniors that it is a less rare phenomenon than they would like to think.

Support staff e.g. nurses also have difficulty in coping with their reaction to baby battering. There exist training courses on children's illnesses in which the importance and requirement to treat a child as part of a family unit is taught, but not all nurses opt for this extra training. Since any nurse may be called upon to look after a battered child, even if only temporarily until it can be placed in a special children's ward, it would appear advisable that all nurse be given some training in the subject. A stunned accusing nurse could cause a parent to arbitrarily remove the child from hospital care, with possibly harmful results, but how could a young eighteen-year-old girl with no understanding of the stresses upon that parent be expected to behave otherwise as she looks down at some poor little bruised infant lying dumb in its cot, knowing that the man or women standing beside her actually hurt it?

The most noteworthy point is that there is no system of even compulsory refresher course for either doctors or nurses, so that theoretically it is possible for half a century to pass before everyone associates with medical care is taught about child abuse, even if such teaching were to start tomorrow. Such pamphlets as those issued by the Ministry of Health may be distributed among all members of staff in some of the more conscientious hospitals but even then it is up to individual members as to whether or not they bother to go through them. As for GPs, if they choose to avoid the subject it is only too easy for them to do so. Certainly the social services receive very few references from GPs of doughtful baby battering cases, and yet most, if not all battering parents and their children will have been examined, sometimes repeatedly, by their family doctors. Occasionally evidence of battering is simply not forthcoming, but sometimes after a child has died various facts came out which prove highly embarrassing to a doctor who did not draw the right conclusion from a variety of factors which to another more experienced man would have clearly hinted at a diagnosis of battering. Once such case, where everybody concerned -social workers, the NSPCC, doctors-were given warning after warning and yet nothing could be done to save the child, will be detailed in the final chapter. The only way to prevent the recurrence of such a terrible blunder is for an intensive period of training to be made mandatory for everyone in the field, and that includes all already-qualified doctors and nurses, however old or experienced in day to day medical matters they may be.

The point of argument can be that a interest in baby battering has suddenly become so widespread, with severe cases receiving such wide media coverage, that it ought to be impossible for an doctor to remain unaware of the syndrome. Yet some doctors still do not accept that baby battering, as distinct from other from of child abuse, even exists. This myopia may be partly caused by the fact that some doctors are uncomfortable with anything that smacks of psychiatry, preferring a nice batch of bacteria one can examine under a microscope. Many times, we hear the phrase used about keenly interested doctors, 'Oh, they've got battered babies on the brain, they see them every where'.

A very common psychiatric explanation of the common refusal to recognize a battered child is that many people cannot face up to the violence in themselves, but it must also be kept in mind that a doctor has inbuilt inhibitions against suspecting his patients. His training has taught him that people expect to come to him in confidence with their illnesses, believing that he will cure them, and that parents with sick children bring them to him in a similar spirit. That the child's illness may have been created by the very mother who has come to him voluntarily and who is now so anxiously holding out her child is ignorant of all he has been taught. He simply does not expect to find that a mother has injured her own child and therefore does not look for signs of abuse.

This issue of secrecy has given birth to much heart-searching among doctors. Doctors may not divulge information given to them by their patients unless those patients have given them signal to do so. Where a parent has admitted to battering but refuses to allow the doctor to pass on what he has told him then the doctor, if he is going to obey those strict medical ethics for which he oothed, has no choice but to remain silent. However such a course is clearly impossible if a child's life seens to be endangered. This problem is being considered by the various medical bodies concerned and no doubt some guidance will be laid down for future code of conduct, but for the present many doctors have to find their own way out of this problem. If the parents can be persuaded to talk to a social worker the doctor's moral problems are over, as social workers are not similarly bound to silence.

Another problem for doctors who understand something of the mentality of battering parents and yet consider themselves bound by the code of professional ethics, is that they will think that these parents are coming to them with an unspoken plea to be stopped from hurting their babies. Few doctors are capable of solving such a problem on their own without the specialized help of supportive agencies, but if the parent emphasise on secrecy the doctor is not supposed to ask for such help! It is small wonder that many doctors prefer to ignore the whole situation, especially when you consider that, in addition to the problem of confidentiality, if in the end the case ends up in court the doctor may well be called on to give evidence, which he will find both time-taking and distressing.

The issue of consideration here is also that most doctors are working to full capacity: how then can they be expected to spare time to investigate doubtful cases of battering and, as important, pre-battering? By pre-battering is Maoist mean a situation where children are chastized heavily but not yet to the point of assault, and where family stress is such that if it were suddenly rose at any time an attack might be made. A doctor may wonder about the origin of one or two injuries, and, knowing the family background, suspect that the brusies are not accidental. The best method is for him to ask for experienced helped immediately, but whether is able to do so depends on many factors. Large numbers of doctors these day, work in a group practice, and some of these have been able to arrange that one or more local health visitors should visit the surgery once or twice a week to talk to the doctors about any social problems about which they are concerned. Old people suspected of under-nourishment, 'work-shy' men pleading non-existent illness, or a low IQ housewife's inability to handle household management, all these can be investigated by a tactful health visitor. Easiest of all from the entry point of view is a situation where a baby is in the house, as the visit will then look like a normal routine checking-up on any problems of feeding or general care. An experienced worker, keeping in mind the doctors's suspicions, should during this visit be able to smell any difficulties, and through repeated calls might well forestall any drastic developments.

The biggest hurdle to such progress is that the very areas most in need of such help are the least likely to get it. In poor districts general practitioners are likely to be over-burdened and overworked while the Health Visitors are probably so busy they have little time to spare for routine visits to doctors' surgeries. Battering parents can be very comfortable, and it takes a perspicacious doctor even to have a hunch that something might be wrong: if they do not have the willing follow-up support of their local welfare services it will not be possible for the great majority of doctors to do anything other than hope for the best.

The inevitable sequel to an unattended 'cry for help' for many of the parents will be a visit to a hospital, bearing a child with fractured limbs or skull. In such a case the casualty officer needs to be highly doubtful. Very few normally-carried-for young babies suffer such injuries. Friedman and Holter found in a recent American research that the type of injury a child suffered had considerable significance. 156 children presented to the emergency room of a hospital were carefully checked, and 10 per cent were examined to have suffered physical abuse. Of the total 156 children, nearly 45 per cent suffered from lacerations, and over 20 per cent had taken in some dangerous substance. About 12 per cent suffered head injuries, while figures for burns, fractures and other limb injuries were between 8 and 5 per cent each. Of those who were doubtful of having been physically abused, however, only one child had suffered lacerations: all the rest fell into the small group with head injuries, burns, fractures and dislocations, abrasions and cuts.

The inference was these made that children with lacerations and ingestions may be regarded as being unlikely to have been battered, but that those with the other types of injury should be checked with particular care. This differentiation in the type of injury may be explained by the fact that most attacks are thought to happen while the parent is physically caring for the child; a knife or some other instrument which could cause laceration is unlikely to be in the parent's hand at such a time; and so any bruises would be of the kind caused by direct physical contact. The hands involved in this survey are statistically small, but further research may well prove them to be valid, in which case they will be useful guide to casualty officers trying to make a snap decisions. It is now being suggested to emergency room doctors by some baby battering experts that every suspected case of battering should immediately be hospitalized for further examination, though whether or not the parents should be informed of the reason is under some dispute.

Solution to the problem here seems to be that everything depends on the hospital set-up. Where a consultant is always available, he will be able to discuss the matter properly with the parents but in some hospitals there may be no one properly qualified in the building. And even in the best-run hospitals consultants are not usually available during the night hours unless specially called out, so that in many cases everything must inevitably be gives under the changed of the emergency doctor. It is a very difficult decision for him to make, whether or not to keep a child in, and whether or not to tell the parents the truth. His problem must be eased as much as possible, and this can only be done by a very clear policy being laid downs by his seniors.

Regarding child battering, deciding when that time has come is one of the most important decisions any doctor has to make. Some hospitals take the advice of psychiatrists, others do not. How supportive the opinions of psychiatrists, are in this situation is something that has not yet been proved, but the general understanding seems to be that most psychiatrists at present still favour a more rapid return to the parents than do some of the other workers engaged in the process, although this Bowlby-inspired reaction does seems to be weakening. Psychiatrists working in the field of child care who occupy the latest information in their reading have probably mostly moved on from the position Bowlby did so much to popularize in the 1950s.

It has been experienced that slightly fewer than 10 per cent of the parents are seriously mentally ill, psychotic or aggressive psychopaths who will not respond to the kind of treatment usually successful with other battering parents. But beyond this 10 per cent Kempe now accepts that there are another 15 per cent who inspite of treatment still cannot be regarded as safe parents. Pollock and Steele write (*in Helping the Battered Child and his Family*): 'Under the best of conditions we would estimate that at least 80 per cent of cases can be treated with reasonably expected result', but the words 'under the best of conditions' probably account for the difference in numbers here. If 90 per cent of the battering parents may be taken to be comparatively normal, (i.e., not psychopathic or psychotic), then perhaps in the future the 75 to 80 per cent success rate may go up, but for the moment it must be borne in mind that in about a quarter of all cases coming to light the child will eventually have to be taken away from its.

Parents while doing this, sentimental assumptions about parents' rights and natural ties must not be allowed to interferer with a decision which should be made by a committee expert enough to be able to ensure as near as humanly possible that a mistake is not made. Such a decision should never be left in the hands of one or two people, whose biases lack of experience may well result in the death of a child saving whose life should be first priority. Helfer has estimated that a child who is returned home after injury without further preventive steps to aid the parents, stands a 25 to 50 per cent chance of being either killed or permanently injured. Since much of the aid given at present is woefully inadequate, this is hair rising to think what is the figures might be even amongst those who are supposed to be receive care. If the committee were to automatically follow up at regular intervals all cases which had gone through their hands, even in areas where the social services labour under almost intolerable strains, such additional attention might make all the difference between life and death for many children.

Of course, some cases of battering simply cannot be proved, and a family may continue under suspicion while 'accident follows 'accident' without any action being taken. It was said by several policemen and women of various cases which they felt certain were instances of deliberate child abuse but which they felt certain were instances of deliberate child abuse but which they had never been able to prove; children would astonishingly fall through narrow gaps in windows which they could not only have reached by clever gymnastics probably-but not provably-beyond their ability; younger children in a family would swallow aspirin or medicine in lethal and sub-lethal doses; small infants would face into nearly boiling baths, for which 'accident' an older child might be blamed. Genuine accidents of this kind do undoubtedly happen, and a policeman's lunch that any particular incident is not accident is not enough reasons for action. Proof of guilt in such cases is very hard to come by. Sometimes three or four children in a family will have such injuries, some of them to the point of death, before action is finally taken. Charge of neglect is all that may be fastened on the parents even then, but in such circumstances this will be enough to separate any remaining children from their parents. Even then no person can be cent per cent certain that all such accidents in the family were not genuinely accidental, the result of criminal carelessness but not of criminal assault.

This have been found that even in more obvious cases of battering the correct diagnosis is not always made or it may be found more convenient to hope the parent has learned his or her lesson and will not hurt the baby again. These are all typical cases some ending in brutal attacks resulting in death. Clearly, not only is better diagnosis needed, but also an efficient system through which hospitals can check with general practitioners and other hospitals if a child has suffered a previous injury. If such a check were automatic for every injury irrespective of explanation then many lives would be saved. In America reporting of all suspected baby battering cases is compulsory, though there seems to be some confusion at present as to who should receive the report. Such a law ought to be passed everywhere without delay. The NSPCC has repeatedly stressed the importance of a national register, and in the light of publicity surrounding the famous Maria Colwell case it seems likely that the NSPCC's advice will at last be taken. Attempts at keeping local registers have been made in some countries, but without legal enforcement most have proven to be very patchy affairs indeed. Sometimes it is the social services who, have tried to organize a register, on which they have mentioned the name of any child suspected of being in possible danger through poverty, severe marital break up or other cause of stress which might disrupts a home. Elsewhere it has a been the Medical Officer of Health or one of his assistants who keeps the register.

If we keep on waiting and watching it will never be possible to save every child from death: there will always be the occasional case where unexpected stress has a sudden and violent effect on the parent of a very small baby with immediate disastrous results. But in most cases there is some warning, time for action to be taken. Where every doctor, every nurse, every health visitor is familiar with specific symptom of battering, the majority of cases, which at present progress through various stages of battering, may be caught in time before unrepairable damage is done. Is that not a worthwhile goal to aim for? A valuable weapon in the doctor's armoury would be an ability to detect the possibility that an as-yet innocent patient might batter any time in the future. Such techniques are at present being explored in America. Though they are still in an experimental stage, but they have already throw up many interesting ideas which should be of use to everyone whose prime aim is to stop battering even before it begins. Such efforts need to be introduced in other countries of the world as well so that we can evolve a world free from child battering.

Section—V

LEGAL ASPECTS

14

INTERNATIONAL CONVENTION ON THE RIGHTS OF THE CHILD: POSSIBILITIES AND PROSPECTS

After the second world war, in the aftermath of the most devastating war in history, along with UNO, UNICEF was created on 11 December 1946 to provide succour to children. Its emergence stemmed from the concern that children would not be adequately protected in the overall relief effort under way in Europe. The international recognition that children need special care was revolutionary at the time.

Towards the end of the postwar reconstruction period, developing countries released from the colonial duties invoked the same principle to demand that children be given specific attention in international cooperation. UNICEF's initial relief mandate was expanded to include the survival and development of children.

Recently, the international stand on children has changed dramatically once again. The idea that children have special needs has created to the conviction that children have rights, the same full spectrum of rights as adults: civil and political, social, cultural and economic. This conviction, expressed as the Convention on the Rights of the Child, entered into international law on 2nd September 1990, nine months than the Convention's adoption by the UN General Assembly. From then awards, the Convention has been ratified (as of mid-September

1996) by all countries except the Cook Islands, Oman, Somalia, Switzerland, the United Arab Emirates and America making it the most widely ratified human rights treaty in history.

After coming into existence, this Convention has produced a profound change that is already beginning to have substantive effects on the world's attitude towards it children. Once a country ratifies, it is bound in law to undertake all appropriate measures to assist parents and other responsible parties in performing their obligations to children under the Convention. Now, 96 per cent of the world's children live in State that are legally obligated to safeguard children's rights. Those rights are comprehensive and all encompasing. The Convention defines children as people below the age of 18 (article 10 whose "best interests" must be taken into account in all situations (article 3). It safeguards children's right to their full potential, and among its provisions are those approving children's rights to the highest attainable standard of health care (article 12), and to express thoughts and receive information. Children have a right to be registered immediately after birth and to obtain a name and nationality (article 7), a right to play (article 31) and to protection from all from of sexual abuse (article 34).

Being remitive to the condition of newly freed countries, the Convention recognize that not all governments have the resources necessary to ensure all economic, social and cultural right immediately. But it forces them to make those rights a priority and to ensure them to the maximum possible extent of available resources. Fulfilling their obligations sometimes requires State to make necessary changes in national laws, institutions, plans, policies and practices to bring them into line with the provisions of the Convention.

Before we start implementing the convention, the first priority must be to generate the political will to do this.

As the drafters of the Convention admitted, real change in the lives of children will come about only when social norms and which progressively change to conform with laws and values. And when, as actors in the process, children themselves know enough about their rights to claim them. The official monitor of this process of change has been made the Committee on the Rights of the Child. Governments are obliged to report to the Committeee within two years of ratification, and every five years therefore, specifying the measures adopted to change national laws and formulate policies and actions. The Committee, made up of 10 experts, collects evidence from NGOs and intergovernmental organizations including UNICEF, and these groups may write alternative reports to that of a government. The Committee and the government then meet to discuss the country's child rights activities and the steps necessary to overcome obstacles.

This process of reporting has proved dynamic and constructive, with the dialogue established helping to promote children's rights. Unfortunately, however, many countries have missed their reporting deadlines, 28 of them by as much as three years, as of September 1996.

The implementations of the provisions of the Convention still remains in its infancy but, as we have noted, the international treaty for children has already started making an impact. As reported in 1996 in UNICEF's annual publication. The Progress of Nations, of the 43 nations whose reports had been reviewed at the time, 14 had incorporated the principles of the Convention into their constitutions and 35 had enacted new laws or amended existing laws to conform to the Convention. And 13 had included the Convention into curricula or courses to begin the key process of educating children about their own rights

Implementation and the Enforcement of Convention

Various enforcement units of convention a round the world, i.e., teachers, lawyers, police officials, judges and care givers, are being trained in the principles and the application of this Convention. Encouraged by the Convention, Sierra Leone has demobilized child soldiers. In Rwanda, UNICEF under the Convention's aegis, has been attempting to move children held in adult detention centres for alleged war offences to special juvenile institutions and has hired lawyer to prefect them. And reforms, changes and improvements continue to accumulate around the world.

The Monitoring of the Convention

Media coverage of the issues has promoted international awareness of severe violations of children's rights. Major initiatives such as the world Congress against Commercial Sexual abuse of Children, held in Stockholm in August 1996, and the International Conference on Child's Labour scheduled for October 1997 in Oslo, receive their impetus from the convention. Highlighting the problems in this way is an essential first step towards their elimination. In a positive step to involve the media in making children aware of their rights, the Asian Summit on Child Rights and the Media, held in Manila in July 1996, invited as wide range of participants in four days of discussions on how to educate, inform and entertain children while also taking into consideration their best interests. UNICEF itself is at a turning point. In its 50th years, the organization has made a mission statement that looks to the Convention as it guiding force. This new mandate has important implications for the work of the organisation. It various steps for children in the past two decades including the year 2000 goals established by the international community the World Summit for Children in 1990, are planned to alleviate the worst aspects of poverty for the majority of the world's children. These goals and agreements must not be carried on in the context of the Convention.

More than four year ago, in September 1996, the Secretary General of the United Nations, Boutros Boutros-Ghali reported to the General Assembly on the development make in meeting the Summit's year 2000 goals for children as the decade for action passed the halfway mark. Larger part of the news is good, with millions of children's lives been saved since 1990.

Still, a lot of remains to be done. More than 12.5 million children under five in developing countries continue to die each year 9 million of them from causes for which low cost solutions and measures such as immunization and antibiotics have been routinely adopted in the industrialized world for 50 years. As long as avoidable death and suffering continue on a large scale in the developing world, child survival must remain the concerns of the Convention, UNICEF and the worked community must not only maintain the commitment to the fixed goals but also look beyond them to social protection and other significant needs and rights not expressly contained in the World Summit Declaration and Plan of Action. The Convention, by expressing and safeguarding all the rights of children, expands the scope of a action required for children and throws a clear shaft of light on paths that extend beyond the year 2000. Some of these will would saving children and youth in conflict with the criminal justice system; others shall ensure the development of the young child, support families, stop the use of land-mines and continues to try to bring about a more justful distribution of resources. It is in this context that The State of the World's Children 1997 report aim at the subject of child labour and it impact on children's development.

The UNICEF Convention on the Rights of child requires families, societies, governments and the international community to take action aimed to fulfil the rights of all children in a sustainable, participatory and nondiscriminatory manner. In realisable terms, this means that the poorest most vulnerable and often the most disadvantaged children in all societies, rich and poor, must have first all call on resources and efforts. The efforts to touch their lives will be complex and will require a sustained attack on the root causes of poverty and underdevelopment.

In an enurement with easily sharable where technology and knowledge worldwide and per capita income, has multiplied many times, there can be no excuses: the rights of all children, including those who are most deprived, can be fulfilled.

At the international level, efforts have been made in its last decade of the 20th century to arrive at a consensus on the way forward on a number of platforms, on human rights, on protection of the environment, on reduction of uncontrolled population growth and on abolishing gender inequality. The avowed aim so sustainable development for all on the ground of social justice and human fulfilment.

True committed intention will now have to be matched with the political will to act and fortified by changes in individual and national attitudes and priorities. An additional $40 billion a year could provide access for the world's people to basic social services such as health care, education and safe drinking water. Two thirds of this could be found by developing countries if they realigned their own budget priorities. Targeting out just one quarter of the developing world's military expenditure—or $30 billion of $ 125 billion—for example, could provide sufficient additional resources to reach most of the goals for the year 2000. A similar shift in aiming at development aid by donor countries could generate much of the rest.

This arrangement has been made in the 20/20 initiative, which calls for developing countries to increase government spending on basic social amenities from the current average of approximately 13 per cent to 20 per cent, and for donor countries to reserve 20 per cent of official development assistance (ODA).

In this manner, the transfer of style of world use of its resources is no longer an appeal to the charity of those with the power and the purse-strings but is a matter of rights and duties. The new era in child rights will still need underpinning by attitudinal improvement, popular pressure and public demands. Wherever opinion polls have been undertaken they have proved that people support the ideas and ideals of human rights, child rights and international solidarity. Part of the task, then, is to transfer this support into action.

Positively speaking on action plane, for the past 15 years, the State of the World's Children has mobilized public and political support for child survival and growth. UNICEF will continue to mobilize, now with the added power and legitimacy of the Convention, because the need for extend advocacy on behalf of the world's children has not diminished, even now, half a century after the need for UNICEF was internationally accepted.

Since policies and enactments at international level are generally made in good spirit. So is the case wrote CRC but ...

There are some practical hurdles also. Accepting treaty commitments under international law often becomes only a gesture, because most of our countries do not accept that international law and domestic law are one system. According to this dualist approach, international law can be enforced domestically, only if treaty components are incorporated into the national legal system. National courts therefore perceive treaty standards as having moral rather than legal authority.

That is the reason why it becomes vital to ensure that the standards set by the CRC are incorporated into the national legal system. In setting about the task of incorporation, we must stand committed to certain basic principles that are enshrined in the CRC. The CRC, like certain other human rights treaties, recognizes the concept of cultural pluralism and diversity. Articles 2 and 3 of the CRC, which can be mentioned as the "non-discrimination" and "best interests of the child" clauses require that States Parties commit themselves to implement the same framework of core rights for all children. Article 2 in particular clarifies that a child's right of life and development, protection from exploitation and aggression and the right to participate in matters that are of importance to the child, consistent with evolving maturity, must be realized for all children within ratifying countries. Aspects such as the child's or the parent's or guardian's birth, economic class, disability, ethnicity religion or gender, cannot be a justification for refusing these rights or liquidifying them.

More importantly, the commonality of the core standards set by the CRC in Articles 24, 26, 27 and 28 must stimulate uniformly applicable policies on the issue of education, health and a safe environment. We can no longer justify different standards in the treatment of children on the basis of a different approach towards nutrition, health, safe environment or education needs of "our children" and "others children". It is difficulty if not impossible to adopt a culturally common approach which would argue that the State had not right to intervene or impose common standards. The articles in the CRC on compulsory education and achieving the highest standards of health, mandate policy intervention by the State to prevent or undermine social practice that would be hurdle to the realisation of those standards for all children.

The CRC to treats children all as indivisible and interdependent. It is not possible to realise the child's right to survival without projecting towards and committing efforts to achieve the rights of development, protection from exploitation and participation. This inevitably means that law making becomes not merely an act for the legislator and the law reformer. Laws have to be implemented properly with a holistic perception of their linkages, and a commitment of the resources required for implementation. It is not therefore possible to prohibit child marriage or child labour by fixing minimum ages by law, without legislative and administrative decisions that provide for compulsory education, provisions for registration of marriage, and the general implementation of relevant socio-economic policies. Resource allocation for education, immunization, nutrition and sanitation, and statutory and regulatory mechanisms to ensure the proper delivery of these services becomes as much a part of law reform action as legislating on minimum age for marriage, employment, and juvenile justice. These social and economic policies can no longer be regarded as issues of political choice outside the realm of law and enforceable rights.

Then the question arises is, this an impractical agenda or framework of international standards for implementation at the national level? In order to answer this question we ought to recognize the social costs of historical experience in law making without providing adequate socio-economic support or making enforcement a possibility. Many developing countries in Asia and Africa face problems of infant mortality, child marriage, maternal mortality, and the aspect of child widows, child trafficking even across national borders for fresh trade and child labour. We are used to consider these children as high risk, exceptional categories who as children placed in tough social and economic circumstances need protection by law. Yet the reality is that these children are a product of our countries helplessness to realise their rights and the right of their families to national resources. When families are given minimal allowance to care for children, when maternity leave is reluctantly granted or perceived as a "benefit" to the working mother, we are encouraging the myth of alleviating poverty and destitution while supporting a welfare payments and benefits ideology. Many of our countries have vagrancy laws that consider poverty as a fault. Juvenile justice laws which deal with neglected street children tell about the need to rehabilitate them, and impose sanctions on parents for their poverty and neglect. Because we do not provide adequate resources for literacy or registration of marriage, we are reluctant to impose sanctions on parents and the family for infringement of laws on child marriage and child labour. We understand the validity of child marriage even as we set a standard of a minimum age of marriage by law. In a vicious cycle the inadequacy of the facilities is used as a justification against imposing sanctions for violations. In the process we do not begin to touch the fringes of the problem of gender discrimination and rejection of children's access, girls in particular, to minimum standards of health and education. We cannot enhance adult female illiteracy of the health of the working mother. Maternity leave laws make it more difficult for a woman to come on equal terms with men for employment. Law making is perceived as ambivalent, and fails to have an impact on these problems.

To right to wrong of past, the CRC focuses on our past failures in recognizing that we should shift from the "poor law" and "welfare benefits" approach that has nourished the jurisprudence of our countries for many centuries. Availability of basic education, health care and a safe environment become the socio-economic rights of all children and their families who are entitled to resources allocation for these purposes. State parties are required to "take measures" to discourage infant and child mortality, combat malnutrition, ensure pre-and post-natal care for mothers as a social responsibility, and make at least primary education compulsory. It is only if these policies can be put in place, that it will be possible to achieve the protection and participation rights of children. A reduction of the level of gender-based and other types of violence in our communities against children can not be expected unless prohibitive sensations are combined with socio-economic programmes that promote responsible parenting and life chances for all children.

The issue of worry is that the concept of people's and children's core right to basic services in the area of health, education and environment is not as radical for national legal systems as it appears. Indigenous norms and even laws often recognised the concept of "community rights" in land. Even the legal systems based on Roman legal system accepted that "the people" had certain rights in public rivers and the sea shore. We already have on the constitutions books of countries, composure education laws, or laws on immunization, hygiene, community health and maternity leave that are often not monitored or implemented.

Nations having written constitutions also have powerful mechanisms for using their chapters on fundamental rights to encourage social action in areas such as health and education. Many of these statute books adopt the typical standpoint in the traditional human rights discourse and treat civil and political rights as enforceable rights and social and economic interventions as enforceable disectives to state policy. However, the Indian Supreme court with its extensive power of judicial review has developed the concept of using public interest litigations to link the directive principles to justifiable fundamental rights. Social sanctions litigation has expanded the scope of Constitutional grievance redress for violation of child rights in areas such as child labour, adoption, children in prison, prostitution and trafficking of manner and children. The right to life has been recently interpreted as broader than a negative duty of the State to refrain from violation of personal liberty. It has been interpreted as a positive duty to provide the basic conditions for survival. These initiatives reflect the same perspective, that special needs in the area of health, education and the environment are inseparable part of the basic justiciable fundamental rights that accompany citizenship. Citizenship laws which discriminate on the basis of gender have been questioned in the courts of Pakistan and Bangladesh.

In this contest the new Constitutional Bill proposed for the Republic of South Africa is unique on the aspect of constitution making for its integration of international law standards on children's rights and for identifying socio-economic needs as justiciable rights. Children's rights to nurturing, basic nutrition and health, are accepted as their particular fundamental rights to basic education and a safe environment. This constitution is also unique in establishing the link between child labour and education, following International Labour Organization norms and the standards of the CRC. Unlike many other constitutions, the South Africa Constitution gives definition to the right to protection from hazardous labour as a right to be protected from labour that is fatal to health and education.

In this way, the CRC provides an incentive to the people, legislators, courts and lawyers to expand the scope of fundamental rights by constitutional Amendments and /or interpretations of the law that link national constitutional standards to duties of their states under international law. In an ethos is created in which there is complete awareness of the CRC, courts and lawyers can be motivated to interpret constitutional and legal standards so as to include the concept of child rights into dispute settlement. Especially in countries that face problems of divisiveness it is important to remember that common legal values have already been enforce by certain processes. Many countries continue to recognize the "choice concept" which allows persons to be governed by State law instead of personal laws based on ethnicity or religion. Certain laws and policies are applicable to all citizens, irrespective of choice. The cords in most countries have used the concept of the "child" best interests in guardianship litigation to forge common standards that discourage gender discrimination, discrimination against nonmarital children and the separateness of personal law than can have a negative impact on children. Constitutional standards already accept equality before the law and even provide for affirmative state action on behalf of women and children so as to realise substantive rather than formal equality.

A remarkable feature of jurisprudence of many countries are gender discrimination and discrimination against non-marital children. With constitutional closes on equality and non-discrimination, the provisions of the CRC can be use to bobby for those areas that have been ignored in law reforms, since they strengthen and relate to the constitutional values of domestic legal systems. Where Judicial discretion is exercised, an understanding of the framework of rights can strengthen dynamic interpretations of law that will give the child access to justice through the law courts and influences other methods of dispute resolution. The absence of a child centred focus in legal proceedings is largely due to the tendency to regard the child as a miniature adult before the courts of law. A child centred approach stimulated by the values of the CRC can help to create spaces for providing the child access to justice even within the constraints of existing laws. It may be disputed that this kind of judicial activism is in consistent with the traditional role of the judiciary as an agency concerned with interpreting rather than enacting law. Yet the judiciary has expanded and expound the content of major areas of law precisely because the arrival at a decision in legal proceedings involves policy options. To day, written constitutions are the basic law of the land, and courts must interpret them to enforce fundamental right's. It is hardly possible to argue that they can not interpret the constitution to encourage realisation of rights.

It is often discussed that the obligation of State to publicise the CRC and the regular country report, as well as the concept of national and international cooperation in enforcing child rights prevents arguments of State sovereignty being used to restrict the monitoring of state responsibilities. Nationally and internationally, the CRC envisages a partnership between many actors and encourages talk and cooperation. Just as it requires and assumes a joint parental and family responsibility, it assumes a shared state and family responsibility for enforcing the rights of children. This concept of a shared commitment designates law making and law enforcement something more than the exclusive preserve of lawyers, judges and law enforcement agencies or their critics. There is infact no places for professional exclusiveness in formulating strategies to enforce and exercise these rights. Since, as we see the massive violations of rights in many of our countries it is easy to lose faith in a strategy of rights and their enforcement through legal processes. Yet a rights strategy has been usually forged through the experience of human anguish in carrying the abuse of power, rather than allow social and economic injustice to continue and spread the terror of violence and disillusionment which impact all our lives, civil society and governments can work together to ensure State, community and family accountability in the use of power and authority. If we can promote accountability and humanism in the process of governance on a agenda of child rights. Based on the value system of this new and significant human rights convention, we will have found a path to improving our past record on rights and move from rhetoric to action. We can then undoubtedly say to children, "you are indeed the wonder tree plant, grown of ruins".

This 21st century is a deeply perplexing age in relation to rights. On the one hand there is a virtual explosion of human rights annotations; on the other hand, there is increasing disregard of rights and cynicism on their future. The proliferation of human rights instruments seems to have caused critics of human rights to make a rights-weariness and rights-wariness. They insist that only a lean and sparse articulation of rights provides chances for their enforcement.

Thus we are in a period where there is a notable increase in recognition as well as violations of human rights, where all struggles articulate themselves in the language of human rights and invoke the "politics" of rights; pushing human rights into bargaining points for the enhancement of power. Even so, the convention on the Rights of the Child , the World Summit plan of Action, and the Jomtien World conference on Education for All, mark triumphant inaugural articulations of human rights. "Human rights", of course, in some has, have tacity included children's rights. But the level of inclusion was never so comprehensive and caring as is the case today. The Vienna Decoration on Human Rights accelerates, in so many ways, the dynamics of the international movement for the enhancement of "respect for the rights of the child to the CRC by 1995 and urges State to suspend "reservation to the Convention" which are "contrary to the objects and purpose of the Convention or otherwise contrary to international treaty law".

Specifically, the Declaration insists that all States, with international cooperation, should:

(a) Fight against "exploitation and abuse of children by addressing their root cause:,

(b) Ensure "effective measures against female infanticide, harmful child labour, sale of children, child prostitution, child pornography, as well as other forms of sexual abuse",

(c) Find out "means of improving the protection of children armed conflicts" and programmes of "aftercare and rehabilitation of children in war zones" and also those in "especially difficult circumstances". The minimum age of recruitment to armed forces is also addressed.

It is a remote possibly and to imagine even the most conscientious critics of human rights enunciation as having any cogent critique of the expansion of child rights. Critics of human rights enunciations must defiulitely respect the achievements of these measures and realise that inaction would be costly. The disregard for of the rights of children, would mean the confiscation of our common future founders:, the world's children. Human rights articulations represent human hope in a brutal and brutalizing world. They devise arenas for the struggle for a just national and international legal order in relation to the child; they mark an insurrectionary protest against the wild uses of power. in the state and society. Even if we fail to achieve our commonly formulated human aspirations, not to try to achieve them is, starkly put, to belie our claim to be and to remain, human. For as state and community which is to the rights of the child can never aspire to be a just society.

The question than arises is what is our appointed historical task? And how do we achieve it? Happily, the agenda for action is now abundantly available. What is required, first of all, is the elimination of adult illiteracy about children's rights. Adult illiteracy about children's rights is prevalent among policy makers, intellectuals, ideogogues, media, persons and even among human rights communities. This illiteracy also makes possible the comprehensive and continual ignorance about connections between the rights of the child and human rights enunciations which are not child-centred and yet affect their and our shared future. Promotion of adult literacy about children's rights is a sine quo non for their attainment. It must be realized at the outset that the problem of adult illiteracy with regarding children rights is as massive, complex and in need of urgent resolution as the problem of general illiteracy discussed at the Jomtien World Conference on *Education for All.*

Moreover, it is important that we acknowledge and develop linkages between the rights of the child and other instruments of human rights. There is no danger in such an effort of losing the focus on children's rights. Rather, awareness and advocacy of such linkages will help us to advance the plan of action union of children's right.

In 1993, WHO had moved the advisory jurisdiction of the International Court of Justice on the use of nuclear weapons by a state in war or other armed conflict as constituting a violation of international law. The World Court accepted the reference and asked all states to make submissions by June 10, 1994. No effort is necessary, I hope, to underscore the critical relevance of this incident to the future of all human rights including children's rights. Whether or not clear so far, the right of all persons, especially children, to immunity from a world with nuclear arms, as a part of the right to peace, is the matrix of all other rights. But there is hardly much awareness of enthusiasm in children's rights communities (indeed, human rights communities in South Asia) on this laudable aspect. Similarly, we have little appreciation of the implications of the Dunkelt text on the life and world of children. It should not necessitate any apologies to seek to review world economic development from the standpoint of children's rights.

Third, therc is also a need to promote awareness of what the Vienna Declaration describes as the "Undoubtedly, the quest for "root cause" is inordinately complex and it would not help to have any reductionist or non-confusing understanding or answer. At the same time, we can not defer action on children's rights until the outcomes of scholarly and scientific engagement comes to existence. It may even be said that the lack of such involvement is among the "root causes" of the plight of the world's children! Whatever the case may be, reorientation of education and research traditions in "children's rights-friendly" directions is a task which ought to be high on our educational policy agenda. Among these "root causes," undoubtedly, is the state the law (both normative and institutional). In India, legislative initiatives for the promotion and protection of children's rights are scarce and their enforcement impoverished; some recent movement does however, point to an emergence of better involvement.

But insofar as rights are to be enforced by courts, the whole nature (and history) of the adjudicatory system and lowering presents itself as among the prime" root causes". For India at least, the need to rethink its adjudicatory system, to retool it, to recreate it is a need which emerges most sharply regarding child rights. If the rule of law (legality) is to have any meaning for tens of thousands of India's children as they develop into "adulthood," then legal education and research, the transaction of the legal profession and court-craft, and the reogranisation of the judicial system should engage the attention of the children's right advocacy in India. In a profound sense, the career and future of a rule-of-law in India remains closely connected with children's formative perceptions about "rights", "law" and democracy". This remains yet to be tested but even so it may be said that a nation determines the reproduction or repudiation of legality by the formative experiences of justice and injustice that it offers to its children.

Lastly, human rights instruments on children's rights stress "participation" as a root value, along with "survival", "protection" and "development". What strategies should be devised to encourage "participation" by children in formulating policies for "survival", "protection" and "development" is indeed, a most critical question. Policy and legal paternalism is the very basis of the movement aimed at the enunciations of children's rights. The ideology of "participation", however, interrogates the institutionalized paternalism of policy, law administration. Even to ask this kind of question may seem to be a king of luxury given the pains and powerlessness of masses of children, especially in many Third World Countries. But it seems that giving children a voice, a forum, empowering their opinion, may accelerate the adult world's speed of progress towards realising their rights. To delink though and action on "participation" in my views, is to contribute, knowingly or otherwise, to a strategy or to a deferment of policies in the context of the rights of "survival", "protection" and development".

Another thing seems imperative that India should develop resources— intellectual, ideological, institutional and praxeological— for continued children's rights advocacy. I know how institutions often become 'traps' or generate a "dead weight" of their own over time. But keeping in mind the nascency of the movement for children's rights, the persistence of historic formations that abuse and exploit children, and the need to accelerate history, some sort of institutional arrangement might increase the capabilities of concerned citizens in their struggle to redeem our common future.

Problems and diseases like Protein-Energy Malnutrition (PEM), Iodine Deficiency Disorders (IDD), Vitamin A Deficiency (VAD) and Iron Deficiency Anaemia (IDA) are the major problems of malnutrition less developing countries, attacking more than half of the young child population. In society, malnutrition in any form is a negative aspect with medical manifestations. The biochemical and medical complexities of malnutrition are handled by the science of human nutrition, while the problem of malnutrition in society demands a much broader approach, requiring sciences, and others.

In the same way, like all other societal problems, malnutrition has a scientific and moral aspect. Science deals with what "can" be done, while ethics deals with what "should" or ought to" be done. It is a scientific fact that iodisation of salt enhances the intake of iodine and reduces the risk of IDD. It is, however, moral question whether or not salt should be iodised. It is a scientific fact that early initiation of exclusive breast-feeding discourages morbidity and mortality among very young children. The extent to which manufacturers should be allowed to distribute free breast milk substitutes in hospitals is again an ethical question. Science and ethics are dialectically related. Scientific discoveries affectethics. For example the new discoveries in nuclear science pose some very difficult ethical challenges. Ethics, on the other hand, may affect scince, such as the way in which human beings may be used for medical experimentation.

To do away with the controversy, both science and ethics progress through the constant interaction between theory and practice. Theory has no value without practice, and practice is useless without a theory. In science statements like "one finds what one looks for" (T. Kuhn) and "nothing is more practical than a good theory" (A. Einstein) reveal the way theory influences practice.

Testing theories in practical situations, often means that the theory needs to be reviewed, i.e. practice influences theory.

To search effective solutions, problems most often reflect current needs. The nutritional needs of young children have been known for a long, time, even if details continue to be discussed. These needs are expressed in qualified daily requirements of energy, protein and micro-nutrients. The definition of thee requirements is a scientific act. Unfulfilled needs pose ethical challenges, depending on how serious the deficiency is judged. When a need is identified as being worthy of sympathy and serious consideration, this need becomes a claim. A need becomes a claim when people find it immoral not to do something about it.

International meets like the World Summit for Children (WSC) and the International Conference on Nutrition (ICN) specified and agreed on a set of nutritional goals. These goals transformed popular nutritional needs into recognised claims. Heads of Governments/States in the WSC and Governments in the ICN promised to attain these quantified goals (objectives) before the year 2000. Rights are more than claims. They are entitlements to something, even if they do not constitute valid claims against any specific individual or entity of society. Most often, however, rights imply duties with the respondent clearly identified. Rights also imply goals. Goals, however, do not imply rights. A goal is a required, but not a sufficient condition for a right. This means that human development goal also, including nutritional goal, for children can be achieved without any rights. Feinberg describes this in a thought experiment "Nowheresville" where most of the human goals were fulfilled but where there was no selfrespect, no dignity, not rights. The full implementation of the CRC requires the achievement of all WSC goals. Moreover, the achievement of goals does not necessarily mean the full realisation of the CRC. The challenge, therefore, is not only to attain the WSC goals but to realise them in such a way that the processes required for the realisation of the CRC are strengthened and speeded up. Such a rights-based approach combines elements from a goal-based and a duty-based strategy. It encompasses a goal-driven, process-conditioning strategy.

It has been by Kant stated that ought implies 'can' -or it is otherwise Utopia.' Rescher (1987) question this statement and recommends a new interpretation of Kant. He argues that if "ought implies can" this logically means that "obligation implies capacity", which in turn is similar to "incapacity removes obligation." This, however seems unacceptable. He puts forth this problem by two arguments:-

One, "to all appearances, an obligation can persist despite an incapacity. We have to be prepared for the prospect of undischargeable duties and unmeetable obligations".

Two, "...incapacity does not actually defeat an obligation, it can, however, negate all blame for a failure to carry it out".

He also recommends a distinction between the weaker mode of 'should' and the stronger mode of 'must'. Based on Rescher's analysis, a choice needs to be made between:

Firstly, 'Absolutistic' rules with "realistic" hopes and

Secondly, "Absolutistic" rules with 'absolutistic' hopes.

If we refer to the above, 'ought' does not imply 'can', while 'must' does. In the ideal world, 'ought' implies 'can', while in the actual world only "must" implies "can." Seen in this perspective the WSC goals represent "realistic" goals with absolute hopes i.e. the goals must be achieve, and they can be achieved.

Complete enforcement of the CRC, on the other hand, should be interpreted as "absolutistic" with "realistic" expectations. Rights are not divisible and cannot be graded; they are absolute. Many goals are "absolutistic: and not achievable. Rescher argues that it is completely rational to pursue unattainable goals.

Though it's been repeated said that rights implies duties and obligations, but most often nobody can be punished if the obligation is not fulfilled. When a right becomes a law, the respondent is identified and if the law is violated the respondent can be punished through the judiciary system. Practice, however, does not necessarily follow from law. There is therefore a need to enforce a law. As number of countries have laws against distribution of non-iodised salt or against aggressive sale of breast milk substitutes but their practices have not changed, because the laws have never been enforced.

WSC and the CRC and can be seen as "social contracts" between the Heads of States and governments and the states themselves and the world's children. More than 300 years back, Thomas Hobbes (1651) defined in his famous Leviathan the concept of a "contract" as, "the mutual transferring of rights" and that "... he that is trusted to perform in time to come, being trusted his performance is called keeping the promise". This warning is now for leaders of governments to keep the promise they gave at the WSC and for states to fulfill the promise they made when they ratified the CRC. Since long, countries are used to being compared on their economic development. Now the time has come when countries should be compared for steps they take to care of their children. Signing the WSC Declaration or the ICN Declaration or ratifying the CRC implies an obligation to give "a first call on resources for children". Only the future will tell who will keep the promise.

Another thing Hobbes mentioned was that "...convenant without the sword, are but words, and of no strength to secure a man at all". What "sword" do we have? Immediate measures that can be way taken is to establish national monitoring systems for the gradual achievement of the WSC goals, which are necessary for the implementation of the CRC.

The historical CRC obliges States Parties:

(a) to disseminate information about the principles and provisions of the Convention to adults and children (Article 42);

(b) to submit to the Committee on the Rights of the Child, through the Secretary General of the United Nations, reports on the steps they have taken which give effect to the rights recognised and on the progress made on the enjoyment of these rights within two years of the ratifying the convention for the state party concerned and every five years thereafter (Article 44/1);

(c) to make their reports widely available to the masses in their own countries (Article 44/6);

(d) to make all legislative administrative, economic and social attempts for the implementation of the rights recognised in the (Convention Article 4);

(e) to make possible that the institutions, services and facilities responsible for the protection of children shall conform, in terms of safety, health, the number and suitability of staff, with the norms established by competent authorities (Article 3/3); and,

(f) to make sure that the best interests of the child shall be a primary consideration in all actions concerning children (Article 3/1).

This is true that it is not an exhaustive list of the obligations that States Parties have undertaken with respect to the Convention. Some duties that States Parties have to perform particularly those which relate to the duty of making booth the Conventional and the reports widely known by the public, have the potential of mobilising the public. The mobilization can leave significant inputs to the material realisation of the rights included in the Convention.

A part from emphasising the economic and social rights of children, the CRC lays down many principles relating to the rights of the child. The legislative, executive and judicial organs of States Parties have to take these principles into account in all activities relating to children. There principles have already been mentioned is the previous pager of the chapter.

Even 50 Years back in the most advanced countries also, the dominant view was that in all actions relating to the child, his or her needs could be best taken case of and met by "adult". If parents did not or could not fulfill their duties in relation to children, the State undertook to place the child in an institution under State supervision or in another family. The child's view was not considered at all and there was little regard for the rights of parents. But today there is a very different approach to the child, and due regard is also paid to the rights and duties of parents. It is accepted in principle that the child has the right to state his or her opinion freely and that his opinion should be properly respected while making decisions concerning the child.

The CRC document of fully reflects this overall change in approach relating to the child. States Parties have the obligation to respect the rights and personality of the child and to incorporate for his or her opinion while they are engaged in legislative programmes relating to the child and preparing the environment in which the child will be able to grow to his or her full personality. This document was signed by the former Turkish Government on September 14, 1990. In order to ratify the Convention, the former Government immediately prepared a bill and submitted it to the Parliament. However, in November 1991 the country had a general election and the composition of the Parliament, as well as the government changed. The consequences were that the provisions of the Turkish Parliament Proceedings Regulation, the bill that would give instruction for the ratification of the Convention, became void.

A new Government had to prepare and present another bill to the parliament. The Bill is presently on the agenda of the Turkish Grand National Assembly for ratification. Attempts are being made by a group of parliamentarians to ensure quick ratification of the Convention. When the Turkish legal system and related practices are analysed in term of the provisions of the Convention, we can reach the following broad conclusion:

(a) As far as some provisions of the Convention are concerned, there is no contradiction at all with respect to legislative arrangements or to legal practices. For instance the child's right to a name and citizenship are guaranteed under the Turkish Civil Code, the Surname Act and the Act on Citizenship, which are all in effect currently. With these acts, it is impossible for a child in Turkey to be deprived of his or her right to a name or citizenship.

(b) For some rights stipulated by the Convention, there are problems relating to practical aspects though no problem exists as far as the legislative frame is concerned. The child's right to education can be cited as an example. In Turkey, the child's right to education can be cited as an example. In Turkey, the child's right to education is recognised firstly by the Constitution (Article 42) and further elaborated by the Basic Law on National education and the Code on Primary Education in a manner fully conforming to Article 28 of the Convention. Under these acts, primary education is compulsory and free for all children irrespective of their gender. Furthermore, the State has the obligation to provide appropriate support to children who are talented but lack the material means to reach the highest stages of education in line with their specific interests and capacities. While these provisions are clearly stated in Laws, there are some difficulties in actual implementation. For example, despite the face that primary education is compulsory and free for both boys and girls according to our Constitution, many families, especially in he region of southeastern Anatolia are reluctant to send their girls to school because of traditional beliefs.

(c) In order to enable our children to benefit from some of the other rights stated in the Convention it is necessary to introduce new legislative arrangements, as well as certain administrative, economic and social measures. Some efforts in this direction have been made.

As we have already said that Article 32 of the Convention recognises the right of the child to be protected from economic exploitation. As per provisions of this article, States parties shall effect all legislative measures in conformity with the relevant provisions of other international measures to provide the following: minimum ages for admission to employment; proper regulation of the hours and conditions of employment; and prevention of the performance of any work that is likely to be hazardous or affect the child's education, or to be harmful to the child's health or physical, mental, spiritual, or social development. It also obliges States Parties to take all relevant administrative, economic and social steps to save children from economic exploitation.

If we make an analysis of the Turkish legal system in term of the right to be protected from economic exploitation, it is seen that the relevant provisions are spread over the various legislations (viz. Labour Act, Apprenticeship and Vocational Training Act, Primary Education Act and the Act on the Duties and Authorities of the Police Force). Same provisions actually contradict each other. The Labour Act stipulates the minimum age for employment as 15 (Article 67) According to the age fixed by the International Labour Organization (ILO) agreements. Nonetheless there are some exceptions to this provision. The very same Act states that children above 13 years can be taken in to employment if the nature of the work is such that it does not impair health, development and school attendance. At the sometime, according to the Apprenticeship and Vocational Training Act, elementary school graduates may be given training at enterprises with the purpose of preparation for an occupation before the minimum age limit fixed. This means that children around 11 or 12 years may be legally employed in lighter work.

According to the legal system, the working conditions of children are also taken into consideration . In the Labour Act, working hours of children must not exceed 7.5 hours and must not interfere with their school hours (Labour act, Articles 67). Before employing children, employers are required to ensure, through a health check-up, that the child's health is appropriate for the job. The health examination has to be done again every six months (Labour Act, Article 30). Employers who do not perform these obligations are liable to be fined (Labour Act, Article 104).

Enactments of this kind which are designed to protect children from economic exploitation, cannot be enforced in-most cases since concerned administrative, economic and social measures have not been taken. Moreover, since the Act, mentioned above do not incorporate children who work in the agricultural sector or in the streets, such children are vulnerable to conditions that are potentially disastrous to their mental and physical health, education and development. Street children particularly are more commonly subjected to physical, emotional and sexual abuse.

For the Provisions of the Convention which require new legislative arrangements and some economic, social and administrative measures, we can give those which are related to delinquent children and others who are abused and neglected. The programme of the previous Coalition Government, in which, gave preference to human rights as well as children's and women's issues. Hence, that Government had, in addition to submitting the bill which provide the ratification of the Convention, prepared another bill which revised the current Juvenile judicial Act. In preparing for the Juvenile Court Bill, the Ministry of Justice considered both the Convention on the Rights of the Child and UNs' Rules for the Administration of Juvenile Justice. The Cooperation programme largely incorporates backward provinces, those which have been prioritised for development and big urban centres.

The rationale behind all this is the fact that these provinces are the ones in which children are harmed much more adversely by such phenomena as poverty, unhealthy urbanization, intensive migration and broken patterns of income distribution.

Moreover, CRC includes special provisions, which cover children in especially difficult circumstances. This category includes children who

— need of protection or special education;

— become subjects of to abuse and neglect;

— become victims of crime, drug trafficking, prostitution and pornography; and

— are workers;

An important question which we would like to raise here in relation to children in need of protection is the change taking place in the overall policies of the Social Services and Child Protection Institution according to the provisions of the CRC. This agency does not consider keeping children with their own families as the priority solution and strives to create supportive institutions for the family and to provide assistance to needy families.

Alternative care such as placing children with relatives, protective family, adoption, etc. is opted only in the most pressing cases. It is now accepted also by the Ministry in charge that institutional care should be the last resort. In spite of this, more than 90 per cent of children who receive protective institutions. We hope that this situation will reverse soon with the introduction of new policies.

Since, the legislative, executive and judicial branches of the State recognise the best interest of the child as a priority issue act in coordination on child related issues, and regard the child not as an "object" but a "subject", we , believe that the realisation of the children's rights will be a relatively easy process. Naturally, the State also has to cooperate with the Children's Rights committee of the UN; international agencies like UNICEF, UNESCO, ILO, WHO and FAO; and international and national non-governmental organizations.

Centuries of criminal neglect, despite protests by humanists, thinkers, and sages in every country, have given place at long last to a gentler thought of juvenile justice and a chastened jurisprudence of the rights of the child. Human rights are inalienable and so are the rights of the child. So long as children are abused, victimized or are not nourished, there is no true humanism in the world. Juvenile jurisprudence, during our heartless century, came to existence after World War I and blossomed after World War II when the UN place stress on the dignity and worth of the child. The Convention on the rights of the Child, represents an instrument of infinite significance which makes it obligators for people everywhere to cooperate for improving the living conditions of children in every country, specifically, the developing countries and to evolve a viable jurisprudence of juvenile justice.

The historic developments like the Universal Declaration of Human Rights and the International Covenants on Human Rights, which together make the magna carta of making, offer rights without discriminating as to age, race, sex religion, birth or other factors. The Universal Declaration of Human Rights truly emphasises that childhood is entitled to special care and assistance. It further maintains that the family, as a fundamental unit of society, should concentrate on children as the new hope of tomorrow and provide all the necessary conditions for their growth, the absence of which would result in the stunting of the community. So it is that Article 24 of the Universal Declaration specifies that:

(i) Every child shall have, irrespective of as to race, colour, sex, language, religion, national or social origin, property or birth to such measures of protection as are necessary for his status as a minor, on the part of his family, society and the State.

(ii) Every child shall be registered immediately after birth and shall obtain name.

(iii) Every child has the right to acquire a nationality.

The children have title to legal protection before or after birth, according to the canons of international justice. But the harsh reality is that the welfare of the child ranks tragically low in the agenda of State action. In todays world, the trauma and torture, the illiteracy and depriviaion the hard labour and gross neglect which are the fate of the Third World's juvenile generation demand sensitive social action, united mass mobilisation and affirmative justice processes. Every child everywhere is as inseparable part of one global family and is entitled to a universal minimum of rights, fullness of expression and development of faculties,

113 nations, by consensus, initiated the Vienna Declaration and programme of Action where the rights of the child and especially of the girl child, have justly received humane emphasis worldwide. The Vienna

Declaration makes a humanitarian summons on nations in the articles relating to the rights of the child. Part D of the Vienna Declaration to causing at the rights of the child must become the locomotive of juvenile jurisprudence. The World Conference at Vienna stressed the principle of "first call for children", and underlined "the importance of major national and international attempts especially those UNICEF for encouraging respect for the rights of the child to survival, protection, development and participation".

Special feature of the Vienna Conference is that it refers to female infanticide, child prostitution, child pornography as well as other forms of sexual abuse and also mentions measures be taken by specialized agencies "to ensure the effective protection and promotion of human rights of the girl-child" and appeals to the States to repeal existing laws and regulations and to remove customs and practice which discriminate against and cause harm to the girl child".

Being part of human world, both childhood and youth are subject to many visible suffering and disabilities. Thus, several conventions and other measures have been included juveniles as part of International Jurisprudence by the United Nations. Each nation must have a special ombudsman for juvenile justice, enjoying power, suo motu, to investigate here cases, render verdicts and take action, including punishment.

In the juvenile field cultural cooperation among nation, acceptance of common values and the introduction of a world watch dog, which will not act an instrument of imperialism, but will operate as a functional and effective Human Rights Commission, will be an urgent desideratum. If the Charter of United Nations and the International Bill of Human Rights are to be considered seriously for humanity worldwide, there is a need to transform the Declarations, Covenants, Resolutions and Programmes of Action from pious values and paper projects into effective commands and operational obligations.

There is no doubt that instruments are a global gain. But shaping children's future with the help of law, and harmonising their lives with the right to health and happy environment has a long way to go. Laws on the books and law in action more after that not occupy different streets. If environmental degradation and betrayal of human health are not corrected by law and affirmative action is neglected by the executive, legislative and judicial wings of the State, there may castigate as treacherous. So what we need is the development of a community conscience in the field of juvenile justice, without which social justice and sustainable development will only be a dream of democracy.

Referring back to the Constitution of India, it states specifically that affirmative discrimination in the form of special provisions for women and children is permissible. Article 39 (e) of the India Constitution as has been discussed shows special concern for children and directs the State to secure conditions in interest of children so that in their tender age, they are not abused nor coerced by economic necessity to enter avocations unfit for their age or strength.

Article 45 directs the State to provide free and compulsory education for all children until they reach the age of 14 years. There is no doubt whatever that these obligations have been violated. There has been a chronic dereliction of assignments on the part of the State. Vast numbers of children have been kept illiterate, uneducated and without the protected against exploitation of childhood such as forced labour and unwholesome activities which condemn them to moral and material neglect.

If the State betrays its obligation, the Court and the people must rise to monitor and correct this phenomena. The needs of Children and our duties towards them have been incorporated in the Constitution and the Resolution on a National Policy on Education has been adopted by parliment. It gives direction to State policy on the Educational needs of children. Now that India is also party to the UN Convention, of the Rights of the Child, goals set out in this document can reasonably be met by judicious and efficient use of the available national resources.

A National Children's Board was though constituted in 1974 and reconstituted in 1981, the majority of Indian children in India belong to the vulnerable section and poor families.

The International Year of the child and the decade have come and gone, statistics have escalated and the dimension of the problem remains frighteningly severe. The Constitutional obligation has not been enforced and although the international instruments, such as the Universal Declaration and the two Covenants and the Convention and Declaration regarding child rights, have persuasive power over the State, their fulfilment continues to be a secondary priority. Nevertheless there has been at least one step forward, the Government is committed to the National Policy for Children which stresses importance of education in Human Resources Development.

The unbreakable circle of child illiteracy, cheap child labour, and poverty cannot be used to deny the child his/her basic right to grow as a full human being. In fact, other countries with repent poverty have performed better. But, India's future, bearing in mind that there are over 20 million children below 14 years of age, depends a lot about juvenile justice in its development dimensions. The NPE is a printed tribute; but if, alongside it, ill-health and illiteracy, child labour, squalor, shanties and infant mortality grow up, the future remains bleak and the country's failure to provide juvenile justice, an unexpected shock. The challenge of the child continues.

At the event of the International Year of the Child in 1979, the Government set up the Gurupadswami Committee to prepare a report on child labour. That Committee notwithstanding, the Ministry of Labour accepted child labour as a "harsh reality", taking the view that eradication of child labour is not an economic feasibility. The culpability of the establishment is aggravated by the fact that, far from taking out children from labour, provision for training of children to labour better, is being organized. To cite example, in 1978, the Handloom and Handicrafts Exports Corporation (HHEC) a Delhi-based Government body, had established training centre to train children between ages seven and 14 to weave carpets. This job been declared hazardous and prohibited by law since the woollen fibres are dangerous for the child's lungs, eye and skin.

These children, after undergoing training eight hours a day for one year, step into the carpet industry for employment.

As has been discussed in the previous chapters during February and may 1983 a series of reports appeared in the newspaper regarding widespread child labour in the fireworks and match factories of Sivakasi, a town in the Ramanathapuram district in the state of Tamil Nadu. This issue of child labour in the sector initiated a national debate on the question of the legitimisation of child labour.

Various redressal unit came up social paediatrics, in the sense of eliminating the infrimities - social, economic and other - of children, has received legal consideration at the hands of our legislatures. Public interest litigation in the area of child-bonded labour has made some change or at least awakened the people to their crime against the tiny population. It is an equally well known fact that trafficking in children is becoming resistant to the law. Cheap labour through mediators middlemen is something blinked at by officials. Girl children often end up in the flesh trade. Indeed, the worst atrocities relate to the girl child. Pimps buy and sell children while the law offers little resistance.

The legislature may undoubtedly, the claim that laws against employment of children have been enacted as partial implementation of the promise of justice to children. The minimum age of employment has been decided by law and hazardous employment prohibited. The period beginning with 1950 has witnessed a spate of legislation based on the Labour Investigation Committee Report (1946). Today it can be said the with confidence that atleast in the eye of the law, the right to life which includes the right to education and development, discourages child labour. This labour not only risks life and opportunity for growth but also denies those freedoms and facilities without which a child is reduced to dwarfism, moronism and penury of creativity. The ILO Convention has gone a long way in the upliftment children's status.

Various enactments like the Plantation Labour Act, the Mines Act, the Factories Act, the Motor Transport Workers' Act, the Beedi and Cigar Workers (Condition of employment) Act, the Employment of child Act (as amended in 1978) carry provisions which are benignly disposed toward children.

But it is said to know that the present priorities of the government ignore the child. The minimum expected was the implementation of the National Labour Commission recommendations of 1969. Scattered parts of legislation are not equal to a uniform code which liberates the child and offers him his entitlement for development.

Issues of child labour, child education, child nutrition, and child development also hold the same fate. As we have seen in chapter on child labour also, the working conditions of child labourers are extremely deplorable causing various physical and mental hazards, depriving children of their childhood, education and blooming all of which constitute their nature rights. Numerous cases of torture, beating, sexual harassment, and other forms of inhuman treatment are heard which are a reflection of the medieval slavery.

Welfare of a child cannot be compromised; a holistic approach to Project Juvenile Justice must look in to the negative and positive aspects, as in the English Children Act. We are not in a position to claim that the Children Act of 1960 and the Juvenile Justice Act of 1986 passed in India are as useful as the English counterpart although the inspiration for both came from the English statues. When we deal with the child we have to deal with parents too, more particularly in societies where divorce is frequent and poverty is undespread. The guardianship of the child must depend upon the interests and well-being of the child also, not only on the personal law of the land.

In he similar manner, the question of criminal responsibility of a child when an offence is committed needs special attention. The question of negligence and delinquency vis-a-vis children is a delicate and sensitive branch of law, and depends very much on concern and commitment for the tender age of the children. In India, more and more crimes are committed by adults using children as instruments. Here we come upon the need for a Penal Code dealing with young persons which comes across the manifold difficulties of the problems of juvenile culpability and curative methodology. Psychiatric inputs may be of great use to the Court to pass appropriate sentences, custodial or non-custodial. After care organizations are also required for careful design, depending on the country and culture and social milieu. Certified schools, industrial schools, children's homes and the like along with foster care, adoption, sponsorship and many more human techniques have to be compassionately created. Our country, there is no adoption law for non-Hindus because religious differences have made it difficult for a facultative national legislation on adoption for others. Intercountry adoption has its own dangers although the Indian Court, at the highest level, has laid down some directives on this aspect. Even so, the fact remains that intercountry adoption deprives the child of is relation to native culture and citizenship and promotes the likelihood of being a second-class citizen in later years in he country of adoption. Cacism, cultural discrimination and the helplessness of the child in a foreign jurisdiction cannot be checked by all that the Supreme Court has laid down.

The best period of Juvenile Justice Jurisprudence arrived in India when the Juvenile Justice Act, 1986 was passed. Prior to that, there were many imitative Children's Acts which when put enforced, produced chaos. The Children Act of 1960 was preceded by the UN Declaration of the Rights of the Child in 1959. Concepts became more purified and juvenile justice was adopted by the UN General Assembly in 1985 followed in India by the Juvenile Justice Act of 1986. These is more scientific and elaborate treatment of the subject in the 1986 law which deals with neglected as well as delinquent children. Prostitution, narcotic drugs and psychotropic substances, observation homes and places of safety are relevant subjects in the juvenile context and are receiving legislative attention now.

In Indian legal work, Jurisprudence of Juvenile Justice is the wayward victim of legislative chaos and statutory slumber. And even when a fine piece has been added to the statute book, meaningful execution is miles away. If inaction is a form of action, the executive is culpable of non-enforcement of the law as any serious student of the subject will support the statement. The tragic irony is that the State Children's Acts continue de facto in many parts of the country, because the Juvenile Justice Act involves various structures, functionaries and expenditures for which the States may not be ready.

Since it is even legally accepted fact was neglected juveniles and delinquent juveniles fall under different categories thus punitive provisions regarding each must therefore be different. Many of miscellaneous matters about duties of parents, appointment of officers, people's participation through Advisory Boards, health care for juveniles and the like, find specific statutory concern in the Juvenile Justice Act. Had this justice legislation been brought into force throughout the country, the protection development correction and rehabilitation of there helpless tiny beings would have received therapeutic jurisprudential attention sufficient to meet Constitution at obligations.

But numerous errors have been committed by the State which cannot be forgiven but those which relate to the welfare of children deserve serious public censure because the child has the first call on the State's resources. Because children are voiceless and voteless they are ignored with impunity by those in power who will be held guilty by those in power who will be held guilty by the future generation.

To overcome all this, the convention on the Rights of the Child is a landmark for human rights, a landmark for children of India and the world, a landmark for human progress and the gradual establishment of universal standards for civilization. The Convention has also become landmark in many more specific respects:

Firstly, in the speed with which the Convention first came into force, less than 11 months after it was adopted by the UN General Assembly, and in less time than any other human rights convention;

Secondly, In the number of countries which have ratified it through there national legislation- now more than 100. Indeed the goal has now been set fair ratification by all countries by the end of 1995 with the objective of making it the first really universal international convention; and

Finally, in the development of a set of international priority goals to meet the basic needs of women and children in the areas of health, nutrition, education, water and sanitation, and family planning. These were adopted in September 1990 at the World Summit for children, just a month later than the Convention came into force. These have by now been converted into National programmes of Action by 92 countries and are in draft or under way in 50 others.

Conclusion thus over 90 per cent of children in all continents (except Africa) now live in countries which have ratified the Convention and prepared a national programme of action to implement its priority goals by the end of the century but the get yet remains to be meet.

Almost 50 years ago Arnold Toynbee, the visionary historian had commanted, "Ours is the first generation since the dawn of history in which mankind dared to believe it practical to make the benefits of civilization available to the whole human race".

The significant provisions encompassing the creation, adoption, ratification and impending implementation of the Convention on the Rights of the Child are major milestones on the march towards the gradual realisation of this vision. It just committed enforcement by the suffering countries can make the objective fulfilled.

15

CHILD LABOUR AND THE LAW

In the chapter on Socio-Legal Concerns Against child labour who have produced information on efforts made by voluntary organisation and legal agencies to set right the wrongs prevalent in the area of child labour at national and international level. But the present chapter *Child Labour and the Law* included in the legal sector presents both a Quick sketch of legal provisions on child labour as well as possibilities of their implementation through pointing out saw hurdles affecting the practical aspect of implementation.

Commitment of the National Statutory Book

India's commitment to the welfare of children is very much reflected by its constitution in the chapter IV on Directive Principles of State Policy. The Constitution makes were quite aware of the requirements of children in need of special care.

Article 15 (3) lays down that "nothing it this article shall prevent the state from making any special provision for women and children".

Article 24 declares that "no child below the age of 14 years shall be employed to work in any factory or mine or engaged in any other hazardous employment".

Article 39 (c) further states that "the health, strength of the workers, man, women and the tender age of children are not abused and that the citizens are not forced by economic necessity to enter avocation unsuited to their age or strength".

Article 39 (f) ensures that "Childhood and youth are protected against exploitation and against moral and material abandonment.

In the same way, Article (45) directs that "the state shall endeavour to provide within a period of ten years from the commencement of the constitution for free and compulsory education for all children until they complete the age of 14 years".

Efforts at the Level of ILO

Basic objective of ILO is the improvement of labour standards throughout the world. It has paid particular attention to the in interests of the employed children. It has sought to achieve its objective of protecting children by approving international standards in the form of "conventions and recommendations". A convention aims to create obligations of binding nature and its ratification requires complete compliance with all its provisions. A recommendation, on the other hand requires provision which are generally the nature of guiding principles for action and may be implemented progressively and in parts. Tilll date, the ILO has adopted 18 conventions and 16 recommendation mainly in respect of children and young persons in regarding their minimum age for entry to employment, medical examination before employment and work during nights. India has ratified 6 of the ILO conventions concerning the employment of children and young persons in industrial and non-industrial sectors.

The declaration made by United nations that "the child by reason of his physical and mental immaturity needs special safeguards ard care, including appropriate protection. The child shall enjoy the benefits of social security. He shall enjoy special protection and shall be given opportunities and facilities by law and by other means to enable him to develop in a healthy and normal manner and in conditions of freedom and dignity. In the enactments of laws for this purpose, the best interest of the child shall be the paramount considerations. The general assembly calls upon local authorities and national governments to recognize these rights, without discrimination on account of national or social origin, property, birth or other status whether or himself of his family".

Indian Statutory Provisions. These provisions have already found briefly descriptive mention in the chapter Socio-Legal concerns Against Child Labour. So, here just renaming the acts, will serve the purpose as we do not need going into details.

I *legal enactments regarding are for employment :* Almost all states regulate employment of children. The minimum age for employment varies from state to state. The relevant statutory provisions are briefly produced below:

(i) *Factory Act, 1948:* The Act forbides the employment of children below 14 years while ILO prescribes 15 years and above for employment in any factory using power and employing ten or more workers, and in an establishment not using power and employing twenty or more workers on any date of the preceding 12 months. To prefect the health of young persons between 14 to 18 years, the Act enjoins surgeon and the certificate will be valid for a period of one year from the date of issue.

(ii) *Mines Act, 1952:* The minimum age of this Act for working in mines above ground is 15 years and at goes with ILO standards also. For underground employment, prescribed age limit is 16 years and above. Along with the above, certificate is also required from an authorised surgeon as in the Factory Act, 1948.

(iii) *Plantation Labour Act, 1951.* Under this Act, a child of 12 years and below (according to ILO 14 years) shall not be eligible for employment in plantation of tea, coffee, rubber or cinchona within an area of 10,117 hectares of more and employing thirty or more persons. A child above 12 years desirous to work in plantation should submit a certificate of fitness which will be valid for the period of one year from the date of issue by authorised surgeon.

(iv) *Motor Transport Act, 1961.* Under this Act minimum age prescribed for employment in any transport undertaking employing five or more workers is 15 years and more. The ILO also recommends the same.

(v) *Beedi and cigarette workers (condition of employment) Act, 1996.* This Act says that no child who has not completed his 14 years, shall be allowed to work in any industrial premises where any manufacturing process regarding manufacture making of beedi or cigar. Is carried on irrespective of the number of persons employed.

(vi) *Employment of children Act, 1938.* To prevent employment of children in inhazardous and unhealthy occupations the Act forbids the employment of children below 15 years as suggested by ILO) in any occupation about transport of passengers, goods or mails by railway, or a port-authority within the limits of a port. The Act rejects the employment of children in railway particularly in construction work, catering services, track and line work as well as cleaning and picking of ash-pits and cinders. It again does not permit employment of children below 14 years in certain less hazardous occupations such as beedi-making, carpet weaving, cement manufacture, cloth printing, dyeing, and weaving, making matches, explosives and fire works, mica-cutting and splitting, shellac manufacture, soap manufacture and canning, etc. It may be informed that the Government of India has another bill to regulate employment of children.

(vii) *Merchant Shipping Act, 1958.* This enactment prohibits the employment of children below 15 years of age in any capacity, on seagoing ships, except (a) in a school ship or training ship or (b) in a ship in which all those employed are members of one family; or (c) in home made ship of less than two hundred tonnes gross; or (d) where such person is to be employed on approved wages and will be in charge of his father or other adult male relative.

(viii) *Inland Steam Vessels Act, 1917.* The Act applies to steam ships ordinarily playing in inland waters. It does not have arrangements for regulating employment of children. The reason for this omission seems to be that it is an old enactment when the community was not aware of the need to have legislation for protection of children.

(ix) *Radiation Protection Rules, 1971.* Under this a child below 18 years of age is not to be employed at places where radiation occurs.

(x) *State Shop and Commercial Establishment Act.* For the implementation of this legislation, different states have their own rules regulating employment and duration of in shops and establishment, restaurants and hotel, etc., to which the Factory Act does not apply. In States of Bihar, Gujarat, Jammu and Kashmir, Madhya Pradesh, Karnataka, Orissa. Rajasthan, Tripura, Uttar pradesh, West Bengal, Goa Daman and Diu and Manipur, required minimum age for employment in shops and commercial establishment is 12 years. In Andhra Pradesh, Assam, Haryana, Himachal Pradesh, Kerala, Tamil Naidu, Punjab, Delhi, Chandigarh, Pondicherry and Meghalaya, it has been fixed 14 years while 15 years in Maharashtra. According to the ILO it is 15 years.

(xi) *The Children (pledging of labour) Act, 1933.* This law prohibits any agreement written or oral to pledge the labour of a child, whereby parents or guardians of these children undertakes to cause or allow the services of the children to be utilised for any employment in return for a payment received or to be received. A child under this Act is defined as a person who is below 15 years of age.

(xii) *The Apprentices Act, 1961.* According to this Act, a person shall not be qualified for being engaged as an apprentice to undergo apprenticeship training in any designated trade category, unless he has completed 14 years of age and fulfils the prescribed standard of education and physical fitness. The minimum educational qualification required is 7th standard but for some jobs it is only 4th standard.

(xiii) *The Contract Labour (regulations and abolition) Act, 1970.* Under this act, the permissible age for the working as contract labour is 18 and above.

The second important aspect of the statutory provisions for the employment of children is the number of working hours or the duration of work. Different Acts have prescribed different working hours. The nature of these restrictions have been mentioned below:

(i) *Duration of work.* Four and half hours per day have been fixed for children under the Factory Act. Similarly, in Mines Act, for the adolescent who does not have a fitness certificate from a surgeon working hours are 4 and a half per day. No limitation on hours of work is prescribed under the Plantation Labour Act, 1951. Seven hours including rest period is prescribed under the Employment of Children Act, 1938. Different working hours have been fixed in different provinces for the shops and commercial establishments under the state acts.

(ii) *Restrictions on weekly hours of work.* No clear-cut limitations have been mentioned for children under the Factory Act, 1948, the Mine Act, 1952 and the Railway (hours of employment) Rules while Forty hours a week for an adolescent and a child has been stated by the Plantation Labour Act, 1951.

(iii) *Regulation of Rest Interval.* The rules regarding rest interval has been prescribed under the Factory Act 1948, and the plantation Labour Act, 1951. The same also made under the employment of children Act, 1938, and state Shops and commercial establishments Acts.

(iv) *Work at Night.* The provision for limitation/prohibition of night work by children and some cases even by young persons is available under the Factory Act, 1948 and the after Act like The Mines Act, 1952, the Plantation Act, 1951. Beedi and Cigar workers (conditions of employment) Act, 1966 and the State Shops and Commercial Establishments Acts. But these provisions very in respect of age and prohibits work during nights.

(v) *Instructions for shift relays and spread over:* Under the Factory Act, 1948, it is written that the period of work of children shall be confined to two shifts which shall not spread over for more than 5 hours a day. Again children shall be permitted to work only in one shift which can be changed for not more than once in a period of 30 days in case previous permission is obtained from the chief inspector of Factories.

(vi) *Dual Employment.* Children are prohibited from working in more than one factory on any day under the Factory Act, 1948.

(vii) *Weekly of.* Every working child under the Factory Act, 1948, Mines Act, 1952; Motor Transport Workers Act, 1961, and Beedi Workers, condition of employment) Act has to be given to a weekly holiday.

(viii) *Protection and Safety.* Under the Factory Act, children are not permitted to work on pressing cotton where cotton opener is at work. Further, the Act of bids the young person to clean, lubricate or adjust any part of a prime-mover or transmission machinery is in working or to clean, lubricate or adjust any part of any machine if it is likely to expose her or him to risk or injury from that part.

(ix) *Provisions of Leave.* The annual leave with wages is given to the working children who have worked for more than 240 days or more during a calendar year a one day for every 15 days of work done by them under the Factory Act, 1948, the Plantation labour Act, 1951. The Motor Transport Works (condition of employment) Act, 1961 and the Beedi and Cigar Workers (condition of employment) Act, 1966. Provisions very indifferent states for children working in the Shops and Commercial establishments.

(x) *Regulation of Wages.* Wages of the child workers are guided by the minimum Wages Act, 1948, and payment of Wages Act, 1936.

(xi) *Rules Regarding Penalties.* Under the Factory Act, the owner or manager of the factory is liable to be punished if found guilty of contravention of the provisions with a punishment of imprisonment upto 3 months of a fine up to Rs. 500 or with both. The adolescents using false certificates and parents or guardians allowing double employment of a child are also liable to be punished. The Employment of Children Act provides for punishment for violation of the provisions of the Act with simple imprisonment extending to one month or fine upto Rs. 500 or with both. Children (pledging of labour) Act, 1933 makes punistive provisious for parents or guardians making an agreement to pledge labour of a child with a fine upto Rs. 50 and in case of an employer with Rs. 200 In the same manner, Beedi and Cigar Worker (condition of employment) Act, 1966 provides for penalty of imprisonment upto 3 months and or a fine upto Rs. 500. The working hours and conditions for young persons and children are given below:

A glimpse of the various Act gives an impression that the government is doing its best to check the exploitation of children by employers and others, but the true picture in the field is otherwise. Various studies and reports by official and non-official organisations have pointed out a poor enforcement and gross breah of the provisions of these Acts by the employers in general and by shops and commercial establishments in particular. There have been an endless debates on various aspects of this problem at various forums. The Law Association of Asia and Western Pacific have not been able to come out with a clear-cut mechanism on the implementation of these acts. Infact, they are in a dilemma. If laws are enforced, on important supplementary family income is needed for the survival of the family and as such laws become on

Table 15.1

Legistation	*Fitness Certificate*	*Maximum hours of work in a week*	*Maximum hours in a day*	*Rest interval*	*Spead over*	*Overtime*	*Night shifts*
Factory Act, 1948	Necessary	Not prescribed	5 hrs	1/2 hrs	5 hrs	Not allowed	Not allowed
Mines Act, 1952	-do-	-do-	-do-	-do-	-do-	-do-	-do-
Plantation Labour Act, 1951 Motor	-do-	40 hrs	6 hrs	-do-	-do-	-do-	-do-
Transport Act, 1961	-do-	-do-	-do-	-do-	9 hrs	-do-	-do-

absolute measure in the present Indian conditions. When the child labour is allowed, the unscrupulous persons and others motivated by a desire for more and more profits fail to resist temptations to abuse child labour. This subject has generated a lot of heat in the minds of various segments of the populations directly and indirectly working for this problem. The concern expressed in various forum has led the Government to think about this problem more seriously.

Guided by these principles, the labour Minister, Government of India (1985) in the meeting of the Child Labour Advisory Committee spoke about prescribing severe penalty for the violation of the child labour laws. Accordingly, the Government made an amendment in the employment of Children Act, 1938 passed both the Houses of the Parliament. If empowers the law enforcing agencies to impose a minimum of 3 months of imprisonment or a fine of Rs. 500 for contravening the provisions section 3 of the Act. The Government of India has also felt that the laws alone cannot prevent child labour and their abuse. Consequently, the Government has mooted ideas for an all-round development of child along with special attention to their requirement. It is being thought that to eliminate child labour if is necessary to focus on the total socio-economic development of those sections of society which is supplying child labour to various sectors and units. Similarly, the Government has proposed to improve the existing working conditions of children at work. In pursuance of these ideas, two pilot projects have been started one at Sivakashi (Tamil Nadu) and another at Bhadohi (Varanasi/Mirzapur of Uttar Pradesh). These projects are to ensure better enforcement of the child labour laws, non-formal education and health care for better development of children working in these places. This is the welcome move because no amount of laws can eradicate child labour and at the same time there is no full justification for the total abolition of child labour in the present existing socio-economic conditions of the country. Because people in general and various organisations and individual concerns did not feel satisfied with measures taken by the Government to regulate child labour, the Government of India has enacted with a comprehensive legislation to counter the various criticism on this front. Accordingly, on 22nd Aug. (1986) a comprehensive bill on Child Labour (Prohibition and Regulation) was introduced in the Rajya Sabha by the Government which was then passed as law route the same name, provides that no child below 14 years shall be employed any of the occupations connected with the transport of passengers, goods or mail by railway, cinder picking, clearing ash-pits or building construction in the railway premises. Child labour is banned in establishments at railway stations, ports, any workshop which undertakes the processes of bidi making, carpet weaving, cement manufacture, cloth printing, dyeing, weaving, manufacture of matches, explosives and fireworks.

Keeping tendencies of children, the Act provides that no child shall be permitted to work from 7 PM. to 8 AM. or overtime. The duration of work of a child shall be so arranged that inclusive of intervals for rest at least one hour) it shall not be more than 6 hours. The violation of the provisions of the bill shall be pusitive with imprisonment ranging from three months to one year or a fine upto Rs. 10,000 or both. Subsequent contraventions will be punishable with 6 months, imprisonment compulsory and it could be extended to 2 years. Any person can file a complaint before the court. However, some contraventions are found in this approach. As Mahajan Krishan (1986) has found the approach of those opposing Child Labour was one of escapism as discussed at the workshop on Child Labour in India organised at the Indian Social Institute on August 9,

1986. He noticed that the Act totally prohibited the employment of any child, who was defined as any person less than 14 in the occupations as mentioned above. But in no-where provides for the rehabilitation of these children pushed out of these jobs. The Directive Principles of State Policy do not permit the union Government to make illusory laws in social justice. By making it illegal to work in key employments which support the majority of Indian families without providing for alternative measures of economic justice at the same time. The result of the Act will be that the majority of children who are employed as mentioned above will have their wages reduced further because of the additional expenditure their employers will have to incur for keeping the labour inspector happy to prevent prosecution.

The drawback of the bill was that it violates the fundamental rights of the child under Article 21 to adequate nutrition, education, clothing and shelter or a decent life. It provides to check abusing children due to economic necessity and to provide opportunities for their proper development. This unconstitutional intention is clear from the fact that it does not even provide that the employer should employ a child below fourteen after having his age determined and certified by the local civil hospital or the primary health centre has been shown. Instead, under section 10 it provided or determination of such age when a dispute arises. Since no child who is working out of "economic necessity" or his parent who send him to work because of such necessity, will be able to fight such legal controversies against an influential and relatively better-off employer. That the framers of the bill have paid no interest to even preventive measures is shown by the fact they have given in terms of fines violating the provisions for keeping registers and putting up notices which constitute the evidentiary basis of all prosecutions. Such a violation under section 14 (3) calles for a penalty of only Rs. 1,000 maximum or a simple imprisonment of 1 month maximum. However, under section 14 (1) the Violation of the total ban on child labour provides for a penalty of a minimal fine of Rs. 10,000 with a maximum of double that amount or a minimum of three months imprisonment which can be extended to one year. If social activists and others make much hau and cry against the labour machinery, a few token prosecutions as provided under the various Bidi Acts, with nominal fines only will get employers off the evidentary hook and thereby save any conviction.

Enforcement of Child Labour Laws

As we have already said in the section on child labour that India is a country with largest number of child workers. Its constitution gives the fundamental rights so children below 14 years not to be employed in any establishment like factory, mine or any hazardous employment. The constitution also requires as a fundamental principle in the governance of the country that children of tender age are not pushed by economic necessity to engage in employments unsuited to their age, strength and they are given opportunities and facilities to develop in a healthy manner conditions of freedom and dignity, and also that children and youth are safeguarded against exploitation. Despite the constitutional commitment and statutory provisions, the social service facilities like health, education, recreation are not adequate for the proper growth and development of the child. Poverty eradication programmes sponsored by the Government may have yielded good results. But a large number of the population are still below the poverty line where their minimum needs are not met. They are forced into the labour market and are not sent to schools. It is a proven fact that poverty is the crux of the whole misery. In various studies also, the majority of employers accepted that children join the labour force due to poor economic conditions of their families. Their parents are not able to fulfil their responsibility to provide them with education, proper care and recreation, etc. Sometimes children are forced to accept work at the early age to meet their family expenses due to the loss of the bread winner. The general tendency of the employers is to get more and more production at limited expenses. Due to varied reasons like abundance, cheaper wages, better out-put, lesser industrial relations problems, etc., employer go for employment of children instead of adults.

Sections 67-68 of the Factory Act, 1948, prevent the employment of children below the age of 14 years. To keep the unit out of the reach of this Act, many employers have divided their set-up in small scale units. Moreover there are a number of units functioning without power but employing 19 employers deliberately. Since these units are not covered under the Factory Act, the employers can employ them easily. More shockingly enough in case of units not covered under the Factory Act, it has been found that not even a single unit has been found that not even a single unit has maintained records or registers of employment regarding their attendance, salary paid, terms and conditions of employment. This situation is not only prevalent in U.P but can be found other states of India as well. Addressing the delegates of the two-day Bonded Labour Conference on 12th Jan., 1986 the Haryana Chief Minister said labour laws were being freely breaches.

In many studies, when employers are asked whether they are aware of the child labour legislation, most of them (91 per cent) deny having knowledge of labour laws. This may be due to their limited knowledge and rural background. Therefore, the employers have divided their working units into different sub-units and it is generally found that employers keep very poor knowledge in urban slum areas. About the sources of awareness of child labour laws, they do not owe their knowledge to readings and formal information.

The information is generally collected from some officers from thc labour or the income tax departments when they came to them to enquire about the production expenditure and the number of workers employed.

The provisions relating to hours of work are also violated as we have seen in some case studies mentioned in the chapter Child Labour in practice. In view of the pitiable conditions of the child labour, the Supreme Court (1986) has asked the Government of Uttar Pradesh to present a Scheme to immediately absorb the child labour in the carpet industry and other non-hazardous occupations. It was also instructed that the scheme must cover the child labour in the district of Allahabad, Varanasi and Mirzapur. This order was passed against a petition submitted by the child workers who had been kidnapped form the Palamu District of Bihar, illegally employed and force to work in the carpet units of Uttar pradesh without food, sleep and wages.

After the passage of child Labour (Prevention & Regulation) Act, 1986, the things began to improve at legal front. But the problem continue under the practicalities. There committed to violate and exploit children at any cost could discover are way or the other. Ultimately, the supreme court of India had in one of its judgement declared very strong steps to be taken for the eradication of child labour for hazardous sector and their rehabilitation including education. The most effective to form severe punishment and high fines for employees violating there orders. In one of the studies conducted in Faizabad District of U.P., children employed in Glass & Bangle Factories had been with drawn and a number of NFE centres had been started all over the state. Again it man found the though things had improved to some extent because adults could find more jobs in factories, but it had also encouraged Child Labour in household sectors for various processes of Choorhi making. Similar consequences have generally found in other sectors &

other states also. Unless and until those involved in the enforcement process are strictly committed and those know as violators are sensitized about the hazards of employment over future lives of children. All legislation will remain only good wishes on papers.

16

PROCEDURAL ASPECTS LAW FOR NEGLECTED CHILDREN

After having gone through the various laws related to children, and same practical aspects regarding their implementation in the previous chapters, the present chapter procedure involved in the implementation just like special legal provision for children, special procedure for their implementation are also required since children are tender young creatures. The first half of the nineteenth century saw no substantial body of law relating to the liability, treatment or welfare of children. Under the common law principle of equality before the law, everyone was entitled to ordinary proceedings in the ordinary courts and hence, no special provision was made for children either. The principles of criminal liability were stated in term of the knowledge of right and wrong. This was applied to children on the grounds that a child under the age of seven could not commit crime and a child between seven and twelve could not commit an crime unless he had sufficient maturity of understanding to judge the nature and consequences of his conduct. In this way, the age of child helped him obtain exemption from liability. If the child did not come within the exemption, his liability to belief was the same as that of an adult. His exemption from criminal liability would lead to his acquittal and the courts could not take further action however much the child might be in need of care or protection. Even in punitive matter, it was fixed by law according to the nature of crime; the age of the offender had no relevance in determining the quantum of punishment.

But the principles of this needed radical changes in the light of the social conditions following the Industrial Revolution. There was quick rise in young offenders and children going wayward who needed to be handled by institutions distinct and separate from the ordinary law courts. This gave births to the idea of juvenile courts for children.

Emergence of Childrens Courts

The Apprentice Act passed in 1850; in India sought to provide for better treatment of children between ten and eighteen years of age. This was followed by the Reformatory Schools Act, 1876, modified in 1897, which provided for special courts which could order three to seven years detention and training rather there convictim. The first move to enact a Childrens Act came from the Indian Jails Committee (1919-20) which recommended special treatment for young criminals and non criminals to reform and rehabilitate them. It suggested, *inter alia,* the setting up of childrens court to hear all cases against children and young offenders, the to hand over a child offender pack to his parents if the conditions at home warranted such a return; and that the commitment of children and young person to jail should be illegal. The law on Children in the various states in the 1920s were a sequel to the Committees recommendations. These law were enacted to provide for (a) the custody, trial, maintenance, welfare, education and punishment of young criminals; and (b) for the protection of children and young persons who are neglected, destitute or in moral danger or in need of care and protection. In 1960 Parliament passed the Children Act setting up the Child Welfare Boards to deal with the problems of neglected children. For the first time two separate institutions were established-Child Welfare Boards for neglected children and juvenile courts for delinquent children.

What is the role of the Children. Acts vis-a-vis neglected children? The prime objective of the legislation is, *inter alia,* the treatment and rehabilitation of neglected children.

Role of Law

On principle, it is the primary responsibility of parents to protect their children from various harm and to ensure that they receive benefits for alround development. Most certainly, parents should be required to feed and clothe their children. They also must comply with laws on child education and against labour. In addition to these minimum requirements, parents should provide affection and a favourable home environment to ensure their childrens physical, mental, emotional and social development. Each childs home should offer him her the best available opportunity to fulfil the potential in society as a civilized human being. In this connection, some think that a childrens bill of rights be enacted to ensure each, child the right to grow up in a healthy home. To put it other way, a child has a moral right and, in addition, should have a legal right to get parental love and affection, learns discipline and guidance and to grow up as a complete mature adult in a favourable home environment.

But the question arise is can we achieve this ideal condition in the Indian context where the majority of children live in state of acute poverty and work to contribute to the monthly earnings of the family? Beginnings had been made before Independence, and certainly after Independence many child welfare programmes were formulated and implemented through child welfare legislation and various agencies.

The state has, under the doctrine of *parens patriae,* a right and an obligation to protect children if their parents are not performing their responsibilities adequately. But the role of the state in term of coercive intervention through laws to protect children has necessarily to be limited, keeping in mind the well-being of children, to regulate certain objectively determinable behaviour and to channelise the activities of same particular categories of children into areas which lead to their proper growth and development.

It is after feared that the legal process set in motion for the protection of children may lead to the curtailment of their individual liberty, though not permanently, and affect parental autonomy. Consequently, the legal intervention of the state, which leads to the timely removal of children from their homes (parental care), should be reduced to the minimum. But, on the other hand, the state should initiate various welfare programmes give generous financial support to NGOs to enhance the living standard of children in their own homes. The reason is that interference of the childs relationship with it parents is painful and the continuity of this relationship is of almost significance to children. Consequently, the removal of a child from the home environment may cause serious psychological damage-damage more serious than what the legal intervention is supposed to check.

The legal support for neglected children in India is found in the Central Children Act, 1960, enforceable in the Union Territories of Delhi, Dadara and Nagar Haveli, Goa Daman and Diu, Lakshadweep and Pondicherry. As of now, all states except Orissa, Meghalaya, Tripura and Nagaland have made laws on children. The Children Acts cover only 197 of the 370 districts in the country. The basic premise underlying the Children Acts is the responsibilities of the state as *parens patriae* to provide protection for children. In fact, the statement of objects and reasons of the Children Bill (Central states this:

> Children are the most vulnerable group in any population and in need of the greatest social care. On account of their vulnerability and dependence they can be exploited, ill-treated and directed into undesirable channnels by anti-social elements in the

community. The state has the duty of according proper care and protection to children at all time...

The very preamble attached to the Central Children Act, 1960, mention that the aim of the legislation *inter alia,* is to provide for the care, protection, maintenance, welfare, training, education and rehabilitation of neglected and delinquent children. Therefore, it has been that the Children Acts deal with two distinct categories of children, namely neglected and delinquent children.

One problem with the law is that the various Acts do not have a uniform definition of the term child. For example, the Bombay Children Act, 1948 defines child as a boy or girl who has not reached the age of sixteen years. The Madhya Pradesh and Uttar Pradesh Children Act fixes the upper age limit as sixteen years. However, under the Central Children Act a 'child' means a boy who has not reached the age of sixteen years or a girl who is below eighteen years. The Central Act, unlike the state Acts, has made a meaningful difference between boys and girls as regards the upper age limit.

There are also laws deal with delinquent children who commit criminal offences. Who is a neglected child? Are the statutory standards of neglect too comprehensive to facilitate legal intervention and limit parental autonomy in bringing up children? Since poverty and neglect are closely correlated in a society like ours, we must question whether sufficient resources exist to make state intervention in family affairs meaningful. The Children Acts (Central as well as State) define the following categories of children as neglected:

(a) one who has no parent or guardian or home or settled place of abode;

(b) a child with no regular means of subsistence or is found destitute:

(c) a child found begging or doing a job which goes against his welfare;

(d) that child in the care of parent or guardian who due to criminal tendencies, or bad habit or madness or disease or cruelty or wickedness or for any other reasons is either unfit to take care or incapable of taking care of the child;

(e) a child who is known to live with a brothel keeper or with a drunkard or is associated with a proven criminal;

(f) a child who takes shelter or lives in a house used for flesh trade or who often visits such places;

(g) a child who is used to intoxicants;

(h) a child who is not beyond parental control or is uncontrollable by any one;

(i) a child who is grossly overworked or ill-treated by his employer.

To deal with the problem of neglected children, the Children Act (Central) provides for the setting up of Child Welfare Boards. The Board is to consist of a chairman and other members, of whom at least one is to be a female, who have special knowledge of child psychology and child welfare. The Board is to act as a bench of magistrates and enjoys powers conferred by the Code of Criminal Procedure on a first class magistrate. The Board while conducting an enquiry under the Act is required to follow the procedure of the Code of Criminal Procedure for trials in summons cases. In a way, the Board exercises quasi-judicial power in respect of neglected children. Decisions are to be made by majority. In the absence of such a majority, the opinion of the chairman is final. The absence of any member does not affect the validity of a decision. Where there is no Board in any area, the powers of the Board are delegated to the district magistrate, or sub-divisional magistrate or any first class magistrate. The powers of the Board may be exercised by the Session Court and the High Court when there is a proceeding regarding appeal or revision or otherwise.

A number of states have taken initiative to the such Boards. The Assam Children Act, 1970, provide for the establishment of Boards but these Acts have not yet been brought into operation. The Kerala Act of 1972 has no provision for the establishment of Boards. Under the other State Acts like Bombay, U.P., East Punjab, Andhra, Saurashtra, Karnataka, Kerala, Tamil Nadu, West Bengal and Madhya Pradesh, the juvenile courts are dealing with neglected children.

Procedural aspects of the Functioning

Children Acts empower any police officer or an authorised person to take charge of neglected children and produce them infront of the Child Welfare Board or Juvenile Court (where there no Boards have been established) within 24 hours. Further, when any police officer in charge of a police station is informed about the presence of neglected children within his jurisdiction, he has to record the substance of such information and send a copy of the entry made to the Board, in case he does not take charge of such children. He is required to send the children to observation homes unless they are staying with their parents or guardians. In no case are they to be detained in the police station or prisons. Otherwise (if they are left with their parents or guardians), the police officer is required to report to the Board.

After getting this report, the Board requires the parents to produce such children and commence the neglect proceedings. As already said, the proceedings before the Board are intended to be informal. No lawyer can appear before the Board except with its special permission. On this matter, the Children Acts present a good compromise in that the Board may permit legal representation in a neglect situation which warrants it. This is as it should be. As neglect proceedings may end up in violating the individual liberty of children, it is imperative that in complicated situation, the children and their parents should ask for legal help. This question of legal representation was examined in England by the Committee on Children and young Persons (Ingleby Committee) which supported it. It stated,

> We do not assert that there is no need for legal representation in Juvenile Courts. On the contrary, there are certainly cases in which the child needs help quite apart from any that his parents and the court can give him.

Legal representation in India, exists as a matter of right in appellate and revisional proceedings. However, we find that the Acts do not have provision for free legal aid which is important in neglect proceedings. As emphasised earlier, neglect and poverty have a close co-relation and hence, lawyers help for children should not be dependent on their monetary resources. It should be provided at state expense. The proceedings are *in camera* before the Board. Only those allowed by the Board can be present and participate in the enquiry. In the interest and well-being of a child, and to present a congenial atmosphere to the child, the Board is to be housed in a separatc building or room away from the ordinary civil and criminal courts. The Acts forbids the publication of the names of the children involved except where the disclosure is in their own interest.

Observation Remand and Children Houses

The Children Acts also provide for short-term and long-term institutions for the care and rehabilitation of neglected children. The short-term institution is variously known as observation home or remand home where children are kept during enquiry by the Boards. During the period of enquiry the children could also be kept with their parents or guardians. However, they should not to be kept with their parents or guardians if the Board feels there is parental or guardian is not shiftable or inadequacy.

The observation home or remand home is envisaged as the venue for temporary care and custody of neglected children when the enquiry is going on. Hence psychiatrists and case-workers conduct the social investigation of neglected children and present reports to the Board for its guidance as well as for the future treatment and rehabilitation of the children. On the completion of the neglect proceeding, if the Board is satisfied that a child is neglected under the Act, it hands over such a child to long-term institutions known as childrens homes (Central Act), 'Certified school' (Bombay), 'industrial school' (West Bengal), etc. till he affains maturity. In special situation, the period of stay may be extended but not beyond the age of eighteen years in the case of a boy or twenty years in the case of a girl. The period could also be decreased by the Board. But in both types of situations, the Board has to record its causes in writing.

The Acts contain detailed provisions for the control and management of these institutions. Superintendents and a Committee of Visitors are designated as managers of these institutions. Annual inspection by chief inspectors and medical inspection by doctors with or without notice to the managers are compulsory. The Acts facilitate the establishment of voluntary homes and fit person institutions which are maintained fully or partly by voluntary contributions. Such voluntary institutions remain under the general monitoring control of government appointed inspecting staff. The government is authorised to suspend or withdraw the certificate granted to private institutions if their performance is not less than satisfactory. Last but not the least, the Act provide for an after-care organisation required to meet the special needs of children leaving institutions. It is envisaged as a centre for rehabilitating them on the completion of institutionalised durations.

Efficacy of Special Houses

What has been the impact of these institutions on children? Though empirical studies are not available for all the states in India, such studies have been conducted for Rajasthan and Maharashtra. These studies have assessed the influence of these institutions on the non-delinquent children who by matter of chance constitute a majority among all the children in these institution. The Rajasthan study observed children who were in institutions while the Maharashtra study interviewed those who had, at some point of time, in these institutions in part. Most of the children had discontinued their education prior to institutionalisation. During the period of institutionalisation, they could carry on with their education which had a definite beneficial impact on their lives. However, their formal education and vocational training were not always useful enough to ensure them jobs after they left the institutions. These studies point out that a fairly large number of institutionalised children had come from broken families. They especially, but also others, required help in many ways to settle in life but the institutions were, more often than not, unable to help.

Apart from there shortcomings, institutions are necessary for socially dependent children. Their management, however, needs to be improved. The educatinal standards of the child-care staff of these institutions should be higher than what it is today. They could be provided with proper training and guidance to enhance their social skills and endeavours for the childrens benefit.

After having gone through the laws, for neglected children, the observation honour & their efficacy, the question arises is state intervention at all justifiable in all types of neglect situations the Acts envisage? The Acts define neglect primarily in terms of parental behaviour or home environment. Generally neglect situations have the these categories of parental behaviour: physical abuse, cruelty, inadequate supervision, and parenting, immoral or unconventional parental behaviour. Since coercive intervention can cause interference with the liberty of children, it is suggested that the statutory definition of neglect should focus more on the specific harm to children than on parental conduct. Further the harm should be serious and be such that the treatment of coercive intervention will do more good than harm. This would mean that certain categories of harm would not constitute a ground for state intervention, though in some individual cases intervention might benefit.

It we look at the type of neglect, one type under the Children Acts is when the child has no settled place of abode. This standard cannot possibly be enforced in the context of Indias rural migrant population, specifically the construction and quarry workers who set up temporary abodes wherever they find work. Another neglect situation is when a child is begging or doing a job which goes against his welfare. Children are provoked to beg or work by poor parents to supplement their small family earnings. The Indian Council of Child Welfare had once estimated that working children (the nation-wide estimate being 10.4 million) contributed 14 percent of the monthly income of families with an income of about Rs. 300. This being so, it would be extremely unjust to expect the lower strata of society to give up child labour until the state is prepared to ensure a substantial improvement in living conditions. Consequently, to bring in child begging and child labour within neglect unless it results severe physical abuse of the child may not be possible in Indian conditions. For example, a child who is heavily overworked or ill-treated by his employer may be protected by coercive intervention leading to neglect proceedings.

One more noteworthy difficulty is that the parameters of 'unit parents or inadequate parent as a basis for commencement of neglect proceedings are vague. What is unfit or inadequate will reflect the value judgements of Boards, social workers and enforcement agencies. Given the vagueness of the parameters, unlimited intervention may be possible. The concept of inadequate parent is hard to define and may comprehend within it may varieties of situation. Inadequacy may stem from poverty-inadequate housing and medical care, poor nutrition; it may be due to drinking problems, mental illness and immorality of the parents. It may be very tempting to full such children out of such undesirable environmental conditions. But in these situations, it may be better for the state to offer services on a purely voluntary basis which the parents may avail of, than the inevitable 'neglect' proceedings which may lead to the ultimate removal of the child from the home environment. One should not ignore the strong qualities of children reared in this environment. They might even be capable of taking care of themselves despite the inadequacy of either both parents or one of them.

Moreover, in the arrangements of extended families, (joint families) the inadequacy of immediate parents may be compensated by the other member of the family protecting the children. The state role of the state should be to support agencies with adequate resources to offer help parents when in need. Do we have sufficient personnel and programmes to allow compulsory neglect proceedings in all types of parental inadequacy? Undoubtedly children should not be reared in inadequate homes. But, is our society able to provide better alternatives for these children? In the circumstances it is advisable to make the social welfare services more effective than now offered to families. The allocation of scarce resources should be to use voluntary services for less serious situations and keep compulsory intervention in more serious one.

Not only this, coercive state intervention in child neglect cases should be confined to circumstances where the child would be harmed specifically:

(a) when the child is orphan and no other member of the extended family willing to take care of him.

(b) when the child has received or is likely to receive physical injury which causes severe impairment of body or death as a result of parental negligence.

(c) when the child lives with prostitutes, or brothel-keepers, or confirmed criminals, or is addicted to intoxicants.

(d) when the child commits criminal offences due to parental pressure.

It is a obvious fact in this situation that the state cannot hope to achieve the well-being of neglected children through coercive measures which should be confined to the minimum. But more and more extensive welfare services should be made available on a voluntary basis to all families. In India at this point of its development, the state should make child welfare an integral part of the Five Year Plan. Steps to be reduce the poverty level of families should be taken seriously to raise the living and environment conditions and the nutritioon level of children. The state should not follow empty ideals at the expense of what is actually attainable within the overall financial limitations.

For availability of more funds, possibly a child welfare cess could be levied to raise resources for the implementation of welfare measures. Parliament could empower the Central Government to impose and collect a child welfare case by way of surcharge on income-tax, corporate tax, wealth tax and gift tax, The proceeds would be credited to a childrens Fund and the Union Government may give grants to NGOs for child welfare programmes. In fact the Central Government proposes to set up a National Children Fund to make possible the implementation of child welfare activities in the country. Voluntary organisation committed to such activities will be able to get grants form the Fund which will have account in all states. The main objective of establishing such a Fund is to ensure that child welfare work does not suffer for lack of resources.

To some up, we can say that the existing statutory standards of neglect are wide and should be limited to situations of particular harm to the child to warrant coersive state intervention..On the other hand, the state should make available extensive welfare services to support neglected children. Further, it should generously give grants to voluntary organisations for child welfare schemes. To mobilise financial resources for this purpose, possibly a child welfare cess could be imposed. In this connection, the Central Governments proposal to constitute a National Childrens Fund is to be welcomed. With these minimum possible, we can realize heaven an earth for neglected children provided the efforts are made whole heartedly.

Section—VI

CONCLUSION

17

CONCLUSION

Child abuse is not specific to any particular culture, community, or region. We have seen it universality and multidimensional nature in the various form discussed in the various proceedings sections and chapters. But the problem is so wide and comprehensive that it is just impossible to cover all froms and aspects of child abuse in any are publication.

Child labour is the most prevalent form of child abuse which is found more or less in all countries of the world proving the universal insensitively of humanity children are employed in both hazardous and non-hazardous sectors despite the fact that law prohibits employment of children below 14 years. in hazardous sector. These little raw looking creatures start carrying responsibilities of their families from the age when they haven't even learnt to speak well. During work, they become victim of cruelty of their employers. Poverty and illiteracy join hands with each other to damage the future of there future builders of nation.

Besides exploitation in Industrial units and other formal establishments, a large number of small children are found the domestic help. Girls are more frequently seen as domestic workers. In closed walls, they are more vulnerable to exploitation most particularly sexual exploitation. And the tragedy of our law is that it does not declare household sector as hazardous one for the children. If we rise above all prejudices, then any employment irrespective of dangerous and non-dangerous should be forbidden for children. But this wishful dream seems to be difficult to come true.

Child in bondage is again are of the worst forms of child exploitation where the so called owner enjoys all rights over the child at the mere cast of some small amount of loan given to the parents/guardians. After 54 years of Independence. Children of their country are still enslaved by their own people. Bondage does not lend to labour only, childrens are same tonnes trafficked to cross state or national border for flesh trade, camel jockeys and other inhuman acts by those known as human beings. Sale of these human beings is again prohibited under law but it is being practiced both through bondage and in trafficking.

Sexual abuse of children is practiced various platforms, on brothels, deserted roadsides and within the house sometimes by the close relatives including parents. Children forced into flesh trade bear the most violent forms of sufferings. Findings of various case studies can shake the conscience of any person with even little score of realisation. Border states like West Bengal are the best representatives of child prostitution. More heartening is that despite there sufferings perpetuated through sex, they are not able to feed themselves three full meals a day while they are lured from their country homes with the assurance they will get good jobs and very lavish styles in cities.

Sexual exploitation in household perpetuate more mental than physical abuse. A child is exploited by those who are supposed to love him and take care of him. Child is not able to understand or infact confused whether the act of that particular family member (abuser) is right or wrong but feels uncomfortable with it. This abuse hardly comes to notice through reporting since abusers are those themselves who should have been reporting to the police otherwise.

A special treatment needs to be given to child battering who has till date been considered a purely western phenomena. But, it is infact prevalent in as well though the nature of it may be different because we in India live under blind ideals of parental obeyance, that a child should never disobey his parents; this is hir duty to rise high in life and their shine the name of his parents even though he is a purer of ordinary intellect only. Parents finding child incapable of fulfilling/his desire victimise him to battering under the pretext of care of their child. A lot of research in west has been conducted to identify factors responsible for battering by parents and remedial measures. A close critical observance of the role of enforcement machinery i.e. police and the medicos has been done. Part played by social workers in prevention and treatment of child battering in also of great importance. Now, the subject has began to draw attention of Indian law workers or social reformers. The subject has also received same treatment in the constitution indirectly. The need is to have a full fledge proper enactment and its serious implementation to counter the problems and legal and social fronts.

Amongst statutory provisions for protection child, the constitution itself and the various enactments make in various arrangements. International conversation at the Rights of Child by UN is a bible for child rights. A number of countries inclouding India has ratified it. A country ratifying it becomes bound to incorporate the provisions of the convention in her national law and their implementation. We, in India have also sought certain legal and social reforms after being a party to the convention. But still a lot needs to be done and we have to go a long way to establish an ideal environment where each child will enjoy its childhood, without economic worries stemming from poverty; education the fundamental rights of all and they will be our future builders in ture sense of the world. All of us should make same commitments an our personal levels to help eradicate the evils performing to children.

Index

D

E

F

G

H

I

J

W

Z